Samuel Harlow

Life sketches of the state officers, senators and members of the Assembly of the State of New York

In 1868

Samuel Harlow

Life sketches of the state officers, senators and members of the Assembly of the State of New York
In 1868

ISBN/EAN: 9783337173814

Printed in Europe, USA, Canada, Australia, Japan

Cover: Foto ©ninafisch / pixelio.de

More available books at **www.hansebooks.com**

LIFE SKETCHES

OF THE

STATE OFFICERS, SENATORS,

AND

MEMBERS OF THE ASSEMBLY,

OF THE

STATE OF NEW YORK,

IN 1868.

By S. R. HARLOW AND S. C. HUTCHINS.

ALBANY:
WEED, PARSONS & COMPANY, PRINTERS.
1868.

Entered according to Act of Congress, in the year eighteen hundred and sixty-seven,

BY S. R. HARLOW AND S. C. HUTCHINS,

in the Clerk's Office of the District Court of the United States for the Northern District of New York.

PREFACE.

LIFE SKETCHES originated in 1866, and the first volume was published in 1867, containing concise records of the lives of the State Officers and Members of the Legislature of that year. Its success justified its continuation the present year. The aim of its Editors has been to make it authentic in its facts and dates, and no pains have been spared to render it so, though occasional errors may possibly be found. It has also been the desire of the Editors, to indulge in no undeserved praise, or fulsome laudation, but to give every man credit honestly for all he is in himself personally, and all he has been able to accomplish, and thus bring out the distinguishing traits of each man. It is possible that some may have been over-estimated, and others not sufficiently credited. But in the main we believe it can be said that the work is reliable in its estimates of character.

A change appears in the editorial management, Mr. BOONE, whose accomplishments contributed so largely to the value of the first issue, being unable to continue particularly identified with it the present season, owing to the nature of his business engagements.

The Editors renew their thanks to many gentlemen who have rendered invaluable assistance in furnishing incidents and dates for the compilation of these Sketches.

They would also acknowledge the kind favors of the Press in 1867, all, without exception, having borne flattering testimonials to the merits of the work. Their publication is unnecessary.

It will be seen that the Sketches of the Members of the Legislature are alphabetically arranged, thus removing the necessity for an index.

LIFE SKETCHES.

REUBEN E. FENTON,

GOVERNOR.

REUBEN E. FENTON, who was chosen Governor of New York for a second term, in November, 1866, was born in Carroll, Chautauqua county, on the 4th of July, 1819. His father is a native of New Hampshire; but the FENTON family is of Connecticut origin. His grandfather resided there until about the year 1777. The Governor is a descendant of ROBERT FENTON, who was a man of note among the early settlers of that State, and one of the patentees of Mansfield, when that town was set off from Windham, in 1703. The family was a patriotic one during the Revolutionary war, and furnished its share of soldiers in "the times which tried men's souls," who did good service in the struggle which resulted in the establishment of our Republican government.

Governor FENTON is the son of a hard-working farmer, and spent his early years on the old homestead. He was an amiable, friendly boy, and a universal favorite among his associates. Whatever was going on in the neighborhood where he lived, he was expected to participate in and lead. When the boys organized for "a training," they invariably placed young FENTON in command; and it is probably owing to this fact, and the military knowledge thus acquired, that before he was twenty-one years of age he was elected to the Colonelcy of the 162d regiment, New York State Militia.

His opportunities for acquiring an education were very limited, but they were well improved. He was a good scholar when he was in the common school, and when, subsequently, he passed a few terms in different academies, he made rapid progress as a student, and won the approbation of his preceptors for his manly qualities and exemplary deportment. He read law one year, not with the view of going into the profession, but to make himself familiar with the principles and forms of that science, under the impression that this knowledge would be useful to him in whatever business he might engage.

At the age of twenty he commenced business, with very limited means, and under adverse circumstances. But the fact did not discourage him, nor turn him from his purposes. The world was before him, and what others had accomplished, young FENTON resolved should be done by him. He went at his work with all the earnestness and energy of his character, and a few years saw him a successful and prosperous merchant. While in this pursuit, he turned his attention to the lumber trade, as an auxiliary to his mercantile business. He was still a young man when he purchased his first "boards and shingles," and as he floated off upon his fragile raft, valued at less than one thousand dollars, there were not wanting those who wondered at his temerity, and the failure of his enterprise was confidently predicted. But nothing could dampen his ardor. He tied his little raft safely on the shore of the Ohio, near Cincinnati, went into the city, found a customer, sold his lumber, and returned to his home with a pride and satisfaction never excelled in after years, though he went the round with profits ten-fold greater. Lumbering became in a few years his principal business; and to such a man, success and competence were but a matter of time. He soon enjoyed the reputation of being the most successful lumberman on the Alleghany and Ohio rivers; but this came only because he wrought it by untiring perseverance and indefatigable energy.

In the business capacity of Governor FENTON, will be found the basis of his success in life; and to the same fact he is doubtless in a great measure, indebted for his political advancement. Uniting superior business qualities with an invincible determination to succeed in whatever he undertakes, he has seldom failed to attain the object of his ambition. He was successful as a merchant; successful as a lumberman; and he has been successful as a politician. His idea is that a man to succeed, should be "always on hand." He was accustomed to fill his store with goods before his neighbors filled theirs; and in the early spring, before "the thaw" was expected, his lumber was snugly rafted on the banks of creeks, ready to take the current and be the first to reach Pittsburgh and Cincinnati. It was not only a pride he felt in being at the head of the river fleets, but experience on different occasions when his readiness and preparation found him the only man in market, had taught him that it was equally profitable.

In 1843, Mr. FENTON was chosen Supervisor of his native town, and held the position for eight successive years. Three of these eight he was Chairman of the Board, though the Board was two to one Whig, while he was a well-known Democrat. But he was courteous and affable, manly and upright, genial and sensible, and his opponents by common consent selected him to preside over their deliberations. What higher compliment could be paid him as a fair-minded and honorable man!

In 1849, his friends tried him for the Assembly, and he came within twenty-one votes of being elected, though the successful candidate was one of the oldest and most popular men in the Assembly district, which was strongly Whig.

In 1852, he was nominated by his Democratic friends for Congress, and elected by fifty-two majority, though the district, from the manner in which it was accustomed to vote, should have given at least 3,000 majority against him. He took his seat on the first Monday in December, 1853, in a House which was Democratic by about two to one. Mr. DOUGLAS, Chairman of the Senate Committee on Territories, in the course of the session was beguiled into embodying in a bill which provided for the organization as territories of Kansas and Nebraska, a repeal of that portion of the Missouri compromise of 1820, which forbade the legalization of slavery in any territory of the United States, lying north of N. lat. 36° 30'. Mr. FENTON, with N. P. BANKS, and quite a number of the younger Democrats, with Col. THOMAS H. BENTON and other seniors, steadfastly opposed this proposition, and opposed the bill because of it. The bill was nevertheless forced through the House by a vote of 113 to 100, and became a law. In the division that thereupon ensued, Mr. FENTON took Republican ground with PRESTON KING, WARD HUNT, GEORGE OPDYKE, and other conspicuous Democrats, and he has never since been other than a Republican.

In 1854, the Know Nothings carried his district by a considerable majority (Mr. FENTON consenting to be a candidate on the Saturday previous to election), as they did a good many others in the State; but, in 1856, he ran on the FREMONT ticket, and was elected, and thence reëlected by large and generally increasing majorities down to 1864, when he withdrew, having been nominated for Governor. He thus served five terms in Congress, each as the representative of the strongly Whig district composed of Chautauqua and Cattaraugus counties, which contains many able and worthy men who were in full accord with its by-gone politics, and to the almost unanimous acceptance of his constituents.

Immediately on entering Congress, Mr. FENTON espoused the cause of the soldiers of 1812, and shortly after introduced a bill providing for the payment of the property accounts between the United States and the State of New York, for military stores furnished in the war of 1812. This measure he continued to urge upon the attention of Congress, and finally, on the 30th May, 1860, had the satisfaction to witness its passage in the House by a vote of 98 to 80. He had a leading place on important committees, and performed the duties appertaining to these positions in a manner satisfactory to all. It is but simple truth to say that he was one of the quietly industrious and faithful members of the House. Nor was he a silent representative. He could talk when there seemed a necessity for speaking. During his Congressional career, he delivered able and effective speeches against the repeal of the Missouri Compromise Act; in advocacy of a cheap postal system; the bill to extend invalid pensions; for the improvement of rivers and harbors; to regulate emigration to this country; against the policy of the Democratic party with regard to Kansas; for the final settlement of the claims of the soldiers of the Revolution; in vindication of the principles and policy of the Republican party; on the Deficiency bill; the bill to facilitate the payment of bounties; on the repeal of the Fugitive Slave Law; on providing for payment of losses by the rebellion, etc.

Mr. FENTON served in Congress nearly to the end of the war for the Union, of which he was one of the firmest and most efficient supporters. Believing the Union to be right and the rebellion wrong throughout, he gave his best energies to the national cause, voting steadily for taxes, loans, levies, drafts, and for the emancipation policy whereby they were rendered effectual. Men of greater pretensions were abundant in Congress, but there was none more devoted, or more ready to invoke and to make sacrifices for the triumph of the Union.

In the fall of 1862, Mr. FENTON's name was favorably mentioned in connection with the office of Governor, but finding Gen. WADSWORTH was to be pressed for a nomination, Mr. FENTON promptly withdrew from the canvass, and yielded to the patriot soldier his warmest support. In 1864, Mr. FENTON was designated as the standard-bearer of the Republican party, and chosen Governor by a majority considerably larger than Mr. LINCOLN's; and two years later, he was unanimously re-nominated, and chosen by an increased majority.

The administration of Governor FENTON commenced at the culminating period of the war, and required the exercise of industry, method, decision, and the power of discriminating, originating and executing. He brought to the discharge of his new position all these forces of body and mind, and proved patient amid perplexities, quick in his perceptions, safe in his judgments, mastering toilsome details, and successfully meeting difficult emergencies. His practical training, his wide experience, his luminous intellect and well-disciplined judgment, saved him from the failure that a man of less power might have encountered. His official relations with our soldiers did not weaken the attachments that had given him the honored title of the "soldier's friend." He was prompt to reward merit, and skillful to harmonize differences that often threatened demoralization and serious injury to many of the military organizations then in the field. Upon the return of our brave boys, Governor FENTON addressed the following letter to the War Committees of the various districts in the State:

GENTLEMEN: The late orders of the Secretary of War for mustering out a large portion of the grand army are being rapidly carried into effect, and it is to be hoped that by the Fourth of July most of the regiments to be discharged under the orders will have reached their homes. In view of this fact, allow me to call your attention to the propriety of celebrating that day in a manner not only befitting the anniversary of the nation's birth, but also commemorating its recent rescue from imminent peril. I need not say that welcome and all honor to the men whose patriotism has consecrated the nation to a new career of greater freedom, whose bravery has given security from strife and perpetuity to our institutions, should be one of the most prominent features of such an occasion. Let us at once demonstrate, by a grand ovation, our devotion to the institutions preserved to us, and our gratitude to those who with heroic constancy, defended them through years of terrible war. I have thought best not to issue an executive proclamation to this end, as I prefer this demonstration should be the spontaneous uprising of the people, eagerly welcoming back the citizen soldiers — our friends and neighbors — from the dangers of the battle-field and the severe duties of military discipline, to peace and the exercise of civil rights under the quiet which their valor has secured. I sincerely hope these suggestions may meet with favor from your people, and that each locality will arrange such a programme as shall, according to its circumstances, best devote the day to commemoration, gratitude and general rejoicing.

Very truly yours, R. E. FENTON.

His judicious course fully commanded public confidence and approval, and at the close of the first year of his term, MOSES H. GRINNELL, WM. M. VERMILYE, JOSEPH B. COLLINS, RICHARD L. TAYLOR, PETER COOPER, JOHN HECKER, MINTHORNE TOMPKINS, ISAAC SHERMAN, J. S. SCHULTZ and many other prominent and wealthy citizens of New York city, addressed to him a letter of thanks, promising him their hearty coöperation and support in his efforts to meliorate the condition of the metropolis. A few months later, when in New York city, thousands of such men waited upon him in person, giving high assurance of respect and approbation. The "New York Tribune" referred to this remarkable demonstration as a proper recognition of official worth and integrity, saying, "This hearty welcome sprang from generous and enduring remembrance of the protection afforded to our municipal rights and franchises, in his judicious exercise of the veto power."

His vetoes of various bills which would have deprived the City of New York of valuable franchises, without compensating advantages, proved so acceptable to the Board of Supervisors of New York county, that the following resolution was unanimously adopted:

Resolved, That the thanks of the Board are hereby tendered to His Excellency, Governor FENTON, for his recent vetoes of various bills passed by the Legislature of this State infringing upon the rights and franchises of this city and county, and we sincerely congratulate the people of the State of New York in having an Executive who possesses the vigilance and fearlessness necessary to correct the errors of hasty and imperfect legislation.

Gov. FENTON's State papers are always compact, cogent and convincing. His vigor of style and strength of diction are admirably illustrated in a letter to the committee that invited him to a meeting held at Cooper Institute, in New York city, in the fall of 1866, for the purpose of ratifying the action of the State Union Convention:

STATE OF NEW YORK, EXECUTIVE DEPARTMENT,
ALBANY, October 13, 1866.

GENTLEMEN: I cannot attend the meeting at Cooper Institute on the 15th inst, to which you invite me; my public duties at the capital will prevent.

The questions now agitating the public mind are of the greatest moment and interest; and they are such as could not be presented to any other people. It will not be forgotten that the gigantic war through which we have just passed was prosecuted on behalf of the government in defense of the supremacy of the ballot. The clearly expressed will of the nation is the supreme law of the land. Against an expression of this will, men honored by large communities with public trusts which they were ready to betray for purposes of guilty ambition, stimulated their States to revolt, and by crafty and dangerous devices, inflamed the passions of their people, until in a spirit of frantic and blind delusion they fired upon their own flag, and enveloped the whole land in the flame of war. The common traditions; the national pride; the sacred oath of fealty; these were all forgotten, scouted, or ignored, and under the ill-starred banner of rebellion, organized armies marched to crush out the grand heritage of American freedom, and to reverse by force of arms the constitutional expression of the popular will. Patriotic men sprang from the various walks of labor and industry, from the schools and colleges, the fields and the workshops; fortunes were thrown into the scale; fireside circles were broken, and every household was made familiar with the perils of mutilation, captivity and death, in that common spirit of loyalty and devotion which prompted the fixed resolve, from the hour that Sumter fell, that the Union our fathers had established should stand, and that the rights and liberties of a free people, secured by covenant, should be maintained in blood. These patriot forces trampled out the fires of rebellion; the principle of popular government was vindicated; and the leaders and armies of the conspirators surrendered, as prisoners of war, the weapons with which they sought the destruction of their country.

To the representatives of these communities who thus organized to destroy our liberties, we are urged to commit, *at once and without guarantees*, the authority to legislate for us; to award justice to the soldiers and sailors by whom they were subdued; to determine whether the public debt shall be paid; and to claim undue preponderance of representation in the national councils, and a disproportionate vote in the electoral college, as a reward for a defeated and treasonable attempt to subvert the government.

Places are now claimed in the Senate and House of Representatives for men who foreswore their allegiance to the Constitution, and held office under the usurpation of DAVIS, and his associate conspirators. Such an assumption is against the common sense of the country. It is plain that on the dissolution of the rebel armies there was no lawful local government in any of the insurgent States; nor was there any power in the people of those States to regain the status they lost by organized rebellion. The State action which they now invoke to excuse individuals from the penalties of personal crime, disabled them as communities from resuming, without the consent of the people on whom they made war, a participation in governing them, by claiming the place abdicated for the purposes of treason. Their right of representation as States being thus practically suspended by their own act, what power is competent to reinstate them in their former relations to the government? Evidently it is not in the States themselves, independent of Congressional sanction or recognition. There is no lawful local executive to call an election, and no lawful local government under which such an election can be made. The Federal government is to determine what shall be the terms of restoration. It is a question for the sovereign power, and with us the sovereign is not the President, but the people. Under the Constitution, the will of the people is to be expressed through its representatives in Congress assembled. The simple duty of the President is to execute their will, thus expressed. By interposing his veto, he may compel them to express it by a two-thirds vote; but it is the will of the people, and not his will which is expressed; and it is not by his vote, but by the vote of Congress, that it has the force of a popular law.

With unerring judgment and forecast, the martyred LINCOLN appreciated the question in its true aspect; and in commissioning loyal men, with the simple powers of military governors, he provided for the present peace; while he recognized in the people in Congress assembled the only competent authority to restore permanent civil government in the insurgent States, under the Constitution they had foresworn, and to determine the conditions under which they should be restored to their practical relations in the Union. Such is the common judgment of the loyal States. Such is the clear conviction and the firm demand of the mass of loyal men North and South. It is a question which belongs to the people, and not to the President — to the law-making power, and not to the agent, whose duty it is to enforce the laws and to obey them.

But it is claimed that the adoption of the amendments proposed by Congress ought not to be made a condition of representation; that however just in themselves, no constitutional safeguard should be provided which has not been passed upon in Congress by the insurgent States. The weakness of this position is too obvious to deceive any but those who advance it. The President is, doubtless, competent to proclaim the cessation of hostilities and the return of peace; but Congress alone can guarantee a Republican form of government to States which have subverted their own governments established under the Constitution.

In the discharge of a high public trust, the present Congress has patiently and laboriously investigated the condition of that portion of the country convulsed by the recent rebellion; and, in a commendable spirit of moderation, it has proposed for adoption, an amendment to the Constitution, so reasonable and appropriate to the existing state of affairs, that its propriety and justice are admitted even by those who oppose its adoption. The plan of adjustment thus presented, is the only one before the people. It has the sanction of an overwhelming majority in the Senate and House of Representatives; it has been heartily and earnestly indorsed by the people of every State in which a general election has since been held; it will receive the unanimous approval of all the States, whose unwavering loyalty bore us triumphantly through the war; it is a noble and magnanimous peace-offering tendered by Congress, in behalf of the people, to the misguided States which permitted themselves to be precipitated into rebellion by bold and reckless leaders, some of whom are now demanding instant and unconditional admission to seats in the governing council of the nation.

Very respectfully,

R. E. FENTON.

To Messrs. F. A. CONKLING, FRANCIS A. THOMAS, OWEN W. BRENNAN, JOHN FITCH, CHARLES A. DANA, Committee.

His views upon the pending issues, were afterward ably maintained in a speech delivered at a large political gathering in Jamestown, just prior to the election of 1866. An unerring test of the correctness of his opinions, and the wisdom of his administration, is furnished in the fact that, during the late canvass, his opponents were utterly unable to assail his official record, while his friends effectively employed the same in his behalf.

The Republican party in 1866 saw the necessity of selecting wise men for its nominees. The more discerning politicians felt that there was reason to fear an unfavorable result of the canvass. Herculean efforts were being made to defeat the party at the polls. A division had been created among those who had theretofore professed its principles. A number of influential gentlemen openly repudiated its ideas in regard to reconstruction. The Philadelphia Convention had produced a schism, which it was feared might prove formidable, if not disastrous. Those who were the most pronounced in favor of the policy of President JOHNSON, were the most earnest in their opposition to Governor FENTON. The questions naturally arose whether this marked hostility might not prove fatal to success, by stimulating the Conservatives to greater effort, and enabling them to exert more powerful influence over the moderate and doubtful portion of the party; and whether a man less likely to be thus assailed might not be stronger. On the other hand, there was to be considered the effect which the leading measures of his administration had produced on the popular mind. His National policy had contributed in a marked degree to the success of the war. He had entered upon his term of office as successor to one who disapproved of many of the principal features of the war policy of the Government, and who had been elected because of his decided views in relation thereto. He had stimulated volunteering, and secured for the State a more just recognition of its rights; had worked clear from the complications in which public interest had been involved by the blundering and incompetency of the Provost Marshal General; and had relieved New York from a large portion of the dreaded burden of the draft. He had done much, with the co-operation of the head of the State finance department, to originate a financial system which rendered the credit of the State stable and secure, and furnished the means to supply the demands of war, without being felt as oppressive. By his keen appreciation of the wants of the soldiers, his tender solicitude for their welfare, and his earnest efforts in their behalf, he had firmly attached them to himself. In his State policy, he had sought to foster all the material interests of the commonwealth; and had reluctantly interposed to the defeat of needed enterprises when their aid would render the burden of taxation onerous, and awaited a more favorable opportunity to join in giving them that aid. He was vigilant in his attention to the commercial wants of the State, both in the great metropolis and through its internal lines of transit. This unwavering devotion to the essential prosperity of the State, elicited confidence and commendation. All the discriminating judgment and forecast of the Statesman had been displayed in a marked degree. These views were impressed on the minds of the representative men of his party, and when the Convention assembled, so strongly did they prevail, and so heavily did they outweigh adverse considerations, that no other name was suggested, and he was unanimously nominated by acclamation. The Democrats entered upon the canvass full of hope. Prominent places were given by them on their State ticket, to Republicans who dissented from the principles enunciated by the Republican party, and nominations of a like character were made for many local offices in various portions of the State. The result showed that Governor FENTON's strength had not been miscalculated. He was re-elected by a majority five thousand larger than that given him in his first canvass.

The year 1867 furnished the occasion for a continuation of a policy which had proved so acceptable, and it is not necessary that we should dwell upon its features.

The absence of all malevolence in the heart of Governor Fenton, and the broad charity of his nature, were displayed during the past year. The remains of the Rebel dead had been left unburied at Antietam. A letter from Governor Fenton, breathing the spirit of loyalty and humanity, decided the committee at once to an act both christian and proper, and in accordance with the spirit of the law of Maryland, which authorized the purchase of a cemetery, and created a corporation to carry out the declared object of burying in it, all who fell on either side during the invasion of Lee at the battle of Antietam. In that letter he took the high ground that it "was a war less of sections than of systems," and that the Nation could confer decent burial on the Southern dead while condemning and sternly opposing the heresies for which they had sacrificed themselves; and that attachment to the Union and devotion to the most thorough measures for its preservation and restoration were not inconsistent with the broadest charity, and the observance of sacred obligations to the dead. This letter accomplished the intended purpose; and the bones of the Rebel soldiers who fell on that memorable field, will be interred as befitting not only a legal obligation, but the highest demands of civilization and our common humanity.

In his message to the Legislature of 1868, Governor Fenton forcibly expressed himself in favor of materially reducing the number of items in the tax lists, and of a re-adjustment of the assessment laws—now so glaringly unequal—in order that every source of wealth might bear its just proportion of burden. He also took strong ground in defense of the inviolate maintenance of the National faith. In his usual terse and vigorous style, he argued against the legality of the Governments instituted by President Johnson, after the cessation of active hostilities, and held that the reconstruction acts of Congress were necessary because the Southern States had rejected, with scorn, the peace offering of the Constitutional Amendment. He eloquently expressed himself in behalf of the rights of the Freedmen, in consideration of his manhood and loyalty, to protection through law, and to the elective franchise.

Governor FENTON realizes that the people have made him their Chief Magistrate, and that they look to him, and to no other person, for the faithful discharge of the duties of the responsible position. He is controlled by no clique —he is the agent of no cabal. He patiently listens to all who desire to consult him, and then follows the dictates of his own good judgment. He has no prejudice so strong, nor partiality so great, as to lead him to do an unjust act.. He is a careful thinker and a hard worker. No man ever labored more hours in the Executive Chamber than he does. Whatever work engages his attention, he attends to it personally, even to the minutest details.

Governor FENTON is a decided radical, and yet he cannot be called an extreme man. There is just enough conservatism in his composition to save him from doing an unwise or rash act. His mind is thoroughly practical. He is a man of decided convictions and fearless in their expression, and yet his manner of address and style of composition are so gentle and courteous as to almost disarm opposition. There are few men whose minds are so well balanced as his.

A more upright man does not exist. Make it clear to him that a thing ought to be done, and he will do it, no matter who may advise differently. He has trod on great schemes and powerful lobbies in this State. He has defended public interest against the rapacity of organized theft. He has escaped the charge of connivance with any of these organized rings. He has won the grateful regard of the Republicans of the State. He has not always satisfied place-seekers, but, in the administration of public affairs, the man is yet to be found who charges him with dishonesty or unfaithfulness.

That the feelings of youth survive in his manhood, and that he cherishes a warm sympathy for childhood, is very pleasantly shown in a letter acknowledging a testimonial of membership to the American Sunday School Union, presented by the scholars of a Sabbath School. In his reply to the Superintendent he says:

"Thank the boys for me and tell them I shall place the gift in my study, that I may never forget in the performance of the grave duties to which I am called, that little children are taking note of what I do, sure that if my conduct can be held up in commendation to those of whom Christ says: 'Of such is the kingdom of Heaven,' it will reach the highest standard of earthly merit."

New York, with entire unanimity, presents the name of REUBEN E. FENTON to the Republican National Convention at Chicago, for nomination to the office of Vice-President. She urges him as combining in unequaled measure the qualifications of the candidate and the qualifications of the officer—the popularity which assures success in the canvass, the ability which makes him equal to the office, and the fidelity which guarantees the maintenance of principle. For years the people have watched his public career with constantly increasing confidence and satisfaction. At the National Capitol he was firm, vigilant and prudent. At the State Capitol he has been a trusty and sagacious leader, always the watchful guardian of the people's interest, and always the defender of popular rights. He is strong with the masses of his party. He is like LINCOLN in this regard; and like him, is a man grown from the people. He has risen to office by no tricks. He commands the esteem of his fellow-citizens, of whatever party. He is worthy to preside over the highest branch of Congress, and in that capacity he would prove a sagacious counselor. And, if that fell calamity should happen, which the sad experience of the country has taught us to contemplate as not impossible, his record and his character give the perfect assurance that, with Governor FENTON in the Presidential chair, the interests of the Nation would suffer no detriment, and the will of the people would not be paralyzed.

The Republican State Convention held at Syracuse, February 5, 1868, composed of three hundred and eighty-four delegates, unanimously adopted the following resolution:

Resolved, That REUBEN E. FENTON is the first choice of the Union Republican party in this State for the office of Vice-President. His early and consistent identification with the cause of human freedom, his patriotic services in Congress, the fidelity and sagacity he has displayed in the office of Chief Magistrate of the State, his earnest and uniform devotion to the wants and interests of soldiers, his popularity as attested by being twice elected Governor over strong antagonists, as well as his great prudence and firmness, give assurance that his nomination would inspire universal confidence and enthusiasm, and be followed by the triumphant success of the whole ticket.

More brilliant men may have occupied the executive chair in our State than Governor FENTON, but it has been filled by no more sagacious statesman, and by no more conscientious man, and such will be the verdict of those who shall impartially write a history of the times wherein we live.

STEWART L. WOODFORD,

LIEUTENANT-GOVERNOR.

LIEUTENANT-GOVERNOR WOODFORD is a native of the metropolis of New York, where he was born September 3d, 1835.

His father, JOSIAH C. WOODFORD, was from Hartford county, Connecticut; his mother, SUSAN TERRY, from Suffolk county, Long Island, in this State.

He was a boy of good promise, whose success in life was foreshadowed by his industry and tenacity of purpose as a lad. Before he was fifteen years of age, he entered the Freshman Class of Columbia College, from which he graduated with high honors in 1854, being assigned the English salutatory address. He then turned his attention to the study of law, in the office of BROWN, HALL & VANDERPOEL, at New York, and was admitted to the bar in February, 1857.

As a lawyer, Mr. WOODFORD was popular and successful, and almost immediately took a prominent place among the younger members of his profession.

In the year 1860, he was a delegate to the convention at Chicago, which nominated ABRAHAM LINCOLN for the presidency. On his return, he entered into the canvass with great spirit, and worked unceasingly for the Republican cause. His eloquence was heard from the rostrum, and his energies were felt in private councils in behalf of the great interests which he was willing subsequently to defend in the field. It was his privilege, after that memorable canvass, to convey the vote of the Electoral College of New York, to Washington. Closely following the honor thus conferred upon him, was his election as Chairman of the Young Men's Republican Committee, of the City of New York.

In April, 1861, Mr. WOODFORD was appointed Assistant United States Attorney, for the Southern District of New York. This was an office of importance, requiring a high order of abilities for the proper discharge of its weighty duties; and Mr. WOODFORD filled it in an unexceptionable manner. After the breaking out of the rebellion, the blockade of the Southern ports rendered necessary the creation of a bureau in that office, for the legal prosecution of the vast number of naval captures made by the government. This bureau was placed in charge of Mr. WOODFORD, whose industry, aided by natural talent and keen discrimination, enabled him to successfully present to the court the intricate questions arising for adjudication. He made the opening argument for the Government, in the case of the barque Hiawatha, which was the first of the seizures under the blockade. The line of Mr. WOODFORD's argument was identical with that followed by the Supreme Court of the United States in its final decision upon the question.

In 1862, after the gloomy retreat of McCLELLAN across the Peninsula, a general feeling of the necessity of renewed action and sacrifice, pervaded the hearts of the people. Mr. WOODFORD hastened to obey the common impulse, resigned his lucrative office, and enlisted for the war as a private. He was immediately elected captain of his company, which was assigned to the 127th regiment New York Volunteers, under Col. WILLIAM GURNEY. Before leaving for the front, he was again promoted to a Lieutenant-Colonelcy. About this time, he removed his residence to Brooklyn. The winter of 1862–3 was spent by his regiment in and around Washington, which was then threatened by the rebel forces; but the life of comparative inaction was interrupted by the siege of Suffolk, Va., by General LONGSTREET. Colonel WOODFORD's command was sent to Suffolk, and subsequently to the Peninsula, under General DIX. He afterward served in the 11th Corps, in the Army of the Potomac, and was then transferred to the Department of the South, where he won for himself distinguished military honors.

When General GILMORE began his extensive operations against Charleston, Colonel WOODFORD, with his regiment, took a prominent part in them. In the spring of 1864, he commanded the several forts on Morris Island, which shelled the city of Charleston so destructively. During the Summer of that year, he acted as Judge-Advocate General of the Department of the South, and, in the early autumn was intrusted with the supervision of the exchange of prisoners at Charleston harbor. But staff duty was not congenial to his taste, and as SHERMAN neared the coast, he applied for leave to rejoin his regiment, and participate in the operations undertaken by General FOSTER, against the Charleston and Savannah Railroad. These operations were for the purpose of creating a diversion in SHERMAN's favor, and preventing Savannah being reinforced from Charleston and Richmond. His request was granted, and he was actively engaged in the movements which followed.

At the battles of Honey Hill, Coosawhatchie and Tulafinny, his bravery was conspicuous, and received marked commendation from his superiors. At Honey Hill his shoulder strap was shot off, and he was slightly wounded in the face. At Coosawhatchie he personally led the charge which made our forces masters of the field. At Tulafinny he commanded an advance Brigade, and for his services here was subsequently promoted to a full Colonelcy, and breveted Brigadier-General.

Just before the surrender of LEE, and after active movements had ceased on the coast, Colonel WOODFORD was temporarily appointed Provost Marshal-General of the Southern Department; and, a short time after, was made the first military Governor of Charleston. It was in this city that the rebellion was conceived and born. The populace, at the time of the breaking up of the gigantic cabal, were filled with hatred and disloyalty. The aristocratic Southrons illy submitted to the dictation of a Northern man. Disloyal citizens on the one hand, and rebel deserters and desperadoes on the other, smouldering buildings, half famished and homeless families, the absence of civil law and a chaotic state of society, all conspired to bring into play the highest order of administrative capabilities.

Under the authority of Colonel WOODFORD, these volcanic elements were harmonized, much to the delight of those who had suffered by the reign of terror. By his courteous but iron firmness, he soon convinced even the disloyal that the best course for them was to submit quietly to the authority of the Military Governor, who had been placed over them by an outraged but vindicated government. Order was restored so perfectly at last, that ten thousand colored people, in the celebration of the Emancipation Proclamation, and weeks before the surrender of LEE, marched triumphantly through the principal streets of the city, with the flag of the Republic floating over them, with banners inscribed with mottoes commemorative of the termination of their bondage, and bearing a coffin emblematic of the death and burial of slavery. It is not to be supposed that the citizens relished this demonstration, but the cool decision of Governor WOODFORD awed them into a state of outward submission; and they well knew, that any molestation would have drawn upon themselves summary punishment.

For the remarkable administrative abilities displayed at this important juncture, he was made Chief of Staff, by Major-General GILMORE. While the city of Charleston was under Colonel WOODFORD's command, order prevailed on all sides; the loyalist felt safe in the enjoyment of his privileges, and the secessionist was forced to admit that the colonel manifested tenacity of purpose to administer justice to all. It was while acting in this capacity that he was commissioned Brigadier-General by brevet, for previous meritorious services.

Subsequently, he succeeded the gallant General GROVER in command of the city and district of Savannah, having been assigned to duty by the President, in accordance with his brevet rank. His administration in that city was also a complete success.

Among the distinguishing acts of his course, was the practical assistance which he gave to the negroes in founding their schools and churches. On every hand he saw hundreds of colored people eager to be taught. They were a distinct and peculiar race that had been shut out from educational advantages for many generations; and he determined that every possible avenue should now be opened to them. How successfully he accomplished his purpose, the gratitude of the negroes testified. He provided an equal number of schools for the black and white children of the city; re-established the police force; lighted the streets with gas for the first time in three years, and demonstrated that he was not only bravely just to the blacks, but wise and energetic in his management of all the civil affairs of the important city that had been confided to his control. He created a revenue which not only defrayed all the expenses of the local government, but also left a good balance to his successor, in the military treasury of the city.

General WOODFORD subsequently reassumed the position of Chief of Staff to the Department Commander; and in August, 1865, resigned his commission, and returning to his home in Brooklyn, resumed the practice of the law.

In October of the same year, he was unanimously nominated by the Republican party in New York city as their candidate for Judge of the Court of Common Pleas; but he decided not to change his residence from Brooklyn (to which city he had moved his family soon after he entered the army), and declined the nomination.

In the Autumn of 1866, and after a canvass in which he visited nearly every county in the State, General WOODFORD was elected Lieutenant-Governor of New York by the Union Republican Party, receiving a majority of 15,024 votes. The Democratic Party were confident of the success of their candidate, Mr. PRUYN, but the ballot of the people gave a sweeping verdict in favor of General WOODFORD.

The Lieutenant-Governor combines with an agreeable appearance and pleasing address, the graces and polish of a gentleman. He is a cultivated scholar, and a close and logical lawyer. His eloquence is of the highest order, and his presence before an audience is strangely magnetic, as thousands can testify who have ever heard him from the political rostrum and in the court room.

As a presiding officer he has been remarkably successful. Courteous but decided in his ruling, his clear, ringing voice is as effective to preserve order in the Senate Chamber as it was to lead his men in the charge. In the selection of his committees for the new Senate of 1868 he displayed a far-sighted wisdom that was applauded by the press and the people of the entire State, and his address of welcome to the Senators was a masterpiece of quiet, but effective oratory. We introduce it here as a fair specimen of General WOODFORD's manner and style:

Senators: It becomes my pleasant duty at the opening of our session to bid you welcome. We stand on the threshold of events upon which the welfare alike of our State and Nation largely depends. Although the harvests of last autumn were abundant; although no pestilence has visited our land, and no organized armed resistance to law exists within our borders, still we must all realize that general anxiety and distrust pervades commercial circles, paralyzing business activity and industrial enterprises; and that all our people await the future with solicitude. It is your privilege as well as your duty to do much towards allaying this alarm. You can labor for the restoration of an absolute and actual economy in public expenditures; an economy which shall be seen in the next tax levy, and thus be appreciated by the people. You can largely insist on a rigid accountability of all public servants. You can arrest hasty legislation, prevent the enactment of needless and cumbersome laws, initiate wise and considerate reforms, and resolutely maintain the existing safeguard of public order and personal security. I know that these are threadbare axioms, and seem but idle platitudes; and, yet, unless we make them actual verities in our official action, we shall not only fail in our duty, but the State will suffer harm. Not only are our people apprehensive in regard to our State interest and legislation; but there is much in our national affairs to awaken patriotic solicitude. Partial disorder and an unnatural, deplorable, but still necessary subordination of the civil to the military law, prevail in States lately in rebellion. The restoration of those States to their just and constitutional relations with the Federal Government, and to their normal condition of self-rule, is delayed by an unfortunate collision between the President and Congress. As Senators of New York, you may not be called upon to act directly upon these questions, and yet, should circumstances arise requiring action, we may remember that the voice and influence of this State is always powerful in the councils of our nation.

Lieutenant-Governor Woodford is the youngest man that has ever been President of the Senate of New York, being now but thirty-three years of age.

HOMER A. NELSON,

SECRETARY OF STATE.

HOMER A. NELSON was born in Poughkeepsie on the 31st day of August, 1829. He acquired his education at the District Schools and at the Dutchess County Academy. When not quite sixteen years of age he entered the law office of Messrs. TALLMAN and DEAN, in his native village, as clerk and student; and in that capacity he afterwards pursued his legal studies in the office of the Hon. CHARLES H. RUGGLES, Vice-Chancellor and Circuit Judge of the Second District of New York, and subsequently in the office of Messrs. VARICK and ELDRIDGE.

He was duly admitted to practice as an attorney and Counsellor-at-law in all the courts of the State of New York, after due examination before the General Term of the Supreme Court of the Second Judicial District, on the 7th day of October, 1850; and in December following, opened an office at Poughkeepsie and commenced the practice of his profession.

His fine legal mind and attainments, and his indefatigable industry and perseverance, soon gained for him prominence at the bar of his native county, a county which has ever been noted for the high character, learning and ability of its lawyers. In 1854, enjoying a practice and a degree of success in his profession rarely so early attained, he entered into a co-partnership with his former preceptor, the Hon. GILBERT DEAN, which continued until the appointment of Mr. DEAN as Justice of the Supreme Court.

Politically, he has always been an active member of the Democratic party. In 1855, he was, by a large majority, elected County Judge of Dutchess county, and discharged the duties of that position with such marked ability, and so acceptably to the bar and the public, that, on the expiration of his first term in 1859, he received a unanimous re-nomination by the Democratic party, and was re-elected by a large majority, notwithstanding all the other candidates upon the Democratic ticket were defeated by majorities ranging above nine hundred. While performing the duties of County Judge, he was also engaged in a large and successful practice in the higher courts of the State. In 1857, Rutger's College, of New Jersey, conferred upon him the honorary degree of Master of Arts. In February, 1859, on motion of Hon. THOMAS EWING, of Ohio, he was admitted as Attorney and Counsellor of the United States Supreme Court.

At the breaking out of the rebellion in 1861, he at once took a decided stand in favor of its suppression by the Government, and was active and strenuous in his advocacy of a vigorous prosecution of the war, addressing numerous public meetings held in Poughkeepsie and throughout Dutchess county, on that subject, maintaining that it was the duty of the people, and especially of the Democratic party, to insist on the perpetuity of the Union, and to resist separation to the utmost power of the Government.

In 1862 Judge NELSON was recommended by the War Committee of Dutchess and Columbia counties, to Governor MORGAN, for appointment as Colonel of the 167th Regiment N. Y. Volunteers, then about to be raised. In accordance with this recommendation he was duly commissioned to raise such regiment, and with characteristic energy at once proceeded to the performance of that duty, establishing his head-quarters at Hudson. Besides contributing liberally of his means, he devoted his entire time to the patriotic work, and with untiring zeal canvassed the whole district for the accomplishment of it. When about six hundred volunteers had been raised, his regiment was consolidated with the 159th, by which number it was mustered into the United States service, and Judge NELSON was commissioned as its Colonel.

In November, 1862, he was elected by the Democratic party, representative in Congress from the 12th Congressional District of New York, running handsomely ahead of the State ticket in his district. At the earnest solicitation of his friends, who believed that his services would be of more value at that crisis in the halls of legislation than in the field, he was induced to resign his commission as Colonel, in order that he might take his seat in the House of Representatives, which he did in December, 1863. He also resigned the position of County Judge, which he then held. In Congress, he served on the Committee on Indian Affairs and the Committee on Unfinished Business.

During his entire Congressional term he warmly advocated and supported all measures for the vigorous prosecution of the war for the suppression of the rebellion. Shortly after the opening of the Second Session of the 38th Congress, he openly announced his intention to vote in favor of the adoption of the Constitutional Amendment for the abolition of Slavery. The adoption of this great measure, which gave liberty to millions, without undue assumption, may be considered entirely due to the vote and personal efforts of Mr. NELSON. The Republican party was united and earnest in its support, and the Democratic party presented an almost unbroken front in opposition; but Mr. NELSON, with a wise foresight, just appreciation, and commendable independence, resolutely refused to act with his party, and by his personal influence induced others to unite with him in giving the measure their support; and had it not been for the vital aid thus rendered, the requisite vote would not have been obtained.

In the Fall of 1865 Judge NELSON was unanimously re-nominated for Congress, but the District having become overwhelmingly Republican, he failed of re-election.

At the close of his term in Congress, Judge NELSON returned to the practice of his profession in his native place, (declining an important appointment tendered him by the administration of President LINCOLN) and by unremitting attention and devotion to it, attained the acknowledged leadership of the Bar of Dutchess County, as a glance at the court calendar of that county at once shows.

Prior to the election of Delegates to the State Constitutional Convention in the Spring of 1867, Judge NELSON's name was prominently canvassed before the people, and he was nominated as one of the Delegates at Large by the Democratic State Convention.

In that body he served upon one of its most important committees—Finance—and in the discussion of the great questions coming before it he took a conspicuous part, bringing to the consideration of the important subjects submitted to it, an ability and attainments which placed him in the front rank of its distinguished members.

Without any previous canvass on his part, but solely on his merits and owing to his popularity as a representative man of the young Democracy, he was, at the Democratic State Convention in September, 1867, nominated on the first ballot for Secretary of State.

The verdict of the State Convention was ratified by the people on the 5th day of November, 1867—Judge NELSON handsomely leading the State ticket and receiving 373,029 votes, the highest number ever cast for any individual in the Empire State.

Affable and pleasing in his address, unpretentious and unostentatious in his demeanor, yet with a quiet dignity and force of character that never fail to win him the place his merits claim, Judge NELSON is generally and deservedly popular. The important trusts which have been committed to his charge, and the eminent position which he now occupies so early in life, furnish another instance of the successful self-made man which is the glory of our republican institutions.

WILLIAM F. ALLEN,

COMPTROLLER.

The present Comptroller, Judge WILLIAM F. ALLEN, was born in Windham county, Connecticut. In 1816, he came with his father and family to reside in Duanesburgh, Schenectady county, in this State, where he passed his younger years. His preparatory studies for college were mostly pursued under private tutors, and he entered Union College two years in advance, in 1825, and graduated two years later, standing high in the honors of his class.

After graduating, he entered the office, as a student of law, of the late Comptroller, the Hon. JOHN C. WRIGHT, of Schenectady, where he spent some time, but finally finished his clerkship in the office of the late CHARLES' M. LEE, of Rochester, one of the most prominent and able lawyers of Western New York, and was admitted to practice in 1829.

Mr. ALLEN went to Oswego to practice his profession in 1830, at first entering into partnership with the late GEO. FISHER, who was then contesting a seat in the House of Representatives. Soon after Mr. ALLEN entered into a law partnership with Hon. A. P. GRANT, then and still of Oswego; and up to the time when he was elected a Justice of the Supreme Court, and of course had to surrender his legal practice, the firm of GRANT & ALLEN was known as one of the most enterprising, able and successful law firms in northern New York.

Mr. ALLEN's success in his profession, together with his sociable and amiable qualities, made him very popular with his party and the public, and he was early looked upon as a very promising young man. Any office within the gift of those by whom he was surrounded, might have been his on his acceptance, but he steadily refused all places, however honorable, calculated to lure him from the pursuit of his profession, or which might be an obstacle to his elevation therein. Under the Constitution of 1821, he was, early in his professional career, appointed to the offices of Master and Examiner in Chancery. In 1842, he accepted the Democratic nomination for Member of Assembly, and was elected. He was awarded the important position of Chairman of Committee of Ways and Means in 1843, a rare compliment to a new member in a body composed of very able men. In 1844, he was re-elected and made Chairman of the Judiciary Committee, a position which his legal acquirements enabled him to fill with great credit.

Something of the rank Mr. ALLEN held during his brief career as a legislator may be estimated from the position he was awarded in an Assembly in which seats were held by such men as MICHAEL HOFFMAN, SAMUEL YOUNG, CLARK B. COCHRANE, HORATIO SEYMOUR, THOS. G. ALVORD and CALVIN T. HULBURD, names then and since prominent among the most distinguished men of New York.

In 1845 Mr. ALLEN was appointed by President POLK United States District Attorney for the Northern District of the State of New York, the duties of which position he continued to discharge until after the adoption of the State Constitution of 1846, when he was elected, for a term of eight years, one of the first Justices of the Supreme Court for the Fifth Judicial District of the State, his associates upon the bench being Hon. CHARLES GRAY, of Herkimer; Hon. DANIEL PRATT, of Syracuse, and Hon. PHILO GRIDLEY, of Utica.

It is as a Judge that Mr. ALLEN is best known, and upon the Bench that he has won the most honorable distinction. It was with much hesitation that the members of the Convention of 1846 created an elective judiciary, but the wisdom of that provision was fully vindicated in the elevation of such men as Judge ALLEN to the Bench. His impartial administration, searching investigations, and convincing decisions, established him to such a remarkable degree in public estimation, that, at the expiration of his first term of eight years, he was, regardless of political considerations, unanimously recommended by the Bar of his District for re-election, and his political opponents, in a district where they had the majority, paid him the extraordinary compliment of a unanimous election. As the first had been, so was the second term of Judge ALLEN, eight years of successful labor. During the last year of each term he, by provision of the Constitution, occupied a seat in the Court of Appeals. There, as elsewhere, he was distinguished for his legal acumen, his discrimination, learning and ability. For sixteen years he was generally acknowledged to be among the ablest, most successful and popular jurists of the State.

On retiring from the Bench, Judge ALLEN went to New York city, where he resumed the labors of his profession. His reputation immediately gave him all the practice that it was possible for him to attend to, and he was entrusted with the management of the most important causes.

Judge ALLEN'S popularity in his own district, and his standing in his party in the State, have made him a marked man. Often has his party made attempts to lure him from his profession. At one time his party in his own Congressional district nominated him for Congress, but he promptly and peremptorily declined. Quite frequently has his name been prominently suggested for the exalted position of Governor of the State.

In 1864, he was appointed by the Secretary of War one of a commission to adjust the matter of credits for recruits due to this State, a matter which had become involved in seemingly inextricable confusion. His associates in this commission were Hon. CHAUNCEY SMITH of Massachusetts, and Hon. JOHN LOVE of Indiana. The duty was discharged in a manner which called expressions of thanks and gratitude from all classes of people in the State.

During the summmer of 1867, Judge ALLEN again removed his residence to Oswego, where he was residing when his party nominated him for the important and responsible office to which he was elected in November last. That a large pecuniary sacrifice was involved in his acceptance of the position no one can doubt. But he surrendered his individual wishes and interests to the judgment of his political friends. His department is one of the most important in the political economy of the State. That the same success and fidelity to the public interests will distinguish him in that position which has through life characterized his public career, no one who knows him can doubt.

In private life Judge ALLEN is genial, friendly and popular. He has been an unwavering, life-long Democrat. He has been for many years a prominent and consistent member of the Presbyterian Church of his own city, and in all the relations of society he sustains the reputation and the character of a consistent Christian and a good citizen.

MARSHALL B. CHAMPLAIN,

ATTORNEY-GENERAL.

MARSHALL BOLDS CHAMPLAIN, Attorney-General of the State, is a direct descendant from the discoverer of Lake Champlain, and is therefore, on his father's side, of French extraction. His mother's family were originally from Ireland. He unites in himself the ease and affability of the former nation with the fervency and ardor of the latter race. His father, GILBERT B. CHAMPLAIN, was a successful physician, who served as a hospital surgeon during the war of 1812, and subsequently, for thirty years, enjoyed an extensive practice in the western part of the State. He was a man of great energy of character, and brilliant and cultivated mind. He died in 1852.

Mr. CHAMPLAIN was born in Stafford, Genesee county, December 22, 1824. In his early years the family removed to Cuba, Allegany county, where he has since continued to reside. His education was confined, so far as scholastic instruction was concerned, to the common schools, except when, for a short period, he attended the Middlebury Academy, in Wyoming county. But what young CHAMPLAIN lacked in the advantages afforded by academies and colleges, he made up by that without which even those aids are useless—a determination to acquire knowledge, and untiring assiduity in its pursuit. His father could not aid him pecuniarily, and he received no help from friends. But the obstacles of poverty were nothing to his will, and the fountain of knowledge could not remain unreached by him.

The young student read law with JAMES A. GUERNSEY, of Pittsford, Monroe County, and Hon. A. S. DIVEN, of Angelica, and at the early age of eighteen was gratified by being admitted to the Bar, and was soon rewarded by a good practice, which rapidly extended throughout Allegany and the adjoining counties. The youthful practitioner was not long in attracting the attention of the leading men in his section, and in January, 1845, he was appointed by the Allegany Court of Common Pleas to the position of District Attorney of the county. He was admitted a Counsellor of the Supreme Court, "*ex gratia*," to enable him to accept the office, which he filled four years. While he held that position, he was of course brought more prominently to the attention of the public. His personal appearance and manner were calculated to impress a jury as but few criminal pleaders are able to do. Of medium height and erect carriage, piercing eye, dark hair, and dark olive complexion, with a countenance expressing intelligence and confidence, when he arose for a forensic effort, not even his youth could prevent a stranger from expecting a superior display of oratorical ability and legal acumen. And no disappointment followed. His voice swelled full and clear, his statements of fact were concentrated, earnest and plain, and as he warmed with his subject, he would become impressive and fervent, playing upon the sympathies and passions of listeners with a master's hand. At the end of four years he retired from the office of District Attorney to the prosecution of an extensive and remunerative practice.

Such marked talents necessarily commended their possessor for political preferment. In 1851, he was prevailed upon to accept a nomination for State Senator. The district was strongly Whig, by a usual majority of 1,500. The previous candidate was JAMES R. DOOLITTLE, now United States Senator from Wisconsin. His opponent was General JOHN A. McELWAIN, of Wyoming county, who was elected by a majority of only 232 votes. Mr. CHAMPLAIN'S popularity having been thus attested, he was nominated the following year for Member of Assembly for Allegany county, and was elected by a large majority. He was the last Democratic member chosen from that county.

The Assembly of 1853 was one of the most important, in the business that came before it, of any that has ever convened. In it, Mr. CHAMPLAIN attained a brilliant reputation. His perceptions were quick and strong; his mind clear and discriminating; his judgment sagacious and prudent; his reasoning logical and convincing. Besides, he soon acquired an intimate knowledge of parliamentary law, and was from the first a ready as well as an able debater. A newspaper of that day of opposing politics, said of him: "He is a young man of much promise and, "unless we much mistake, will yet distinguish himself "among the public men of the State." He was a member of the Canal Committee, and made a vigorous speech in defence of the canal policy of HORATIO SEYMOUR, then Governor of the State. The occasion of his first participation, in any marked manner, in the proceedings of the House, was an interesting one. On the discussion of some finaucial resolutions the excitement ran high, and one member refused to vote when his name was called. The Speaker, Hon. WILLIAM H. LUDLOW, at once ordered him under arrest. General BURROUGHS, of Orleans, who led the opposition, thought to avail himself of the occurrence to intensify the feeling, widen a breach in the majority, and compel the Speaker to resign. At the opening of the session the next morning, he offered as a privileged question, a resolution of censure, declariug the act of the Speaker an exercise of arbitrary power, unwarranted by the laws and Constitution of the State, and supported the resolution in a speech of great force. Mr. CHAMPLAIN responded in defence of the Speaker. It was off-hand, but clear and irresistible in its exposition of parliamentary law. Before his speech, it seemed that the combination of factions, supported by the able effort of Mr. BURROUGHS, would be successful, but Mr. CHAMPLAIN turned the tide, and the Speaker was sustained by an almost unanimous vote.

No more significant evidence of the estimation in which Mr. CHAMPLAIN was held can be given than the position assigned him in the corruption and impeachment proceedings of the session. He was Chairman of the Select Committee ordered to inquire into the conduct of the State officers, and submitted a report which resulted in a resolution impeaching Canal Commissioner JOHN C. MATHER. His speech in support of his resolution exhibited great research, eloquence and power. We make short extracts, showing at once what he regarded as the hope and danger of our institutions. Would that its admonitions might be more generally heeded! He said:

"New York has a mission to perform. It is to advance this Republic to the highest position of national glory, or to sink it to the lowest depths of national degradation. New York shall mould the destiny of this empire. Her morals, her policy, her public order, and her justice and liberty shall impress and give direction to the American Republic.

"Sir, I have nearly done. I do not demand the condemnation of JOHN C. MATHER—I have no right to demand it—you have no power to grant it. Were I his enemy, which I am not, were all the hate, personal or political, rankling in any human bosom against him, concentrated in my own; and did I stand upon this floor to gratify that hate, and blast his earthly hopes, I would not dare to demand more than his trial—a fair, impartial trial. I do not know that he has an enemy in the world—whatever of party hate and party asperity may exist elsewhere, I implore you to let it not enter these halls. We have a consolation in the reflection that if we adopt this resolution, we shall commit his case to a tribunal high above such unhallowed influences. While on the one hand we throw around the case of the accused a generous and noble sympathy—while we guard with vigilance private right and personal liberty, we must remember that we have no tears to weep over buried hopes; that we cannot twine myrtle to decorate the funeral car of a declining political reputation—that we cannot lay in a common grave the sacred trust committed to our hands by the laws and Constitution of our country. But seventy-seven years have gone down the rapid tide of time since

'The bounding isles of the dim woods rang with anthems of the free.'

"Have we proved the duration of our system of free government. Need I refer you to the republics of the Old World. We are familiar with their fabled history, we have read of their splendors, their glories, their trophies, their temples, their triumphal arches, the free spirit of liberty that pervaded them, their decline and their ruin. How they crumbled and passed away in the melancholy drama of destruction. One startling truth has been recorded o'er the ruin upon the sacred cenotaph of time. History tells us that 'all the illusions of ambition realized, all the wealth of a universal commerce, all the achievements of successful heroism, or all the establishments of this world's wisdom, cannot secure to empire the permanency of its possession.' * * * *

"If property is invaded, if laws are violated, if personal liberty is compromised—the people appeal with a firm confidence to the Courts—the judicial tribunals of the land. If the judgment seat becomes corrupted, its ermine sullied, they appeal to the Assembly. If public officers are guilty of a dereliction of official duty, if public laws are disobeyed and the public weal neglected, they come with strong reliance upon the purity, the firmness of the People's Assembly. There is no other tribunal to which they can appeal. Here in the jury box of the grand inquest of the commonwealth, their dearest hopes are centered. Here shall be the last great struggle between that confiding people and the destroyer—the corrupting moneyed power, which is filing off the iron bars of your Constitution. Here is the palladium of their liberties. Here that liberty if ever subverted, shall be cloven down."

The resolution of impeachment was adopted by more than a two-third vote.

Mr. CHAMPLAIN was selected by the Assembly as one of its Managers, to conduct the trial before the High Court of Impeachment. JOHN K. PORTER was selected as counsel for the Managers. They were opposed by Hon. RUFUS W. PECKHAM, Hon. JAMES T. BRADY and Hon. JOHN H. REYNOLDS, who appeared as counsel for the accused. Mr. CHAMPLAIN took an important part in the debate. His argument in regard to the general law governing impeachment cases is so cogent and able that we make liberal extracts from it. Events which have recently excited the country, impart to his remarks fresh interest. He said:

"All power is inherent in the people. They have granted to their immediate representatives, the Assembly, the right of impeachment. This branch of government is nearest to them, and reflects their wants, and will the more vigilantly guard their rights. It is a power *to accuse;* to say what acts in a public officer are sufficient in turpitude to demand his removal from office; what acts disgrace the official and dishonor the State. The Constitution gives this tribunal simply the power to try the fact and pronounce the judgment. If you have jurisdiction of the officer, then the duty is solemnly enjoined to try the accusation preferred, and if proven to be true in point of fact, to declare the judgment.

"The Constitution does not vest the power to impeach or accuse conjointly in the Assembly and the Court. It is exclusive with the Assembly. If the Court may revise and modify the articles of impeachment, or strike out accusations, what is it but a reversal of the action of the Assembly, and an exercise of the function of impeachment? We claim it would be a usurpation of a constitutional prerogative of the Assembly and an invasion of the solemn rights of the people. No Court can despoil the popular branch of the Legislature of this power. Judicial opinion, the waves of partizan prejudice, or passion, may beat upon it in vain, but they cannot subvert it. It is founded in the Constitution itself, and upheld by the spirit and power of a free-born people. As a precedent, such an adjudication is full of danger. Suppose that the People by their verdict, which would be the judgment of the highest tribunal in the world, should reassert this prerogative; that, rising in their primitive power and energy, they should affirm that the right of impeachment is vested alone by the Constitution in the Assembly, acting through their immediate representatives, they place the promulgation of that constitutional right in the solemn form of an impeachment against the judges who have invaded it! This tribunal could again usurp a jurisdiction they do not possess; again invade the prerogatives of the House; again mutilate the record of accusation; again strike out the articles that impugned them, declare their own immunity and beat down in the dust the constitutional power of the People and their Assembly; and thus the order and harmony of the government would be subverted. The great bulwark of the people, reared against vice and corruption in the government, would be annihilated, and a revolution only could apply the remedy.

"Sir, standing here in the highest tribunal of the commonwealth, whose humble agent I am, the dictates of a high duty compels me most solemnly to protest against the exercise of this power. Its usurpation now and in this case, may not fix the public attention or arouse the public fears. The event may pass from the public mind like the fleeting clouds upon the horizon, but a conviction weighs upon me that the time shall come, and come as swiftly as the engendering corruptions of the age can bring it, when this sacred principle of constitutional right in the Assemby will be vindicated by the recuperative power of the people. The fair fabric of civil government may totter to the fall. The absence of public virtue in government officials may enshroud all in gloom. The darkness of political decay and ruin may o'ershadow the land. But this great principle regenerated, breaking forth like the bright effulgence of morning, shall dispel the darkness, and give back to the People's Assembly the high prerogative of which they had been despoiled, and restore to a violated Constitution its departed splendor.

"This brings me to the examination of the question raised by the counsel, whether an act to be impeachable, must be an indictable offense. We shall maintain, that by the Common Law, to which the counsel has appealed, by the usage of Parliament, by all the authorities upon this subject, it is not necessary *that an act in order to be impeachable, should be indictable as a crime at Common Law, or by any Statute.* We can follow the counsel in his argument, until he refers to the Common Law, to define impeachable acts, and then we choose to refer to one branch of that Law, and he to another. He goes to the provisions of the Common Law, which define indictable crimes—felonies and misdemeanors as such. We prefer to go to that portion *which defines what shall constitute impeachable crimes and misdemeanors;* and we claim that the Common Law of impeachments, the usage of Parliament, clearly establishes, from the very nature of the proceeding, that the act for which an impeachment may be instituted, need not consist of an *indictable crime.*"

Citations of several cases follow.

"It will be perceived that these cases fully establish the doctrine that an impeachment may be preferred for a usurpation of power, for an excess of jurisdiction, and as Mr. Justice STORY says, for neglects or malversations in office. What those neglects or malversations *shall be is not defined,* and I think the counsel will no where find by the authority of any tribunal that the precise class of acts of official misconduct, which are impeachable, have been specified. They cannot be laid down, for the reason that it is a matter which cannot be exactly defined. It may vary with the varying interests of the community, or the changing policy of government. The right is reserved to the impeaching body to judge for what sort of misconduct or for what magnitude of misconduct an impeachment may be preferred. When the policy of a government becomes fixed, whatever is opposed to that policy, whatever acts in a public office, conflict with and affect adversely the public weal, those acts become impeachable. The officer is bound to support the laws, the policy, the prosperity, and the honor of the government he represents. When he neglects this, or acts in direct conflict with them, then he forfeits his trust, he violates the compact under which he accepted the franchise, and becomes liable to be removed by impeachment."

"The theory of this motion is not only that the official who is upon trial, has usurped an important prerogative, not only that he has been guilty of a gross excess of official power, but that the dark outline of his acts has been filled up by corruption—foul corruption. This is conceded by the motion; and it at the same time asserts that he is not liable to trial or removal, We charge him, in the first five articles, with having awarded contracts for $6,000,000 of work. His counsel come before this tribunal and say, this was a usurpation of power; he had no right to do it. They strike from around him all semblance of law, all semblance of official authority. They concede, that in the usurpation of that power, and in its exercise, he disgraced his office and was guilty of corruption. And yet, the startling and monstrous doctrine is advanced, that the State is powerless to dissolve its connection with this delinquent. Mr. Justice STORY says that it is the purpose of an impeachment to withdraw from the hands of an official a trust that he has betrayed. It is the purpose of an impeachment to take back from an officer, an office that the people have conferred upon him, when, by any act in the exercise of that office, usurped or not, assumed or not, indictable or not, he has shown himself unworthy longer to hold it. Why, sir, it seems to me that if this doctrine is to be maintained, disgrace and infamy, long and lasting, may be inflicted upon the fair escutcheon of a State or Nation, with no power in the government of either, to rid itself of the unworthy official. Shall it be said that a conspiracy, a corruption, under even an assumed power, is not a disgrace to the officer? Shall it be said that it is not official misconduct? Shall it be said that it is not dishonorable? It is dishonorable to all to whom honor is dear. Shall it be said that an officer may not show himself, by the manner in which he executes an unconstitutional law, entirely unfit to execute a valid law? Why, sir, crime in the conduct of high officials, has but to be ingenious and studiously avoid the inhibitions of criminal law, by steering clear of an indictment, and according to this doctrine the State would be utterly powerless to discharge from her temples the unworthy official, or dissolve her connection with him. It is not enough that the commonwealth has suffered a deep pecuniary injury. It is not enough that a dark cloud has been thrown athwart the pathway of her advancement in public glory. It is not enough that the generous sensibilities of her citizens have been deeply wounded by her dishonor. But you are called upon, solemnly to declare that she cannot divorce herself from the unworthy agent who has betrayed her; that she must, although struggling to avert the catastrophe, become an accomplice in the crime, by continuing the official character of the criminal."

The Court denied the motion against which the argument of Mr. CHAMPLAIN had been directed.

Mr. CHAMPLAIN's coolness and skill on the floor, with his superior abilities, secured for him the acknowledged position of leader of his party in the House. It was during this session that dissensions began in the Democratic party. The inaugural address of President PIERCE was the occasion for a development of this division. Resolutions indorsing the Inaugural were introduced, but they were deemed too faltering and cold by others, and additional resolutions more full and hearty were offered. These were sustained by Mr. CHAMPLAIN in an eloquent impromptu speech, which was copied by the leading Democratic papers of the country, and elicited the warmest encomiums from the friends of the President.

Mr. CHAMPLAIN has always been a consistent Democrat. His first participation in politics was in 1844, when he took the stump for JAMES K. POLK, as he also did in 1848 for LEWIS CASS. He has supported every Democratic candidate for the Presidency since that time. He was admitted to the Supreme Court of the United States in 1858, on motion of Mr. BLACK. He was a delegate to the Charleston Convention in 1860, supported DOUGLAS, and was chosen to present the claims of the New York delegates.

In 1861, upon the withdrawal of Hon. LYMAN TREMAINE as candidate for Attorney-General, Mr. CHAMPLAIN was substituted. In July, 1862, Governor MORGAN appointed him a member of the War Committee of his Congressional District, and in conjunction with Hon. MARTIN GROVER and Hon. WILKES ANGEL, the duty was well and faithfully performed. He was again nominated for Attorney-General in 1863. In 1864, he was a delegate to the Chicago Convention, favoring the nomination of Gen. McCLELLAN. In April, 1867, he was elected a Delegate at Large to the Constitutional Convention of this State, where his participation in the debates exhibited the same finish, clearness and power which has always characterized his efforts. His speeches upon the Rights of Naturalized Citizens, Suffrage, National Banks and in Defense of Personal Liberty, attracted wide attention for their forcible declaration of his sentiments on those subjects. That upon "Personal Liberty" has been extensively published in Democratic papers from Maine to California. He was elected Attorney-General in the fall of 1867. His popularity in his own section of the State was attested by the fact that in the town in which he resides he ran 150 ahead of his ticket; in the county about five hundred, and largely also in the adjoining counties.

Fearless, able, firm and upright in public life, Mr. CHAMPLAIN is also honored in private life. As a neighbor and citizen, he is honored; his social qualities render him a favorite in society, and his kindliness of heart, manifested in practical deeds of love, have attached him to the more humble.

WHEELER H. BRISTOL,

STATE TREASURER.

Mr. BRISTOL was born in Canaan, Columbia County, New York, January 16, 1818. He had none of the advantages of education except such as were derived from the common schools of the country. During his boyhood he devoted his time to agricultural pursuits. At the age of eighteen he left home and became engaged with an engineering party upon the construction of the Utica and Schenectady railroad. Upon the completion of that work he went to Ohio and was engaged in various kinds of business until 1847, when he became engaged upon the construction of the New York and Erie railroad, where he remained until 1854, when he was appointed Assistant Superintendent of the Ohio and Mississippi railroad at Cincinnati, and continued upon that road until 1857, when he became one of the firm known as the McCallum Bridge Company in Cincinnati, and has continued as such during the past ten years, spending most of his time in the construction of bridges in the Western and Southern States. In 1863 and 1864, he was engaged in re-building bridges for the Government, which had been destroyed by the confederate army to impede the progress of our soldiers. Among the prominent bridges re-constructed were the bridges at Bridgeport, Alabama, and London, Tennessee, and many others in the same States. In 1853, he was appointed by Governor SEYMOUR to fill the vacancy in the office of State Engineer, caused by the resignation of W. J. MCALPINE, but business arrangements compelled him to decline the appointment. He was nominated upon the

Democratic ticket in 1853, for State Engineer but the election resulted in the success of JOHN T. CLARK, the Whig candidate. The Democrats of Tioga county nominated him for Member of Assembly in 1863 and 1864, and although defeated in both elections, he ran largely ahead of his ticket, reducing the usual majority of 1,200 to about 350. He has held the office of Supervisor of the town of Tioga for the past two years, and was the only Democratic Supervisor in the county.

Mr. BRISTOL has always acted with the Democratic party. He gave liberally towards the support of the Government during the war, and sustained the Administration in its efforts to maintain the Union. He has always been steadfast and firm in his devotion to the Constitution, and opposed to every infringement of this heritage of the Nation. Possessed of ample means, mainly the result of his own remarkable energy, his liberal hand is ever open to the poor, and ready to help forward the enterprise of his neighbors. Whatever is of public interest finds in him ready coöperation. Though largely engaged in business, both in Cincinnati and Owego, at which latter place he has extensive iron works, he yet finds time to take an active part in all matters of local interest, political and social. He is a vestryman in his parish church, and gives to it a sincere interest and most liberal support, though not a communicant. The beauty of his residence at Glen Mary, near Owego, the former home of N. P. WILLIS, and named by him, is not more attractive than the hearty hospitality that generously awaits those who visit it. His character is read in his fine frank face, as a man who despises sham. He is outspoken and fearless, never courting popularity, and in consequence possessed of the more. He is untiring in energy, and courageous in what he believes to be his duty. Of the high estimate in which his character is held as a citizen and man by those who know him best, no stronger assurance could be given than the vote of his county, which is strongly Republican, where he ran largely ahead of his ticket in the late canvass.

He was elected Treasurer of the State of New York in November, 1867, on the Democratic ticket, by a majority of 48,000. His known integrity is a guarantee that he will discharge his duties faithfully and honestly.

VAN RENSSELAER RICHMOND,

STATE ENGINEER AND SURVEYOR.

VAN R. RICHMOND is a life-long engineer. He is thoroughly conversant with all the duties of that position on the canals. He was born in Preston, Chenango County, in January, 1812, being the eldest son of OLIVER RICHMOND. His father was a farmer, who died in 1853, at an advanced age. The son was educated at the Academy in Oxford, Chenango County, receiving a first rate practical business education.

Mr. RICHMOND, on attaining his majority, became engaged upon the Chenango canal, then in process of construction, and received from the State the appointment of Chairman in the engineering force. He remained on this canal, gradually rising in point of rank, until 1837, when he was appointed Resident Engineer on the Erie canal, and took up his residence in Lyons. In 1842, he was placed in charge of the entire Middle Division, under JONAS EARLL and DANIEL P. BISSELL as Canal Commissioners. He held this position until 1848, when he resigned, in order to accept an appointment on the Oswego Railroad.

About this time, the Canal Board decided to run a line for the enlarged canal from Jordan to the Cayuga Marshes. This work, including the aqueduct across the Seneca river, will be recognized as one of the most important along the entire canal. The Board, appreciating the necessity of having the most accomplished engineer to design the construction, after canvassing the merits of every man in their employ, and, in fact, of all the leading engineers of the State, selected Mr. RICHMOND as the man to whom the trust could be most safely confided. The value of this choice will be the more readily understood, when we state that the Board was Whig in politics, while Mr. R. had never been anything else than a Democrat. He accepted an appointment so flattering, perfected his plans, including the aqueduct, submitted them and they were approved. They still remain, the most telling evidences of the skill, capacity and genius of their designer. Having satisfactorily arranged the plan, Mr. R. resigned in 1850.

He was at once tendered, and accepted, the office of Division Engineer of the Syracuse and Rochester direct railroad, which he held until 1852, when he was again appointed Division Engineer of the Middle Division of the Canals. A Whig Canal Board was again elected in the Fall of 1853, the Hon. JOHN T. CLARK being chosen State Engineer. Very persistent efforts were made to secure the removal of Mr. RICHMOND, but Mr. CLARK turned away the most powerful influences, deciding to retain his services, a fact than which none could bear stronger testimonial to his personal fitness and worth. The American party assumed control of the Canal Board in 1856, and at once removed Mr. R., for the only time in his life. He thereupon retired to his home in Lyons, where he resided until January, 1858, when, in obedience to the voice of the people, as expressed in the election of the preceding Fall, he entered upon the discharge of the duties of the office of State Engineer and Surveyor. He acquitted himself to the entire satisfaction of the business public during the two years of his term, retiring with honor and additional credit. He was again elected in 1867. He is of course rendering entire satisfaction to the public in the method of his administration.

Of Mr. RICHMOND's superior abilities as an engineer we need not speak. The tributes to his capacities which we have recorded are a sufficient attestation. He is also industrious, upright, faithful and energetic. He is of a tall and slender form, but is nevertheless capable of much physical endurance. His complexion is fair, hair light, eyes light blue. In short, he is an athlete, in mind and body.

PATRICK H. JONES,

CLERK OF THE COURT OF APPEALS.

Mr. JONES is a gentleman of slight proportions, but plainly possessing powers of great endurance. He has a mild, calculating eye, a pleasant face, and a courteous, modest mien. He was born in the county of Westmeath, Ireland, November 20th, 1830. At the age of seven he was sent to a grammar school in the city of Dublin, where he remained for three years; and, in 1840, at the age of ten, he came to this country with his parents, who settled on a farm in the county of Cattaraugus, New York. He was sent by his parents to the Union School at Ellicottville, then presided over by Professor LOWELL, of Middlebury College, Vermont, where he was well grounded in the common branches of school studies. In 1850, being then twenty years of age, he became connected with a leading journal of this State, and traveled through the Western States as its correspondent. He subsequently became the local editor of the "Buffalo Republic," and one of the editors of the "Buffalo Sentinel."

The pursuits of a journalist do not appear to have been congenial to the tastes of Mr. JONES, for, in 1853, he began the study of law in the office of Hon. ADDISON G. RICE, at Ellicottville, New York. Three years afterward, Mr. JONES was admitted to the bar, and commenced the practice of law in partnership with Mr. RICE; he continued this partnership until the outbreak of the Rebellion, when, like so many of his profession, he left the desk of a lawyer to enter the army, in which he was destined to rise to distinction. Much of the interest of this sketch, of course, centers in his military career. It was his bravery which brought him so early into prominence, and secured his elevation by the voice of the people to high official position, as a spontaneous testimonial of approbation and thankfulness for services rendered to his country.

He entered the service in 1861, as Second Lieutenant in the 37th Regiment, New York Volunteers, commanded by Colonel J. H. McCunn, now one of the judges of the Superior Court of New York city. His regiment was attached to the army of General McClellan, and Lieutenant Jones served throughout the whole Campaign of the Peninsula, and was present at the battles of Williamsburgh, Fair Oaks, and the battles of the celebrated retreat to Harrison's Landing. For gallant conduct during this campaign, Lieutenant Jones was successively promoted Adjutant and Major of his regiment, before the close of the Peninsular campaign. That the services of Lieutenant Jones' regiment, during these battles, were important, and the fighting severe, will appear from the fact that it formed a part of the command of the gallant Kearney, who fell at Chantilly. Major Jones was commissioned Colonel of the 154th Regiment, New York Volunteers, in October, 1862. This regiment was raised in the counties of Cattaraugus and Chautauqua. Upon its arrival at Washington, Colonel Jones assumed command of it, having just left his old regiment, the 37th, in which he had so gallantly earned his promotion. He soon afterward reported to General Sigel, whose command at that time formed a part of the Army of the Potomac. Upon the retirement of General Burnside in the new organization of the army, Colonel Jones' regiment was a portion of the command of General O. O. Howard, under whom he fought at Chancellorsville, where he fell severely wounded, fighting amidst the rout of his corps. He fell into the enemy's hands during the battle, but was soon after exchanged. In the meantime, and while he was recovering from his wounds, General HOWARD's corps, the 11th, and SLOCUM's, the 12th, were ordered to the west under HOOKER, to relieve the starving army of THOMAS at Chattanooga, recently driven by BRAGG from the field of Chickamauga. Colonel JONES rejoined his regiment the day before the battle of Chattanooga, having hastened thither as soon as the nature of his wounds would admit, and thus had the honor of being present at that great battle which effectually turned the tide of rebel victory in the west, and plucked from BRAGG the laurels won at Chickamauga. Soon after the corps of HOWARD and SLOCUM were consolidated by order of General GRANT, and formed thenceforth the 20th corps under General HOOKER. In the new organization, Colonel JONES was assigned with his regiment to the division of General J. W. GEARY (present Governor of Pennsylvania), a sagacious and skillful officer. He commanded a brigade under General GEARY during the terrible and glorious campaign of Atlanta, and in the great march of SHERMAN to the Atlantic; and entered Savannah in triumph, on the 22d of December, 1864, in the van of the army. It is well known that General GEARY's vigilance was rewarded on the occasion by the discovery of the evacuation of the city by the enemy. He entered Savannah while the rest of the army were sleeping. Colonel JONES was stationed with his brigade in the city. For services during the campaigns of Chattanooga and Atlanta, he was promoted to the rank of Brigadier-General, upon the recommendation of Generals HOOKER and HOWARD, approved by General SHERMAN himself. After the great review at Washington, active service being over, he resigned his commission and retired to civil life. He recommenced the practice of law, on his return home. He was elected on the Union Republican ticket of 1865 to the position of Clerk of the Court of Appeals, and entered upon the duties of the office January 1st, 1866. In their discharge he has secured the particular approval of the legal fraternity, who have found him ever attentive and obliging, and faithful to his trusts.

Such is a short account of the interesting history of this gentleman. So many men of the present day, fresh from the fields of strife, are so worthy of admiration, that it seems almost invidious to eulogize any particular one; but we cannot refrain from adding that Mr. JONES' course, from boyhood to the present time, has been marked by integrity of purpose and bravery of spirit. Born in a land where the oppression of hundreds of years has not been able to crush out the longings of the people for liberty, and coming to a country where every man is a sovereign, and where eagerness for distinction, wealth and power, is remarkable, he has, in reality, "won his way" in a praiseworthy manner.

SENATORS.

A. BLEECKER BANKS.

A. BLEECKER BANKS, the Senator from the Thirteenth District, was born in the city of New York March 7, 1835. His father, DAVID BANKS, is one of the oldest business men of New York, having established a law book publishing house in that city as early as 1802, and soon after connected with the same a branch house at Albany, the capital of the State. These establishments are now carried on by the sons of the founder, the present Senator being at the head of the branch house at Albany.

Mr. BANKS was educated to business, and at an early age became familiar with all the various branches of trade connected with printing and publishing books. The character of the business in which his father was engaged brought him in contact with men of the highest reputation, and made him familiar with authors whose works must continue to remain the standard of law literature for many generations to come. The influence thus exerted over his mind was not lost. It tended to shape his future course and inspired him with an ambition to make his own influence felt among those with whom he might be called upon to associate. At the age of nineteen he entered Columbia College and enjoyed the benefits of that renowned institution. In 1857, when but twenty-two years of age, he assumed the management of the Albany publishing house of BANKS & BROTHERS, and became one of the partners. In 1860 he was the Democratic candidate for the Assembly in the Second District, Albany county. The odds were vastly against him, but his popularity was such that he cut down the large Republican majority of the previous year to 265. In 1861 he changed his residence to the Third, or what is better known as the City District, and was again put in nomination for the Assembly. This effort proved a success, as he was elected by a majority of 447. He was one of the youngest members of the House that year, but from his knowledge of public men and measures, took rank at once as a man of influence; and although in a political minority was accorded places upon important committees.

In 1867, after a residence of ten years in Albany, his friends brought forward his name as a candidate for Senator. After a somewhat active canvass, he was nominated for that office by the County Convention, and was elected over CHARLES H. ADAMS, his popular opponent, by a majority of 1,166. Two years before, the district now represented by Mr. BANKS, elected to the same position LORENZO D. COLLINS, Republican.

Senator BANKS does not make pretensions to oratory. His power to influence men lies in his activity, his keen discernment, quick judgment and careful analysis of character. He is ready to give his energies in aid of public enterprises, and uniformly acquires the position of a leader in whatever he undertakes. Always a favorite among those who know him best, he cannot fail to become popular with his associates in the Senate, and with the widening circle of acquaintance to which his position must introduce him.

GEORGE BEACH.

GEORGE BEACH was born July 26, 1817, in Winchester, Litchfield County, Connecticut — the natal soil of many of the most prominent New York State politicians — and is now in the 51st year of his age. His father, a plain, substantial farmer, was one of that now almost obsolete class of clear-headed, sententious men, quite numerous half a century agone. He evidently transmitted to his children many of his excellent and decidedly practical traits of character.

The circumstances of Senator BEACH's parents being moderate, his childhood was not luxurious, nor surrounded by many advantages. In 1825, like "the march of empire," westward he took his way, with his father's family, to the Catskill Mountains, where, (land being not only cheap, but the area so extended as to admit of cultivation on three superficial sides), he soon became inured to the laborious duties of a struggling farmer's son — occasionally attending a common district school — but farm labor in summer, and lumbering in winter, monopolized his youthful years.

Early manifesting a taste for political life, upon the attainment of his majority, he at once took a commanding local position, and represented his town (Jewett) for four years in the Board of Supervisors of Greene County, besides holding several minor town and county offices. He was a prominent and active member of the New York delegations to the Democratic National Conventions, in 1860 and 1864. In July, 1863, he was appointed, by Governor SEYMOUR, Colonel of the 86th Regiment, National Guard, State of New York, and, in the fall of the same year he was elected to the State Senate, from the Greene and Ulster district by 1,500 majority. In July, 1867, he was appointed, by Governor FENTON, Brigadier-General of the 8th Brigade, 5th Division, National Guard, State of New York, and in November, 1867, he was re-elected to the present Senate from the same district by a majority of 2,016.

He has ever been an old-school Democrat, of "the strictest sect," and was never known to deviate a hair's breadth from the path of political fealty.

Senator BEACH took an active part in the proceedings of the Senate during the sessions of 1864–5. He was a member of some of the most important committees, and, by his untiring energy and strict attention to his duties as a legislator, although largely in the political minority, was instrumental in procuring the passage of several bills of both general and local importance. His record was so satisfactory to his constituents that he would have been returned to the following Senate, only for the reason that the nomination (on the principle of rotation) belonged to Ulster county. But at the last election, when it was the privilege of Greene county to name the candidate for Senator, he was the unanimous choice of the delegation. In the present Senate, he is a member of the Committees on Militia, Roads and Bridges and Poor Laws.

As a speaker, Senator BEACH is not ornate, though most convincing and impressive. Utterly discarding the flowers of rhetoric and rotund periods, he does not, like an illustrious Senatorial predecessor, "defy the English language," but exhibits the workings of a rough-hewn, practical mind, which has arrived at its common sense conclusions after close scrutiny, and liberal observation, and dexterously delivers its points and convictions with positive force.

Mr. BEACH possesses the most genial social qualifications, which, with his amiable, positive character, and native shrewdness, promote his popularity among all classes.

He resides in Catskill, Greene county, where he is at present engaged in mercantile pursuits.

JOHN J. BRADLEY.

Senator BRADLEY is the representative of the Seventh Senatorial District, comprising the Eighteenth, Twentieth and Twenty-first Wards of the city of New York, a district which embraces more wealth than any other district of the State. He is a native of the city of New York, and was born in the Third Ward in March, 1831. He will therefore be thirty-seven years of age before the close of the present session. His parents were Irish, and came to this country from Ireland in 1827.

Mr. BRADLEY was educated at the grammar school of Columbia College. At the age of sixteen, he entered into the employ of the importing house of GEORGE PEARCE & Co., as a clerk, where he remained for five years, occupying, most of the time, the most confidential position in that house. He then engaged in the livery stable business at the corner of Fourth avenue and Eighteenth street, and is now one of the most enterprising livery stable proprietors in the city of New York.

In 1855, when twenty-four years of age, he, at the urgent solicitation of the Democrats of the Eighteenth

Ward, became a candidate for Councilman. The district was considered a forlorn hope, but Mr. BRADLEY was elected by a majority of three votes, and held the position for three years. In 1857, he received the nomination for Alderman in the Fourteenth Aldermanic District, and was elected by a large majority. His course, while holding that position, was such as to meet the commendation of business men of the district. In fact he was one of the most influential members of the Board.

In 1861, he was nominated by the Democrats of the Sixth Senatorial District, then composed of the ninth, fifteenth, sixteenth and eighteenth wards of the city of New York. This was the first year of the war. Both wings of the party united in his support and, although the district was the stronghold of the Republican party in the city, Mr. BRADLEY was elected by a handsome vote. The Republican party, however, ran two candidates, Mr. MANNIERE and Mr. SMITH, enabling Mr. BRADLEY to secure his election by a plurality of about one thousand votes. He took an active part in the Senate during the sessions of 1862 and 1863, making one of the most attentive and industrious members of that body. He served on three committees, being chairman of the Committee on Public Expenditures, a position to which he was assigned by Lieutenant-Governor CAMPBELL, and was also a member of the Committees on Claims and on Indian Affairs.

In 1866, he was nominated by Mayor HOFFMAN, and confirmed by the Board of Aldermen, as President of the Croton Aqueduct Department. The incumbent of that office held on to the position, claiming the right to do so under one of those clauses in the tax levy, which the Republicans placed in that bill at the close of the session of the Legislature of that year. A mandamus being refused by the courts, Mr. BRADLEY gave up the contest.

During the last campaign he was nominated by Tammany Hall, as the representative of the Seventh Senatorial District. The Mozart and Democratic Union factions of the Democratic party, nominated JOHN HARDY, a young man who has heretofore shown himself a man of great strength before the people in one portion of the district. The Republicans united on CHRISTOPHER PULLMAN, who had made considerable reputation in the Board of Councilmen. The contest in the district was a spirited one, and one of the most hotly fought of any district in the State. Mr. BRADLEY not only came out successful, but lacked only fifty-eight votes of receiving a majority over both of his opponents.

In person Senator BRADLEY is of medium size and height; has light brown hair, blue eyes, and fresh countenance. He is a gentleman of considerable wealth, which he has accumulated by his superior business attainments and strict attention to whatever he undertakes.

SAMUEL CAMPBELL.

The village of New York Mills lies in the lovely valley of the Mohawk and Sauquoit. There are three factories, the "Oneida," the famed "New York Mills," and the "Burt Stone." For a mile and a half skirting each side of the fine hard road, are the school houses and churches of the village, the grounds and residences of the factory owners, and the homes of the operatives. In summer, New York Mills is very attractive; it is one of the sights, in Oneida county, which strangers go to see. The houses of the workingmen are neat, convenient and healthy, most of them standing back from the road, with yard in front, garden in rear, and half hidden by foliage. Sobriety and good order at all times prevail.

It is hard to realize that this factory people, with their comfort, temperance and intelligence, their books, Sunday observances, and winter lectures, their freedom from the "clemming" of crowded Europe, are working at the same business, and were originally, very many of them, of the same nationality as the men and the women made familiar to us by Parliamentary reports and debates, by poets and novelists—the men and the women of ELIOT, Mrs. GASKELL, CHARLOTTE BRONTE, JOHN BRIGHT and CHARLES KINGSLEY. The good standing of New York Mills is due to the character of the employés, which has always been high, and to the regulations and example of the employers.

The memory of BENJAMIN WALCOTT is honored in many places, but nowhere more honored than among the working people, for whose interest and happiness he was zealous and responsible. The ovation given him some years ago, on his return from the Old World, was a striking evidence of the love that was borne him; the whole population turning out to give him joyous welcome. His ideas have, in the main, been carried out by his successors, his son and SAMUEL CAMPBELL, the stranger, whom, thirty-five years ago, the elder WALCOTT welcomed within his gates.

SAMUEL CAMPBELL was born at Tarbolton, Ayrshire, Scotland, in 1809. In his boyhood he had the advantages of those schools for which his native land has been renowned through Europe, since JOHN KNOX returned from the feet of CALVIN, and Scotland broke forever with Rome. He came to America in 1831, and pitched his tent in New York Mills. He began his new life, as a workingman, in the employ of MARSHALL & WALCOTT. He had an iron frame, great working power, mechanical skill, ready adaptation of means to ends, quick perception of defects and remedies, and he rose steadily and rapidly. He made many valuable improvements in machinery. In 1847, he became a partner in the company. From that time his business career has been upward and onward. The hands and brain of Mr. CAMPBELL have been ceaselessly at work, and with large results in many directions. And now, in his advancing years, he has the joy to know that his ample fortune has been won by honest labor of head and hand, without a stain on his character or reputation, and with a full discharge of his duties to employés, to community, to family and to country.

Mr. CAMPBELL has given much attention to agriculture. A fine farm is attached to his residence, and he has imported and raised some of the best stock—Ayrshires, Durhams and Alderneys. His herd of Ayrshires is the best in the country. His stock has often won for him the first prizes at State and county fairs.

Mr. CAMPBELL married, in 1833, the lady whose virtues and whose pleasant ways cheered him during his long years of toil, and who still presides over his household. A large family of sons and daughters have grown up around him; his eldest son is Consul at Bayonne, France. The residence of the Senator is on an eminence far back from the road, in the centre of fine and variegated grounds, and overlooking a wide and lovely landscape. The rooms are high and large, the hall and staircase of unusual breadth and sweep, and all around are memorials of his motherland.

Mr. CAMPBELL was a Whig, afterward a Republican, and always a devoted son of his adopted country. As Supervisor of Whitestown and member of the War Committee of Oneida county, he worked with all his might during the war and for the war. His liberality went forth in every conceivable direction. We had intended to give his benefactions, so far as known to us, but the list is too long; we have no room for it; and a statement of what we know would do but partial justice to an open-handed patriotism most rare and honorable. The Union party showed their sense of his nobleness in this regard by appointing him a Delegate to the Convention, at Baltimore, which nominated Mr. LINCOLN for his second term, and by the large majority which sent him to the preceding Senate. The manner of his nomination was very complimentary. Dr. L. W. ROGERS, of Utica, a man who knew him well, prefaced the presentation of his name to the Convention by the following address.

"Mr. PRESIDENT—I rise to name a candidate for Senator, who is well known to the members of this Convention—so favorably known that he needs no word of eulogy from me. He is a man of large experience in business, and well acquainted with the wants and condition of the district; a Democrat in the true sense of the term, who sympathizes with the common people, and aims to improve and elevate them; a patriot, who stood by the country in her day of trouble, laboring without ceasing, and contributing without stint to furnish troops for the Union army, and to support our brave soldiers in the field; a man whose character for personal and political integrity is without reproach and above suspicion; a large-hearted, liberal gentleman, whom none know but to love, none name but to praise—SAMUEL CAMPBELL, of Whitestown."

The strong sense of Mr. CAMPBELL soon mastered the details of a Senator's duty; and, in his quiet, unobtrusive, but effective way, he has accomplished all that he or his constituents desired. His discharge of the duties of his position was so satisfactory to the Republicans of the district that his name was unanimously presented by the nominating convention, and he was re-elected in 1867. His integrity was so entirely unassailable and unquestioned, that he was selected by the presiding officer of the Senate for the important, responsible and delicate position of the Chairmanship of the Railroad Committee. He will stand the ordeal safely. There will not be even so much as the smell of fire on his garments. The attention is naturally drawn to him as he sits in the Senate, and the eye of the stranger lingers on the fine head, flowing beard, white hair and bright, cheery face, surmounting the broad shoulders and stalwart frame of SAMUEL CAMPBELL.

WILLIAM CAULDWELL.

WILLIAM CAULDWELL, Senator from the Ninth District, was born in New York City on the 12th of October, 1824, and is consequently in the 44th year of his age. His father was a native of Scotland, and his mother, like himself was born in the metropolis. Like so many men who have carved out by personal industry and indomitable will, a reputation, and secured a competence, Mr. CAULDWELL had only the benefits of a common school education. Early in life he began to learn the trade of a printer; and this, probably as much as anything else, was the basis of his future success. He is now one of the editors and publishers of the New York Sunday Mercury, one of the most widely circulated journals in the Union, having become connected with it in 1850.

Senator CAULDWELL has always taken an active interest in politics, and yet has often refused many offers of political advancement. A resident of the town of Morrisania, in Westchester county, he has aided in making it one of the most prosperous and noticeable places in the State. For eleven consecutive years he has been its Supervisor, chosen often without opposition, and always by an overwhelming majority. He has also taken a deep interest in the cause of public education, serving for nine or ten years in the board of education of his town. In short, his name is connected with almost everything pertaining to the prosperity of his section of Westchester.

Mr. CAULDWELL was presented for the position of State Senator last fall, not entirely with his own consent. But once nominated he entered into the canvass with spirit, and was elected by the largest majority ever before given for any man in the district, which comprises the counties of Westchester, Rockland and Putnam. Mr. CAULDWELL is and always has been a Democrat, and enjoys, in no restricted way, the confidence and esteem of his associates. Among the members of the Senate there are few who possess a more practical mind, or bring to their aid a more extended experience.

ORLOW W. CHAPMAN.

Senator CHAPMAN, representing the Twenty-fourth District (Broome, Tioga and Tompkins counties) is one of the younger members of the Senate. His age is 35 years. He was born in Ellington, Connecticut, on the 7th of January, 1832. His father CALVIN CHAPMAN, was a farmer. Young CHAPMAN, having acquired a good ordinary education at the Ellington Academy, struck out another path, and began by teaching a district school at Tolland, Connecticut, when he was 17 years of age; and during three succeeding winters he taught at East Long Meadow, Massachusetts. Entering Union College in this State as a sophomore in 1851, he was graduated with his class in 1854, though he had occupied a part of his time in teaching. Subsequently he was engaged at Fergusonville Academy, Delaware county, as Professor of Languages. In 1856, Mr. CHAPMAN began the study of the law, with ROBERT PARKER, formerly a partner of the Hon. AMASA J. PARKER, and finishing his course removed to Binghamton, where he was wholly unacquainted, in 1858, and established himself in the practice of his profession. Among the men of talent and reputation practicing law in Binghamton at that time were LEWIS SEYMOUR, GILES W.

Hotchkiss, afterward member of Congress, and the late Hon. D. S. Dickinson. The young lawyer rapidly gained position, and in the summer of 1862, in accordance with a petition of the bar of Binghamton, he was appointed District Attorney, for the unexpired term of George Northrup, deceased. In the fall of the same year he was elected to fill the office, and in 1865 was re-elected, leading his ticket. At the time when he was chosen Senator in November last, one year of his official term as District Attorney remained to be filled. Politically Mr. Chapman has always been a staunch Republican.

Mr. Chapman's time has been almost exclusively given to the duties of his profession, and to public duty; but he has occasionally found leisure to engage in literary labor. While studying law he was chosen poet for the occasion of an anniversary celebration of the Zeta Phi Society of Delhi, and in 1866 was selected as orator by that society on a similar occasion. His oration was repeated by request in Delhi in 1867. He has also lectured at intervals before lyceums, &c., and for the benefit of schools. During his practice, he has been an occasional contributor of articles on political and other topics for the press.

As District Attorney, Mr. Chapman's record was singularly good. His faithfulness and ability were conceded, and were conspicuously shown in many important cases. In an unusual number of these he was successful. Only two indictments found during his official terms were quashed.

As a citizen and public officer Mr. Chapman enjoys universal esteem. He resides permanently in Binghamton.

In the Senate he is chairman of the Committees on Literature and Erection of Towns and Counties, and is also a member of the Committees on Claims and Roads and Bridges.

THOMAS J. CREAMER.

Senator CREAMER is the youngest member of the present Senate, and, perhaps, the youngest man that has ever held a seat in that body. He is of Irish descent, and was born on the 26th day of May, 1842, and is, therefore, in his twenty-sixth year.

Mr. CREAMER may truly be termed a self-made man, having, by his own energy and perseverance, worked his way to the present prominent position he occupies in the councils of the State without the advantage of a collegiate education, which many of our public men have had, and without even the privilege of a common school education, which most of the young men of the present time possess. He has, nevertheless, by close application and untiring energy, fitted himself for the duties of the high position which he now holds, far better than most men upon whom a small fortune has been expended in academical training.

At the age of ten years he left the public schools in the city of New York, and engaged as an errand boy in a dry goods establishment, where he remained several years.

Few have ever started to fight life's battles at an earlier age, and few men have achieved the same success within such a short period. Mercantile life did not suit his tastes, and he resolved upon a change to that of a professional. The profession of law being more in accordance with his turn of mind, he applied himself diligently night and day to his studies, and at the age of twenty-one was admitted as a member of the New York Bar. Soon after this he commenced taking an active part in politics, and was elected a member of Assembly in the fall of 1864, polling the largest vote ever cast for a candidate in the district. In the Legislature of 1865, he took an active part in the debates on all questions relating to the city of New York, and delivered several able speeches in opposition to the establishment of commission government. He served during that session on the Committees on Claims and Roads and Bridges. He was re-elected in the fall of 1865, by over 2,000 majority, and was one of the most active members on the Democratic side during the session of 1866. He served on the Committees on Railroads, Claims and Engrossed Bills, and won for himself while a member, the friendship of even his political opponents by his straightforward and manly defense of his principles. During that session he was a strong advocate of a change in our militia law, in order to place the old fogy generals on the retired list, and did more to bring about the desired change than any other member of the Legislature.

Mr. CREAMER was re-elected in the fall of 1866 by an increased majority, no one in the district being willing to run in opposition to him. In the session of 1867 he served on the Committees on Insurance and on Privileges and Elections, and also was a member of the Grinding Committee. He was chairman of a committee to investigate the affairs of the Pacific Mail Steamship Company, and made a very able report to the Assembly in connection with the same. During the session he developed a talent as a legislator far better than at any former period, and was universally acknowledged as one of the most upright, efficient and capable members on the floor.

Few men in the Assembly commanded that universal respect and confidence of all connected with the Legislature as did "TOM" CREAMER. During his career in the Assembly not a breath of suspicion has ever been raised against him—he has passed through all the temptations and trying ordeals of three sessions, and that too when, according to general report, corruption was the rule and honesty the exception. In the fall of 1867, Mr. CREAMER was unanimously nominated by the Tammany Democracy of the Sixth Senatorial District, comprising the tenth, eleventh and seventeenth wards of the city of New York, and was elected by a majority of 12,500, the largest majority ever received by a Senator since the organization of the State. In the Senate he is a member of the important Committee on Municipal Affairs, serving also on the Committees on Engrossed Bills and Grievances, and although the youngest man in that body he has already taken a prominent position, and is one of the most influential members on the Democratic side. Mr. CREAMER is a good general debater, and though not gifted with that plethora of language which characterizes many of our public men, yet he is possessed of those more essential qualities of a practical and successful legislator—a clear and attractive manner of presenting a question, concise and logical method of exposition, quickness of perception both as to his own position and opportunities, as well as those of his opponents. He is an argumentative and forcible speaker, carrying with him that earnestness which is almost certain of conviction; has thorough knowledge of parliamentary rules, and a personal bearing to all with whom he comes in contact calculated to rally strong support. He is a firm friend, adhering with great tenacity to those whom he classifies as his personal friends. Mr. CREAMER is a member of the Tammany Hall General Committee in New York, and with the same care in the future as in the past, is destined to win still higher honors and wield an important influence in the politics of his city and State.

He is above the medium height, standing nearly six feet, slim built, and weighing about one hundred and sixty pounds, dresses with scrupulous care and good taste, has dark brown hair, dark gray eyes, light complexion and gentlemanly manner. He is unmarried, but too young to be classified in the list of bachelors.

RICHARD CROWLEY.

Mr. Crowley is one of the youngest members of the Senate, and was elected to the place which he now holds in that body, before he was twenty-nine years old. He was born at Lockport, New York, December 14th, 1836. His father and mother came to this country from Ireland; they settled on a small farm, when Mr. Crowley was ten years of age. His life, until he became twenty-one, was like that of most farmers' sons, of small means, made up mostly of working on the farm, during the summer months, and attending the common school in the winter season. As an exception to the above mentioned educational advantages, he attended the Union school at Lockport, two terms. During the years that he spent on his father's farm he had access to a tolerably good school district library; and also studied Latin, and pursued a course of reading under the teachings of a friend. He had a great taste for history and biography, which he fully gratified. When he was twenty-one he left home and commenced his fight with the world. He worked his way to the West, as far as Kalamazoo, Michigan, and " hired out" to teach a country school, in an adjoining town. While thus employed, having purchased a copy of Blackstone's Commentaries, he devoted his spare hours to the study of them. When his school term expired, he traveled through several of the Western States, and then returned to Lockport. In the spring of 1857, he entered the law office of GARDNER & LAMONT, practitioners in Lockport, devoting a portion of his time, however, to general reading and the study of Latin, rhetoric and mental and moral philosophy. The succeeding winter he again engaged in teaching, in order to replenish his exchequer; and, in the spring, resumed his professional studies in the office of L. F. & G. W. BOWEN, where he remained until 1861, when, having been previously admitted to the Bar in Lockport, he commenced practicing, after having formed a partnership with E. J. CHASE, Esq., a brother of Hon. S. P. CHASE. He was admitted to practice in the Supreme Court of the United States in January, 1865, Chief Justice CHASE, presiding. Mr. CROWLEY has had entrusted to him many cases of importance, concerning property and crime; and has proven himself an able advocate and counsellor. In early life he took a deep interest in political matters growing out of the repeal of the Missouri Compromise, and the Kansas and Nebraska agitation. The result of his reasoning was a determination to attach himself to Republican principles. He has never before held any public office, except that of City Counsel for the city of Lockport. When first elected to the Senate, in the year 1865, his vote was very flattering, especially in the county of Niagara, wherein he received over four hundred more votes than any other candidate on either the State or county ticket, although some of the most popular men in the county were in nomination. He was re-elected in 1867, and was very properly honored by the Lieutenant-Governor with the very responsible and arduous position of Chairman of the Committee on Municipal Affairs. No higher evidence of the value placed upon his character, integrity and ability could be given.

Mr. CROWLEY has made achievements that are certainly remarkable. What he now is, cannot be due to ancestry, for like CICERO, when jeered at concerning his name, he has felt that he must make his own name, if he would have a place for it in the great hereafter. He is a living exemplification of the truth: "*Perseverantia omnia vincit.*" He is the son of a poor man; by his own personal efforts he has risen from poverty to be an ornament to the Niagara Bar; and the high esteem in which he is held, may well be envied by young men who have been surrounded, all their lives, by much more advantageous circumstances. As a speaker and debater he is far above mediocrity. His language is elegant and forcible, sometimes almost severely chaste, and his voice is distinct in utterance.

LEWIS A. EDWARDS.

Senator EDWARDS represents the First Senatorial District. He was born on Gardiner's Island, in the town of East Hampton, Suffolk county, June 18, 1811, and is a direct descendant of WILLIAM EDWARDS, one of the original settlers of the town, who came from Ipswich, Massachusetts, about the year 1648. Mr. EDWARDS' educational advantages were limited to the ordinary district schools.

In February, 1828, by the destruction of the homestead and effects of his parents by fire, he lost everything, except the clothes he wore. The effect of this disaster was to direct his steps toward the city of New York, where in the following spring he took the position of a grocer's clerk.

In 1832, he was appointed collector of wharfage under the then existing firm of WM. C. TAYLOR & Co., and afterward under the late MICHAEL SANDFORD. The manner in which he discharged his duties secured the hearty approval of all who were cognizant of his integrity, faithfulness and energy. At the decease of Mr. SANDFORD in 1846, Mr. EDWARDS was intrusted with the closing up of the very extensive business affairs of his late employer, and has continued in the management of the affairs of this valuable estate to the present time.

Mr. EDWARDS became the successor of Mr. SANDFORD in the wharfage business, and in connection with his associates became the lessee of nearly all the wharves belonging to the corporation on the North river side of the city. And about this time he became considerably interested in the building and employment of vessels in the coasting trade. He prosecuted his business with tact and assiduity until 1853, when, in consequence of nearly all the wharves having been leased by steamship companies, he abandoned the avocation and returned to Suffolk county, settling at Orient, a very pleasant place, situated near the eastern extremity of the north branch of the island.

Mr. EDWARDS became associated, in 1861, with Messrs. LAWRENCE, WATERBURY & Co., of New York, and commenced the manufacture of fish oil and guano, on Long Beach, contiguous to Gardiner's Bay. Their works deserve more than a passing notice, being the largest of the kind on the Atlantic coast, giving employment (including fishermen) to sixty men. The oil is manufactured from the menhaden or mopfunken, and as many as nine millions and a half have been worked up in one season by them. In 1866, Mr. EDWARDS put up a branch manufactory on Hog Island, Hancock county, Maine, which was in operation the past season. The successful management of such an extensive business demonstrates Mr. EDWARDS to be a man of peculiar and marked talent, enterprise and foresight.

Mr. EDWARDS is a Democrat, and cast his first vote for ANDREW JACKSON for President, and believes and has adhered strictly to the principle laid down by that statesman, that a man has not the right either to seek or decline office. He was placed in nomination for the office of Senator last fall against his wishes. He was elected by a majority of 3,836, to succeed Hon. N. B. LA BAU, Republican. Mr. EDWARDS is a man of unassuming manners, who attends to his duties as Senator quietly and with despatch. Although in his first term, and his only experience in a legislative body, his long and varied business habits are a sufficient guarantee that he will, in due time, make himself acquainted with the ordinary routine of legislation, and commend himself as one who will be measurably successful in all the practical duties of his position. He will never retard nor mystify the business of the Senate, by an undue indulgence in talk; and hence, as a working, energetic, and cool Senator he will not be likely to get far astray.

CHARLES J. FOLGER.

CHARLES JAMES FOLGER, Senator from the Twenty-sixth District, is a native of Massachusetts, in which State he was born on the 16th of April, 1818. His ancestors were sea-faring men; masters of vessels sailing out of Nantucket, and his early boyhood days were spent in the wild and free associations of the coast life, which possesses so much of romance and adventure. When he was a little more than twelve years of age, he removed with his parents to Geneva, in this State, where he has resided since, except when at intervals engaged in the study of law elsewhere. He entered Geneva College in 1833, and graduated in 1836, with the honors of his class. In October of that year, he commenced the study of the law, in the office of MARK H. SIBLEY & ALVAH WORDEN, at Canandaigua. The influence of such a preceptor as Mr. SIBLEY, upon a mind so receptive and active as that of his young friend, could not fail to be beneficial, and, undoubtedly, a large share of the great practical success he has since attained in public life, is to be attributed to this association. He also read law in the office of BOWEN WHITING, at Geneva, and with JOHN M. HOLLEY, at

Lyons. In 1839, he was admitted to practice at the Bar of the Supreme Court, General Term, at Albany, and in May, of the following year, entered upon the pursuit of his profession at Geneva. His advance was rapid and honorable. A fine personal presence, a studious analysis of all the rules and practices of law, a mind fully stored with classic lore, and with the very best productions of the jurists of all countries, and a persuasive style of eloquence, were the elements of a sure and honorable promotion. In 1844, he was appointed — under the old Constitution — Judge of the Ontario Court of Common Pleas. He held that office for one year, and discharged its duties with general satisfaction, and then resigned. He was also Master and Examiner in Chancery until the Chancery Court was abolished by the adoption of the Constitution of 1846. In 1851, he was elected County Judge of Ontario county, and held that office for four years. In 1861, he was elected to the Senate, being re-elected in 1863, 1865, and again in 1867.

Mr. FOLGER has acted with the Republican party from the period of its organization, and has always been a conspicuous and able defender of the principles it was established to maintain. His influence in his own particular section of the State has contributed largely to the great popular predominance of Republican principles. Upon the Forum, through the Press, and as a Legislator, his voice has always been earnest for equal rights and justice to all. Almost uniformly chosen a representative in the State Conventions of his party, he has contributed largely to give shape to its general policy. His address as temporary Chairman of the Syracuse Convention in 1865, will long be remembered by those who heard it, as a model of eloquence, vigor and terseness.

In the Senate, Mr. FOLGER is a recognized leader. His opinions are always treated by that body with marked respect, and even when he is compelled to dissent from his peers in judgment, he receives from them the credit due to sincere convictions and great ability. As Chairman of the Judiciary Committee, which he has held in the past and present Senates, much of the most important business of the Legislature passes through his hands; and his extensive legal knowledge, his great skill in research, his wonderful powers of analysis, and his untiring industry, have made his services in this capacity of almost incalculable value. Without derogation of the claims of other gentlemen upon the Committee, it is safe to say that all will pronounce this tribute to his personal usefulness entirely just and deserved.

The estimation in which Mr. FOLGER is held by his peers may be judged from the fact that during the session of 1865, he was unanimously chosen President *pro tem.*, to serve during the absence of the Lieutenant-Governor, Hon. THOMAS G. ALVORD. This high compliment has been renewed at the opening of each succeeding session, and without a dissenting voice. Senator FOLGER was a prominent member of the recent Constitutional Convention, and was Chairman of the Judiciary Committee of that body.

The chief characteristics of Mr. FOLGER, as a Senator, are his great industry and his unbending integrity. He is thoroughly devoted to the duties of his position, and labors incessantly, both upon the floor and in committees, to perfect and elaborate legislation. The importance of this fact is best understood by those who know how great are his resources of legal lore. Nobody ever suspected him of favoring a bill or advocating a scheme from the impulse of selfish or mercenary motives. His mind is preeminently that of a statesman. He regards all questions from the broad, general stand-point of public expediency and justice, and is able to bring to his use the lessons of history and the experience of centuries in determining his own views.

As a speaker, there are few among the many eloquent men in the State, who possess so much or such varied power as Mr. FOLGER. He is a native orator, whose innate abilities have been wondrously increased by a thorough education and severe discipline. He never addresses the Senate without fixing its attention, and always utters ideas which are certain to illustrate the subject in hand. His wealth of imagery is sometimes surprising, and the readiness with which it is employed in giving charms to the most commonplace topics, makes him a most desirable ally and a formidable opponent. He is uniformly dignified and affable in debate; but the trenchant vigor with which he disposes of an antagonist is frequently inimitable. Never making speeches for "effect;" always confining himself to the topic immediately under discussion; and grouping facts, figures and fancies with the skill of a master, he has achieved a position beside the master intellects of the State, and will long be remembered after he shall have left the Senate Chamber, for — we trust — higher honors and richer spheres of usefulness.

In personal appearance, Mr. FOLGER is commanding and graceful. His features wear the stamp of intellect, and advertise the gentlemanly suavity which is a predominant trait in his character. His voice has that peculiarly melodious inflection which is always ascribed as one of the graces of the native orator. He is cool and self-possessed under every circumstance, and never finds himself in a situation for which he has not adequate resources. Nobody would suspect him of having approached, within a decade, the forty-nine years he wears so well.

HENRY WEBB GENET.

Senator GENET was born in Wethersfield, Connecticut, February 27th, 1828. His father was JOHN M. GENET, a native of France, who came to America during the troubles which ensued upon the French Revolution. His mother was a native of Ireland, who emigrated to this country, in childhood. Mr. GENET, the elder, removed to Albany when his son was about one year of age, and went into commercial business, near the river. HENRY attended school in Albany, for several years, and then taking a fancy for the life of an agriculturist, was placed upon a farm in the town of Moreau, Saratoga county, where he remained four or five years, diligently prosecuting his literary studies, during the winter months. When about sixteen years of age, he left the farm, and entered the Glens Falls Academy, where he remained about a year and a half, when he went to the city of New York, where his father was then residing.

When about nineteen years of age, he entered the University of the city of New York, at which he remained two years, and then entered the law office of Mr. HASTINGS, in that city, and was, in due time, admitted, finishing his preparatory studies in the office of McCUNN & MONCRIFF. He was, in early life, an enthusiastic admirer of HENRY CLAY, and, during the life of that great man, naturally acted with the Whig party. On the dissolution of that organization, he joined the Democracy, with which he has ever since coöperated. In 1857, he was elected on the Democratic ticket to the Board of Councilmen from the Twelfth Ward of New York. The following year he was elected Alderman, and re-elected two years after, being chosen President of the Board, during the last two years of his term. In 1861, he was elected to the responsible office of County Clerk, the duties of which he faithfully discharged during the years 1862, 1863 and 1864.

During the three most important years of the war, viz.: the years ending January 1st, 1864, Mr. GENET, as President of the Board of Aldermen, was, *ex officio*, a member of the War Fund Committee, of which the Mayor of the city, and the President of the Board of Councilmen, were also *ex officio* members. Every one remembers the constant and valuable aid rendered by this organization to the National Government, during the dark era of our history, and there was, on the Committee, no one who privately, or in his public capacity, was found more ready to support every measure dictated by patriotism, than Mr. GENET; and his votes will always be found in favor of the most lavish support, in blood and treasure, of our threatened Nationality.

Mr. GENET represented the 21st Assembly District of New York in the Assembly of 1866. He was closely attentive to the business of the House, and took interest in all matters of general legislation. His genial warmth won for him many friends, who sustained him in matters affecting his own district, in which he took a special and lively interest, resulting usually in success. He was a most efficient worker. He was elected to the Senate in 1867, his constituents elevating him to a higher sphere in evidence of their appreciation of his services. Mr. GENET is a thorough politician, of potent influence, and is popular outside of his own party for his lack of narrow and exclusively partisan notions.

WILLIAM M. GRAHAM.

Senator GRAHAM was born in the town of Minisink, Orange county, September 8, 1819. His paternal ancestors came to this country from Ireland, while those of his mother were Holland immigrants. In his qualities of mind and person, he combines the excellent characteristics of these two nations. He has all the solidity, industry and persistence of the Hollander, with the genial warmth, unselfish benevolence and patriotic ardor of the intelligent Irishman. He received an academic education at the Montgomery (Orange county) and Ridgebury (New Jersey) Academies.

Mr. GRAHAM'S business life has been confined to that of banking. He entered the Middletown Bank in 1841 as Teller, and in 1844 was made its Cashier. It was in this institution that he achieved a reputation as a financier of superior qualities—an inflexibly honest banker, and a faithful and laborious officer. He necessarily acquired an intimate acquaintance with the business men of Orange and other counties, who were won by his courtesy and fair dealing, and esteemed him for his personal worth and capacities. After twenty years of faithful service in this institution, he was (in 1860) chosen President of the Wallkill Bank, which position he still holds, retaining the approval of all for his careful discharge of his responsibilities, his uprightness and sound judgment.

Mr. GRAHAM has but once before held public office, and the large majority by which he was then chosen was practical evidence of the appreciation in which he was held. In 1857, he was elected County Treasurer of Orange county, and re-elected at the close of his first term. During the six years that he discharged the duties of the office, he showed himself not unworthy the trust reposed in him. He entered the canvass for Senator in 1867 under serious disadvantages. The district in which he was nominated, and which he now represents, had for three successive terms sent to the Senate Hon. HENRY R. LOW (well known to many of our readers), the last time by a majority of 551. Mr. Low's prestige was, therefore, against Senator GRAHAM. The political revolution which swept over the State might not have carried with it men less known for sterling integrity and business capacity. But he was so strong in the confidence of the people that he gave additional impetus to the tide in his own district, and was chosen by a majority of 633. Mr. GRAHAM is not a man who has either the disposition or the art of holding the Senate from the dispatch of business by fine forensic talent, but he has those other and higher qualities of a successful legislator — attentive application to business, discriminating perception, and careful, quiet and persistent management. His clear judgment is highly appreciated and sought after, especially on questions of finance. Lieutenant-Governor WOODFORD but gave appropriate recognition at once to his powers and uprightness, when he placed him on two of the most responsible Committees in the Senate—those of Banks and Railroads.

Senator GRAHAM's private and social life adds to his honor. The friends of benevolent and humanitarian movements rely upon him as a wise counsellor and willing contributor. The sick and wounded heroes of the late conflict with armed treason, had their sufferings frequently relieved by his kind offices. He has always been a firm Democrat, but never a bigoted partisan.

MATTHEW HALE.

The original head of the American branch of the HALE family was one THOMAS HALE, who came to Newbury, Massachusetts, in 1635. Hon. ROBERT S. HALE, late member of Congress from the Sixteenth District of this State, is a brother of the Senator.

Senator HALE was born at Chelsea, Orange county, Vermont, June 20, 1829. Going through a good academic course of instruction he entered the University of Vermont, and graduated at the age of twenty-two. He then commenced the study of law with the firm of KELLOGG & HALE, at Elizabethtown, Essex county, New York, and pursued his studies until he was admitted to the bar in 1853. Shortly after, in connection with a brother, he opened an office in Poughkeepsie, and commenced practice, soon establishing a promising business. After a time this partnership was dissolved, and his brother removed to St. Paul. Mr. HALE then formed a new copartnership with Mr. A. B. SMITH, of Poughkeepsie. This partnership existed for three years. While in Poughkeepsie Mr. HALE became much interested in politics, entering with enthusiasm into the first campaign of the Republican party, and made speeches in support of FREMONT.

In 1859 Mr. HALE was led to change the sphere of his professional labors from Poughkeepsie to New York city, forming a copartnership with LOT C. CLARK, of that city. This business arrangement continued for five years, at the end of which time he removed to Elizabethtown, where he entered into a law partnership with Honorable A. C. HAND (whose daughter Mr. HALE had married), a lawyer of high distinction in that place, and R. L. HAND, a son of the Judge. The Senator is still a member of this firm.

The first political office ever held by Senator HALE was that of Supervisor of Elizabethtown, which he held during the years 1864, '65. In the Spring of 1867 he was with great unanimity selected as one of the candidates of the Republican party to represent the Sixteenth District in the Constitutional Convention. The Democratic party of the district nominated opposing candidates against the three other candidates on the Republican ticket, but constrained by their high regard for Mr. HALE, and their confidence in his integrity and sound principles, they not only declined to nominate a candidate against him, but they indorsed his nomination and placed his name upon their printed ballots. In the Convention he was made a member of the Judiciary Committee. In this sphere of extended usefulness his enlarged ideas, his clear logical statements, his evident desire to establish sound principles regardless of mere partisan ends and aims, his faithfulness in labor, his ability as a speaker and his courteousness as an associate, all combined to make him one of the most respected and admired members of that body, in which was comprised so many of the intellectually strong men of the Empire State. He did not speak often, but when he did, what he said had energy and force and was to the point. His speeches on the separate submission of the Suffrage question and on the Judiciary article were most able efforts, and were listened to with the greatest interest.

The fine reputation made by Mr. HALE in the Constitutional Convention, naturally led the Republicans of his district to make choice of him as a candidate for the office of State Senator. This was done without his knowledge, and the announcement of the fact was to him a great surprise. He was elected by a majority of 1,436. He is a member of the Senate Judiciary Committee, and Chairman of the Committee on Claims.

Senator HALE does not descend to the low tricks of partisan warfare, but in the advocacy of such measures as he approves, relies upon argument rather than management. Such men do not seek office nor manipulate primary meetings, nor "run" conventions, nor make partisan bargains. The people respect them for their attachment to principle, and the bold and faithful advocacy of political doctrines to which they subscribe; and this respect impels them to put such men in office. Senator HALE has another characteristic of the high toned gentleman and the man of honor. He does not deal in personal abuse nor bandy partisan squibs; there is no bitterness or biting sarcasms towards political opponents in his language. He is also conservative in his views; he is a safe man, and seldom or never does a rash or imprudent thing, or one out of season. His fairness and honorableness of word and deed to political opponents have elicited words of praise even from Democratic organs such as the New York World, which most truthfully spoke of him as "one of the best men in the Convention," and characterized his speeches in that body as "among the most interesting made."

JOHN F. HUBBARD, JR.

Senator HUBBARD was born in Norwich, Chenango county, October 14, 1822. His father, JOHN F. HUBBARD, Sr., who is still living at the date of this sketch, ably represented the Sixth Senatorial District, under the preceding Constitution, from 1828 to 1836.

The present Senator received an ordinary academic education, and afterwards read law, but never entered upon the practice of the profession.

After some years spent in editorial life, he received, in 1847, from Hon. W. L. MARCY, an appointment in the War Department at Washington. He remained in that city, holding various subordinate positions in the Government service, until about 1854, when he resigned, and again took up his residence at Norwich.

In 1860 he was chosen a delegate to the Democratic National Convention, held at Charleston, from the then Twenty-first District of this State, and participated in the proceedings of that body.

In 1866 he was appointed Assessor of Internal Revenue, by President JOHNSON, for the Nineteenth District of New York, but not being confirmed by the United States Senate, his time as Assessor expired on the 4th of March following.

In the fall of 1847, he was, unexpectedly to himself, nominated for the office of Senator, to represent the Twenty-third District, and was elected by a majority of 247 votes. His competitor was Hon. DANIEL WATERBURY, of Delaware county. At the same election the Republican majority on the State ticket in the district was 52; the year previous it was 1,421.

In politics Senator HUBBARD is and has been all his life a decided Democrat. He is at present the editor and publisher of the Chenango Union, printed at Norwich, one of the best edited and managed country newspapers of the State. He is a careful politician, bold and undisguised in his political sentiments, yet affable in his personal address. He is energetic and of sound practical talents, and gives every evidence of becoming a sagacious and successful legislator.

WOLCOTT J. HUMPHREY.

Mr. HUMPHREY is a gentleman who has had considerable experience in the political affairs of the State. For twenty years or more, he has taken deep interest in public matters, and has served the people in various positions of responsibility and trust. His ability and fidelity have been recognized by a re-election to the Senate, under circumstances which rendered it one of the highest expressions of confidence which can be given. A few days preceding the election, he was made the object of a malicious personal attack by a disappointed legislative schemer, with the avowed purpose of defeating his re-election. The polls opened on election day, leaving him no defense against the trumped up charge of corruption other than the confidence of his constituents. It was under such circumstances that he was again elected. The Grand Jury of Albany county heard the case after election, but as there was no evidence substantiating the charge against him, dismissed the complaint and refused to find an indictment.

This suffices as a complete vindication. During the present session he is Chairman of the Committee on Commerce and Navigation, and a member of the Finance Committee, two of the best positions in the Senate. He is also Chairman of the Committee on Joint Library.

Mr. HUMPHREY's birthplace was Canton, Hartford county, Connecticut. He is forty-nine years of age. His father, grandfather and great-grandfather were natives of the same town. The original head of the family in this country were two brothers, who came from England, in the sixteenth century, and settled in Massachusetts. From them have descended the numerous branches of the family, which may now be found in every State in the Union.

Mr. HUMPHREY's father concluded, in 1818, to remove from the locality where his family had dwelt for so many years, and decided to make the town of Sheldon, Genesee county (now Wyoming), his future home. This section was then the "far West," and when we consider the primitive facilities for travel which then existed — when the long, tedious journeys of the hardy pioneers were performed on horseback or in lumbering wagons — and when it is known that his father had the good old-fashioned family of fifteen children to look after (afterward increased to seventeen), it will be readily believed that the change was one requiring a good deal of New England *grit* and perseverance. But the exodus was accomplished, and a new scene opened in the lives of the whole family.

Senator HUMPHREY's early education was acquired wholly in a common school; but, by extensive travel through the States, and much mingling with the bustling business world — "keeping his eyes and ears open" the while — he has stored his mind with a large fund of practical knowledge and information. When twenty years old he entered the military service of the State; and, in 1840, was elected Colonel of the 9th Regiment, 8th Brigade, New York State Artillery. In 1844, he resigned his commission and gave up all connection with military affairs. He married, in 1841, Miss AMANDA MARTINDALE, a daughter of Major WILLIAM S. MARTINDALE, of Dorset, Vermont, a lady of excellent domestic qualities.

At different times Mr. HUMPHREY has held various town offices; and during the year 1850, was Marshal for taking the census in six of the towns of his county. In 1849, '53 and '60, he was appointed Postmaster, and, after serving awhile, as many times, resigned; his second resignation took place when TYLER proved himself recreant to the party with which he was identified. In 1850, he was elected to the Assembly, and was returned in 1851. His political talents and constant activity gave him a leading position in that body. The latter term he served as Chairman of the Committee on Railroads, and reported the Central Railroad Bill, authorizing the railroad consolidation, and establishing the existing restrictions. He was also selected by the caucus to take charge of the Prohibitory Liquor Law passed at that session; and he made an able speech in its behalf.

Some time in 1855, Mr. HUMPHREY removed to Bloomington, Illinois, where he was instrumental in securing the return of the late OWEN LOVEJOY to Congress, against Judge DAVIES. He was, we believe, President of the Convention that nominated Mr. LOVEJOY. After residing in Bloomington three years or thereabouts, he returned to Wyoming, and resumed business at North Java, from which place he removed to Warsaw, in 1864, where he now lives. During the war, he was enrolling officer for the government, and was mobbed, by foreign opponents of the draft, while in the discharge of his duties.

Mr. HUMPHREY was first elected to the Senate in 1865, from the Thirtieth District (Wyoming, Livingston and Allegany), by 5,240 majority over the late Judge HASTINGS, of Livingston. An excellent position was given him, on the committees, he being a member of the Committees on Railroads, Internal Affairs and Printing, and Chairman of the Committee on Roads and Bridges. He ranks as a faithful worker, and one of the best debaters among the non-speech-making Senators. His political views were Whig, so long as there was a Whig party, and he became a member of the Republican party when it was formed. He has been farmer, merchant, and tanner by turns, and is extensively engaged in the latter business at present. He is a gentleman of fine presence, and great nervous energy, of warm friendships and good impulses, and possesses talents of a high order, as a political organizer and an indefatigable worker.

GEORGE NELSON KENNEDY.

GEORGE NELSON KENNEDY, Senator from the Twenty-second (Onondaga and Cortland) District, is a native of Marcellus, Onondaga county, New York, where he was born September 11th, 1822. His paternal grandfather emigrated from Ireland in 1760, and his maternal grandfather was an immediate descendant of the Puritan settlers of New England. Both were active participants in the Revolutionary struggle, as soldiers in the army of the young Republic. His mother's grandfather was killed in the battle of Saratoga; and both his grandfathers were also engaged in that conflict. His father, in early manhood, removed to Marcellus, and was a farmer in moderate circumstances. In 1831 he removed, with his family, to Skaneateles, in the same county, where he remained three years, in order to give his children the advantages of the academy at that place. When GEORGE was eighteen years of age, he was thrown upon his own resources, and his fortune and honorable career have been achieved through his own unaided exertions. Throughout his life he has adhered strictly to the principles of honor and comity that mark the true gentleman, and has aimed to live for the good of, those about him rather than for self-aggrandizement.

Mr. KENNEDY began the study of the law with EDMUND AIKIN, a lawyer at Marcellus; was admitted to practice in the Court of Common Pleas of Onondaga county, in 1842, and to the Supreme Court two years later. He remained at Marcellus, engaged in the practice of his profession, and doing an extensive business, until 1854, when he removed to the city of Syracuse, his present place of residence, and entered into a law partnership with CHARLES B. SEDGWICK and CHARLES ANDREWS, forming the firm of SEDGWICK, ANDREWS & KENNEDY, which has been and still is a leading law firm in Onondaga county, and one of the foremost in the profession in the Fifth Judicial District. Mr. KENNEDY has a prominent position at the bar of Onondaga county. He has been an active, energetic practitioner; and to his credit, it is said by his professional compeers, that no more honorable adversary is found in the legal ranks of Central New York. He is able both as counsellor and as advocate; he is a sound adviser in the office, and a strong, convincing speaker before the court and the jury. Since he has resided in Syracuse he has devoted himself assiduously to his profession; and for more than half this period he has been engaged in a majority of the important legal controversies that have claimed the attention of the courts of Onondaga county.

Mr. KENNEDY cast his first vote for JAMES K. POLK for President, in 1844. Four years later he was a member of the Buffalo Convention, which nominated VAN BUREN and ADAMS as the Free Soil candidates. Subsequently he acted with the Democratic party until 1854, when he was among the earliest of those, who, impelled by a sense of duty and patriotism, disconnected themselves from that organization, because of its favoring the extension of slavery over free territory, and joined the Republican party, to whose principles he gave an earnest and efficient support, and with which he has since steadfastly acted. Until his election as Senator he held no public station. He had several times been pressed for nominations by his party, but waived his claims to subserve what he deemed its best interests. For several years he was at the head of the party organization in Onondaga County, holding the chairmanship of the Republican County Committee, the duties of which he discharged with ability and thoroughness, and thereby did much to secure the proud success of his party in that locality. When a candidate for Senator, the best evidences of his personal popularity were afforded in the vote he received, which was greater than that of his party for the State ticket in the Ward, City, and County where he resides.

During the war to suppress the rebellion, no citizen was more earnest and laborious in prosecuting the work of raising troops for the Government, and in providing means of support for the families of absent soldiers, than Mr. KENNEDY. His voice was heard at the war meetings in city and country, and his means were liberally given to aid the cause of the nation. Few men who did not actually participate in the strife of the battle-field, did more for his country than he; and his work was done without ostentation — his aid was extended without parade.

Mr. KENNEDY has achieved a gratifying professional and pecuniary success. The practice of his profession, to which he is enthusiastically devoted, has secured to him a handsome competency, and his other business operations have been uniformly successful. He has the proud satisfaction of knowing that he has been, in the fullest degree, "the architect of his own fortune." He possesses all the attributes requisite to the attainment of high success in legislative bodies. His ability as a speaker, his thoroughness as a business man, his uniform courtesy and manliness, combined with unremitting industry and rare energy, are qualities that indicate for him a bright and honorable career in the halls of Legislation.

ABNER C. MATTOON.

Senator MATTOON represents the Twenty-first Senatorial District, composed of the counties of Oswego and Madison. He was born in Locke, Cayuga county, in 1814. Senator MATTOON's has been particularly an active business life. At quite an early age, he went to Rochester, where he remained until years of manhood, when he went to New York city and entered into commercial pursuits. His business in New York was of such a character as to require frequent trips to the then "far West," the Mississippi river being then considered in the same light by the pioneers, as the "*Ultima Thule*" of the ancients. While yet a young man, Mr. MATTOON spent several winters on the steamers of the great "Father of Rivers," and at the various towns which line its waters, advancing the interests of the house he represented in the commercial metropolis. The time thus spent gave him an experience and a knowledge of business and men which has been of great use to him all his subsequent life.

In 1844, Mr. MATTOON removed to the then village of Oswego, the principal port upon the southern shore of Lake Ontario, with the prosperity and growth of which he has ever since been closely identified. From an unimportant town, he has lived to see the village of his adoption expand into a point of great commercial importance, rating, in fact, in the year 1867, the sixth port in the Union in volume of receipts for foreign customs; New York, Boston, Baltimore, Philadelphia and New Orleans alone exceeding it.

On removing to Oswego, Mr. MATTOON entered the employ, as agent and managing man, of the firm of BRONSON & CROCKER, at that time the oldest, and one of the most extensive and respectable commercial houses on all the northern frontier. Subsequently opening a commercial house of his own, he has ever since been very extensively engaged in the forwarding business, in grain dealing, in milling, boat building, and in kindred pursuits, his business relations extending to nearly all points in Canada, and to the extent of the great lakes west.

Activity has always characterized Senator MATTOON in his relations to society. His own city, during the last twenty years, has taken a leading position in educational matters. The efficiency and success of its schools, and the excellence of its system of education, have given it a deserving prominence among all the cities of the Union. Senator MATTOON has been one of the most active members of the Board of Education of Oswego, almost uninterruptedly since its first organization. He has several times been its president. Through his efforts in the Legislature, an appropriation was obtained for the support of a "Training School" for the teachers of Oswego, which has since grown into a most flourishing and successful State Normal School, and which is educating and training hundreds of teachers annually to go out into the State and the Union, prepared to introduce and practice the latest and most approved methods of imparting primary instruction. Of the local Board for the management of this school, Senator MATTOON has been from its organization one of the most active members.

Senator MATTOON was an early advocate of the temperance cause, and in 1854, when political action was proposed in his district, he was the temperance candidate for Member of Assembly, withdrawing, however, before the election in favor of the Hon. D. C. LITTLEJOHN, the Whig candidate, who was elected.

Senator MATTOON has always been an active politician. In early life he was a SEWARD Whig. At the winding up of the affairs of the Whig party, Mr. MATTOON for a time was identified with the "Americans," and was their candidate for member of Assembly in 1855, in opposition to Hon. ORVILLE ROBINSON, the Democratic candidate, who was elected and became speaker.

Senator MATTOON, since its organization has been an active and influential member of the Republican party. He was an energetic supporter of President LINCOLN's administration and of the war against rebellion. In 1862 he was the Republican candidate of his district for member of Assembly and was elected. His experience and pursuits pointed him out as peculiarly fitted for the position, and he was made the Chairman of the important Committee on Commerce and Navigation. He was also upon the no less important Committee on Canals. Being re-elected the following year, he was awarded the position of Chairman of the Canal Committee, and was also upon other important committees.

In 1867, he was nominated by the Senatorial Convention of the twenty-first District, and was elected by a very large majority over General ROBERT C. KENYON the Democratic candidate. In the Senate he is Chairman of the Printing Committee, and also a member of the Canal and other committees. His Senatorial career bids fair to be an active, influential and honorable one.

LEWIS H. MORGAN.

This gentleman represents Monroe county, which forms the Twenty-eighth Senatorial District. He resides in Rochester, where he has long been regarded as one of the leading men in the highest society of that intellectual and cultivated city. He is descended from New England ancestors, of whom those on his father's side settled in Massachusetts in 1636, and those on his mother's as early as 1631. His grandfather, THOMAS MORGAN, was born in Groton, Connecticut, in 1742, from which place he removed in 1792, with his family, to the Cayuga Lake, where he established himself as a farmer, and where he died in 1815. His father, one of eight children, was eighteen years of age at the time of the western movement. The expedition of General SULLIVAN, in 1779, against the Seneca and Cayuga Indians, had attracted public attention in an unusual degree to the beauty and fertility of the lands in Western New York, and particularly of the inland lake region between the Onondaga and the Genesee, which led soon after to a large emigration from the New England States. The only roads west of Utica were the Indian trails, and the only mode of emigration into the interior was by means of batteaux up the Mohawk, thence across the Wood-creek portage, into Oneida lake; from which the outlets of the Cayuga and Seneca lakes were reached. At this time a dense forest of heavy timber overspread the entire region, in the subjugation of which the first settlers were forced to contend with innumerable hardships. The rapid development of this inland lake region of Western New York, by the hardy class of New England men who were the pioneers in its settlement, has hardly been surpassed in any of the newer States. As early as 1804 a newspaper was published at Aurora, Cayuga county, which at that time, as the seat of the Land Office, was one of the most important points in Western New York. As population advanced westward, this office was removed first to Canandaigua and afterward, we believe, to Batavia. With the completion of the Erie canal, in 1825, Western New York ceased to be a new country, and began in turn, to furnish emigrants to the Western States. There is no part of American history more striking or more fruitful of suggestion than the great movement of population from New England westward to the Mississippi, during the fifty years between 1790 and 1840. The number of new States formed within this period, the cities and villages founded, the public works conceived and executed, and the commerce inaugurated, in the brief space of half a century, are without a parallel even in American history.

Senator MORGAN's father, Hon. JEDEDIAH MORGAN, was bred a farmer, but engaged quite early in mercantile pursuits. After his father's death, he became the proprietor of the homestead, near Aurora, and devoted himself chiefly to agricultural pursuits during the remainder of his life.

Before the completion of the Erie canal, the market for farm products was limited. At an early day the farmers of Western New York devoted their principal attention to sheep culture as the most profitable staple they could produce. Wool was then worth a dollar per pound, whilst a bushel of wheat would bring but half that sum. Flocks of twelve and fifteen hundred sheep for a single farmer, were not uncommon along the east shore of Cayuga lake. With the completion of the Erie canal, grain became the staple of the farmer, and sheep culture declined to a subordinate position.

In the year 1823, Mr. JEDEDIAH MORGAN was elected a member of the State Senate from the Seventh Senatorial District; in which capacity he served in 1824, 1825, and 1826, when his failing health admonished him to resign. He died at Aurora, December 10th, 1826.

It was during his senatorial term that the "famous seventeen" removed DE WITT CLINTON from the office of Canal Commissioner. When the vote was taken but three Senators were found on the side of CLINTON. McINTYRE, MORGAN and one other. In politics Mr. MORGAN was a CLINTONIAN, and a warm advocate of the Canal policy of the State.

His son, the present Senator, was born November 21, 1818. When eight years old his father removed to the village of Aurora, where he resided until 1844, when he removed to Rochester. His education was commenced at the Cayuga Academy, located at Aurora, in which he remained until sixteen years of age, when he entered the law office of DANIEL WRIGHT, and studied law for a year; then entered Union College, and graduated in 1840. Resuming the study of the law in Rochester, he was admitted to practice in 1842, and commenced practice in Rochester in 1844, and continued in such practice for twenty years until 1864, when he retired from the profession.

With a well cultivated mind and a natural tendency to investigating and philosophical modes of thought, Mr. MORGAN's attention was early called to the study of our native Indian tribes, and especially of the powerful Six Nations, whose seat of empire was in Western and Central New York. He studied them carefully in their historical relations, and especially with reference to the structure and principles of their civil and domestic institutions. In the course of these studies he examined and surveyed many of the ancient traces of Indian occupation in the western part of the State; and in 1848 he communicated to the Regents of the University a paper urging the formation of a museum of Indian antiquities, to illustrate the aboriginal era of our history, and to show the progress and condition of the useful arts among the tribes. The earlier reports of the Regents upon the condition of the State Cabinet, contain several elaborate and fully illustrated papers from his pen, upon the ancient earth-works and modern arts of our Indians, and a large part of the collection of aboriginal utensils and relics in the State Museum, was made by him.

In 1851, Mr. Morgan published a volume entitled "The League of the Iroquois," in which he gave the matured result of long and careful researches into the true nature of the institutions, civil, social and religious, of that famous confederacy of tribes, whose history is so closely identified with our colonial annals. Of this valuable work, the North American Review, the highest of our critical journals, said in July, 1865, in an article on the Indian tribes: "Among modern students of Iroquois institutions, a place far in advance of all others is due to LEWIS H. MORGAN, himself an Iroquois by adoption, and intimate with the race from boyhood. His work, The League of the Iroquois, is a production of most thorough and able research. Though often differing widely from Mr. MORGAN's conclusions, we cannot bear a too emphatic testimony to the value of his researches." In the recently published life of Dr. FRANCIS WAYLAND, long President of Brown University, we find a letter from that eminent scholar addressed to Mr. MORGAN, in which he says: "I have just completed reading, for the second time, your

League of the Iroquois. I cannot forbear the pleasure of thanking you for it. It is the most remarkable book of the kind I have ever seen. * * * It is in all respects to me a most surprising book, and ought to be in every public library in the world. Men ought to know that such a race as this has lived." FRANCIS PARKMAN, the brilliant historian of "The Conspiracy of Pontiac," "The Jesuits in North America," and other works of the highest character in our early history, bears equally emphatic testimony to the value of Mr. MORGAN's book, to which he constantly refers as an authority of the greatest weight in all that relates to the Iroquois.

In the course of his studies of the Indians, Mr. MORGAN's attention was strongly drawn to their peculiar system of family relationship, and to the terms which they employ in addressing their relatives and kindred. In pursuing his investigations, he made long journeys to the West and visited the tribes of the Great Plains and of the Upper Missouri. He found everywhere among the aborigines a strongly defined and peculiar system of relationship, of which, in the course of his studies, he detected unmistakable traces among the barbarian nations of the Old World. This led him to enter upon a series of investigations, extended to nearly every nation of the globe, by means of letters and carefully prepared circulars addressed to our missionaries and consuls in foreign countries. The results of this vast and laborious correspondence, which was carried on for many years, have been embodied by Mr. MORGAN in an extensive and elaborate work entitled "Systems of Consanguinity and Affinity of the Human Family," which the Smithsonian Institution has accepted, and has now in course of publication. A committee of eminent ethnologists, to whom it was submitted for examination by the Secretary of the Institution, pronounced it a work of great value, contributing original and important additions to the science of ethnology.

While sojourning in the Lake Superior region, where he usually spends the summer months, Mr. MORGAN made a special study of the habits of the beaver, the result of which he has given to the public in a beautifully illustrated volume, entitled "The American Beaver and his Works," of which LIPPINCOTT & Co., of Philadelphia, are the publishers. The book adds largely to our knowledge of the natural history of this most intelligent and interesting animal, about which so many fables have been related, and of which so little has been hitherto accurately known.

In politics he was a Whig, until the formation of the Republican party, by the vote of which he was elected to represent the Second District of Monroe county in the Assembly of 1861.

As a lawyer, Mr. MORGAN, for nearly twenty years, stood high in his profession at Rochester, and having acquired an ample competence by its successful practice, retired from the bar to devote himself to scientific and literary pursuits. Socially and personally he is one of the foremost of the citizens of Rochester, where he is held in universal esteem for his fine talents, his scholarly acquirements and his spotless purity of character.

LORENZO MORRIS.

The name of MORRIS is one of the most familiar in the history of the government and public service of this State. It was borne by one of the most distinguished of the revolutionary associates of Washington, and has been prominent in many departments of action. In leading movements of progress, and in legislation, it has never been forgotten by the people; and at this day it is identified upon the map of the State, by territorial designation, in that part of the State where individuals of that name were best known, most cherished and honored.

The present Senator from the Thirty-second District, was born August, 14th, 1817, at Smithfield, in Madison county. His father, DAVID MORRIS, and his mother, yet live, in advanced years, in Chautauqua county.

That corner of the State which a few years since seemed so secluded and remote — the county of Chautauqua — has taken and maintains high rank, having grown to opulence in the possession of whatever gives prosperity, and in political power it has, in the government both of State and Nation, made itself influential. But it had to pass, before attaining that eminence, through its wilderness age. When Senator MORRIS removed thither with his parents, it had those incidents of an American new land life, which determined to energy of character those who fixed their fortunes in its early day. Its education is only of the productive school, and mingled with it was the daily task of the culture of soil that, but a brief interval previous, was under the dominion of the Indian.

Senator Morris had the advantages of school and afterwards of academy, and while thus fitting himself for the more intricate problems of life, he was engaged in that preparation of the country for all the purposes of civilization, which in our American phrase, we call "clearing it." While thus educating both mind and body, he formed the friendship of the Hon. Emory F. Warren and the Hon. Thomas A. Osborn, with both of whom afterwards he connected himself professionally.

The profession of the law, which in our country has such fascination for all men who study, and out of their study learn to reflect and reason, had its attractions for him, as he found real life coming out before him, and he devoted himself to it, and was admitted to practice in 1841.

Coming to the bar at a time when a Mulett, a Marvin, and a Burnell made the Chautauqua Bar one of the strongest and most eloquent in the State, he has reaped the advantages in practice that observation and contact with great legal minds necessarily give, as is evidenced by his standing at the bar of his county where he is best known, and by his election from a district where the Democratic party have heretofore polled less than one-third of the popular vote. A few years subsequently, he removed to the county seat and made permanent place for himself in his profession. From 1854 to 1860, he was Postmaster of Fredonia.

His political judgment being with the opinions of the Democracy, he has shared the varying fortunes of that party. It was a test of no ordinary force to the political life, to be constantly surrounded by a powerful majority opposed to his opinions. It is honorable to the fidelity and ability with which Senator Morris held those views of public duty, that in the crisis and extraordinary circumstances of the election of 1867, his friends should have made him their standard bearer, and the result fully justified their judgment, as he was elected in a district then for the first time choosing a Democrat.

Quiet and thoughtful, observing closely and proving his judgment in that way which is of all others the wisest, after practical waiting for evidence, Senator MORRIS at once becomes a valuable member of the Senate of New York. In that body he is a member of two of its most important Committees, those of Judiciary and Literature.

It is a gratification to see the old names of the State reappearing in its annals. It has in it something of that steadfastness in which our institutions have been, it was feared, deficient; nor is it the less interesting as found in this instance, in the representation of the most distant of our districts, when in older days it was most intimately connected with those of the sea-board and river.

HENRY CRUSE MURPHY.

TIMOTHY MURPHY, grandfather of the Senator, emigrated to America, from Ireland, in the year 1769, and settled in Monmouth county, New Jersey, where he married MARY GARRISON, granddaughter of RICHARD HARTSHORNE, of Middletown, for several years member of the Council, and Representative of the Assembly of that Province. On the breaking out of the Revolution, the above mentioned TIMOTHY MURPHY warmly espoused the American cause, and took up arms in defense of those principles which he cherished, and transmitted to his descendants. He left eight children, four of whom were sons, viz.: WILLIAM, JOHN GARRISON, FRANCIS and JOSEPH.

JOHN GARRISON MURPHY married CLARISSA RUNYON, of Princeton, New Jersey, and settled, about the year 1808, in Brooklyn, where he died in 1854, in the seventieth year of his age, leaving two sons and four daughters.

HENRY C. MURPHY, the eldest of these children, was born in Brooklyn in 1810, and has ever since been a resident of that city. After receiving a preparatory education, he entered Columbia College, from which he graduated in 1830. He then commenced the study of the law, with the late PETER W. RADCLIFFE, of New York, and was admitted to the bar in 1833. In the year following, he married Miss AMELIA GREENWOOD, daughter of RICHARD GREENWOOD, of Haverstraw, Rockland county, New York. Though applying himself assiduously to the duties of his profession, Mr. MURPHY found time to bestow on literary and political subjects, and was a frequent contributor to several periodicals of the day. He thus early became known in political circles, in which he has since occupied a foremost position.

At the time Mr. MURPHY entered public life, the State of New York had been long pursuing, in regard to its moneyed interests, a policy which had placed the banks, in every section of the State, under the control of petty monopolists, created by political favoritism. A convention of the young men of the day assembled at Herkimer, in 1834, to which Mr. MURPHY was elected a delegate. On its organization, he was appointed Chairman on Resolutions, and then, for the first time, exhibited that foresight and energy of character for which he has since been distinguished. He took occasion at once to introduce in the Committee, and subsequently in the Convention, a resolution denouncing the above policy, although the patronage which it created had been distributed for the benefit of his own party. Violent opposition was made to the adoption of the resolution, but it finally passed, with some modification. It was, however, never permitted to see the light, having been suppressed in the official report of the proceedings of the Convention. Still it had its effect. The fact that the resolution had been suppressed, soon became known. The New York Evening Post, then edited by the late WILLIAM LEGGETT, and many other journals, exposed the unfair proceeding, took up the doctrine, and gave it a strength and popularity which resulted, in a few years, in the utter prostration of the system of monopolized banking in the State of New York.

Mr. MURPHY was, soon after, appointed Attorney and Counsel to the Corporation of his native city, and, consequently, became familiar with the nature and operation of municipal corporations generally. In 1842, he was elected Mayor of Brooklyn. During his administration, he introduced a system of retrenchment, which actually kept the expenditures of that city within its income. He commenced this retrenchment by the reduction of his own salary. Before the expiration of his term of office as Mayor, he was elected member of the Twenty-eighth Congress, and took his seat accordingly in the House of Representatives, in 1843. Although one of its youngest members, he at once occupied a high position in that body; and, on the Tariff question, advocated a system of duties for revenue purposes only, and thus incidentally indorsed the doctrine of free trade.

On the question of the annexation of Texas, he was in favor of the measure, but advised its postponement, in order that Mexico might be afforded an apportunity to give her assent, and that more unanimity might be secured thereby in favor of it in the United States. In view of the events which have since transpired, the wisdom of this recommendation must be admitted. On other questions of public policy, he took an equally prominent position; and, with ability, opposed the alteration of the Naturalization Laws, and demonstrated the inconsistency of such a measure with the genius of our government, and its bad effects on the settlement of the public domain. For the splendid Dry Dock which has been constructed at Wallabout bay, the port of New York is entirely indebted to Mr. MURPHY's zeal and perseverance.

The most notable position in State politics which this gentleman has occupied, was that of member of the Convention which assembled in 1846, to frame a new Constitution for this State. Here he brought forward several important provisions, some of which were eventually incorporated into that instrument. His course on this, as on most occasions, met the approbation of his constituents, and on his return from the Convention he was again elected to Congress by the largest vote ever previously polled in his district.

On the accession of Mr. BUCHANAN to the Presidency Mr. MURPHY received the appointment of Minister to the Hague. Identified, as he had long been, with the efforts made to rescue from oblivion the early history of our State, particularly that portion of it which relates to its first colonization by Holland, the selection elicited general approval. When the rebellion broke out, Mr. MURPHY was still Minister of the United States to the Netherlands. It was exceedingly important at the time, that the governments of Europe should be correctly informed of the precise facts of the case, and of the real relation of the States to the Federal Government, in order that foreign powers might readily see and adhere to their well-established line of duty. Accordingly, Minister MURPHY addressed to the Government of the Netherlands, an elaborate exposition of that relationship, and clearly pointed out the absolute supremacy of the General Government in all matters committed to it by the Constitution, and the equally absolute rights of the States over all matters not delegated to the United States by that instrument. He seized the opportunity to show, at the same time, that the rebellion owed its origin chiefly to sectional hate and the ambition of the leaders. This paper was printed at length in the Diplomatic Correspondence of 1861 and 1862, and was highly praised by men of all parties. Upon his return to the United States, he announced his determination to uphold the National flag against secession, and was immediately elected to the Senate of the State as a Union man. At the State Convention of the Democratic party, in 1862, he was chosen temporary Chairman, and insisted that all citizens, without distinction of party, should support the Administration in putting down the rebellion. In the annual oration before the Tammany Society, on the 4th of July, 1863, he took no less patriotic ground in behalf of the Union. Indeed, he was no less zealous in acts than in words; for mainly by his exertions, the Third Senatorial Regiment — the 159th New York State Volunteers, Colonel MOLINEUX — was raised, and the bounties paid to the men, without calling upon either the State, city or county authorities for that purpose. Such, in brief, is the history of his action in regard to the rebellion.

Mr. MURPHY has been elected four times to the Senate, for successive terms, and is now in his seventh year of service in that body. He has taken a conspicuous part in all important debates and discussions, and particularly distinguished himself in his efforts to repeal the bill in regard to ecclesiastical tenures, and to establish the quarantine in the lower bay of New York — measures which he successfully carried through. He also was in favor of sustaining the different internal improvements throughout the State, without regard to the section where they were proposed, provided they contributed to the general prosperity. Having always been a strict constructionist, Mr. MURPHY voted against ratifying the Amendment to the Constitution of the United States abolishing Slavery. He holds that, as the Federal Government is one of delegated powers exclusively, and as the subject of slavery was not embraced in the Constitution, and was to be disposed of only by the States where it existed, the power of amendment is necessarily limited to the subjects embraced in the Constitution, and does not legitimately apply to that of abolishing slavery.

Senator MURPHY is the acknowledged representative of his party in the Senate. In 1867, he received the nomination for United States Senator from the Democratic members of the Legislature. He was a leading member of the Constitutional Convention just held, and took prominent part in all its proceedings.

In debate, Senator MURPHY always speaks extemporaneously; in argument, he is close and logical; in manner, earnest and apparently severe; and, when he warms to his subject, history, precedent and analogy, all seem to rise unbidden to fortify the positions he assumes. In private character, he possesses, in an eminent degree, all the essential elements of a high-toned and honorable gentleman; and no public man has, probably, passed thus far through the trying ordeal of a legislative career, so entirely free from the taint of corruption. Though eminently a practical man, taking a deep and active interest in public affairs — a man of the people — he is a scholar, " and a ripe, good one." To the gratification of this taste, Mr. MURPHY has given much of his time and means. During his travels, at home and abroad, he has accumulated one of the finest private libraries in America, and possesses the full power to appreciate and enjoy it; and however much he may win honor and fame as a public spirited citizen, or a successful political leader, his claims as one of the *literati* can never be lost sight of, and will constitute his most enduring fame. Mr. MURPHY's contributions to literature are of a very valuable character, and include a number of translations from the Dutch language, of which he is a perfect master.

ASHER P. NICHOLS.

HENRY WARD BEECHER, in one of his literary lectures, made the assertion that a peculiarity of Yankee blood was that it ran to brains. The remark betrays the BEECHERIAN vanity and class pride, and yet there is much force in it. The descendants of the Puritans, as a race, are probably ahead of all others in natural intellectual powers and capacities. One need hardly refer to census reports or statistical tables to convince himself that a very large share, at least of the intellectual men of our country, are of New England birth or parentage. In this connection it is interesting to note the fact that a large number of our State Senators are of New England birth, and that Vermont can claim the honor of being the native place of five of them. Of these five, Senator NICHOLS is one.

Mr. NICHOLS was born in Whiting, Addison county, Vermont, and is fifty-two years of age. Having obtained an excellent education, he commenced the study of law with Judge CLINTON, at Buffalo, in this State, to which place he removed in early life, and where he now resides. He is one of the first lawyers of that city, and is greatly respected and esteemed. At one time he was a law partner of Judge CLINTON. At present he is associated with Mr. ROBBINS, of that city, and the firm of NICHOLS and ROBBINS has a high standing at the Buffalo Bar. This is all we have been able to learn of his personal history.

Senator NICHOLS ever since attaining his majority, has acted with the Democratic party; but he has not been a managing politician nor a party operator. Like many other people of New England birth, he does not think it honorable or manly to seek office. His whole course in respect to politics has been that of disinterested attachment to, and support of, political principles involved in National, State and Municipal governments. By no other person could have been uttered with a better grace the declaration, when expressing his surprise to the Committee that waited on him to inform him of his nomination for the position he now holds, that "I regard it at all times an honor to serve the people, but have certain peculiar notions on the subject. But it has always been my belief, that when the people really desired the services of an individual in any capacity, they would make their wishes known, in which case it would become the duty of the man honored by their choice to throw aside all personal preferences, and devote himself to the public interests. Therefore I feel honored that you have selected me for this important nomination, which I gratefully accept."

He has never before this held any political office. He was elected to represent the thirty-first Senatorial District by a majority of 1521 over JAMES SHELDON, Republican. In 1865, a Republican Senator was elected by a majority of 743. He is a member of the Committee on Canals.

Senator NICHOLS, though a staunch Democrat and no trimmer, is not a rabid partisan. He does not, as some do, give all his mind to politics, for, beside his law business, he has a love of general literature. He is pleasant and easy, and yet dignified in his manners, and has the highest esteem and confidence of his associates.

JOHN I. NICKS.

Senator NICKS was born at Rhinebeck, in Dutchess county, in the year 1822. He is of English descent. At an early age he was left to fight his own way through life. His advantages of early education were extremely limited; a few months in the rude common school of the day was all that he enjoyed. A necessity more immediately pressing, than a brilliant, or even an ordinary education, made imperative demand on his time and energies. He must work—and so was apprenticed with Messrs. NEAR & HENDRICKS, at Red Hook, New York, to learn the art and mystery of a tobacconist. He afterward, before he was of age, carried on a little business in that line, in Brooklyn, from whence he removed to Ithaca. At this latter place, he was, for some time, foreman of a large tobacco factory, and also carried on business for himself. In 1847, he removed to Elmira, at which place there was then no establishment of the kind. Mr. NICKS' resources were small, and he opened business in a modest way; but constant success, from the first, attended his enterprise. For years past, his business has been larger than that of any similar establishment in Southern New York.

Mr. NICKS early took a prominent interest in politics. The first political office held by him was that of Supervisor from the Second Ward in the village of Elmira, in 1851, having been chosen by the Whig party. He was afterward, for several terms, chosen Trustee of the village, also member of the Board of Education, and Chief Engineer of the Fire Department. In 1864, when Elmira was made a city, he was the candidate of the Republican party for

Mayor, but failed, by a few votes, of an election. In 1865, his name was again used, and his election secured by an unprecedented majority. In 1866, he was re-elected by a handsome vote, in spite of very determined opposition. His term expired in March, 1867. In the prompt, intelligent and satisfactory discharge of the duties of Mayor, he has displayed his marked executive talent. Under his administration, numerous reforms and improvements have been inaugurated, until the business matters of the city have been reduced to the same thorough system which ever characterizes the prudent management of his private affairs.

In 1862, when the present internal revenue system was inaugurated, Mr. NICKS was appointed by President LINCOLN to the office of Assessor for the Twenty-seventh District of New York. To the management of this office he brought the same characteristic ability which has marked his discharge of every public as well as private duty. Out of chaos he produced system and order, and ranked, at Washington, among the best officers of his class in the country. No decision of his was ever overruled by the Department. The duties of this office he was quietly pursuing when Mr. JOHNSON commenced his gyrations "around the circle." Mr. NICKS, like hundreds of other Republican office-holders, was true to principle. He kept on the even tenor of his way, pursuing precisely the same course which he would have pursued under ordinary circumstances. He neither courted martyrdom nor hid from the wrath of the "powers that be." In August, 1866, after the adjournment of Congress, the Republicans of Elmira invited their able and faithful Representative, Hon. HAMILTON WARD, to address them on the political issues of the day, at Ely Hall. Over this meeting Mr.

Nicks was invited to preside. On taking the chair, among other remarks he made the following:

"LADIES AND GENTLEMEN:—You are all aware that I am now filling a small office in the gift of the Government. But if to hold that office I must sacrifice my principles, I say begone with the office. I say to you, and desire it may be heard and understood throughout the length and breadth of the land, that principle is, and ever should be, above office. When I, in my boyhood, learned to love that great man, HENRY CLAY, I was taught by him that it was 'better to be right than President.' I say to you, ladies and gentlemen, of this platform sent forth by Congress, that in looking it over carefully, I feel that I can indorse every word of it. I feel that it is asking but little of those men who have combined to destroy our Government to submit to the policy of Congress. I care not for the position in which this may place me, so long as I feel that I am acting upon principle, fearless of all considerations."

This was but a few days before the Philadelphia Convention. Within a week, the head of Assessor NICKS rolled in the basket. On the evening of the day of the telegraphic announcement of this fact, the Republican citizens of Elmira, to the number of three or four thousand, marched with music and banners, to the residence of the Mayor, and saluted him in honor of his adherence to principle. The demonstration was a spontaneous and heartfelt expression of popular sentiment. A few days afterward, when the office of Senator for the Twenty-seventh district was made vacant by the resignation of Canal Commissioner HAYT, the public voice suggested Mr. NICKS as his successor. In the nominating Convention, held at Corning, each delegate from Chemung, Steuben and Schuyler, as his name was called, rose in his place and designated him as the candidate of their choice. The nomination thus made was ratified by the people, by a larger majority than was ever before received by any candidate in the district.

In the last Senate Mr. NICKS served on the Committees on Canals, Grievances and Retrenchment. He was renominated and re-elected by a flattering vote. He serves the present term on the Canal Committee, and as Chairman of Roads and Bridges, and Poor Laws.

Affable, attentive to his duties, wise and firm in his course and judicious in his management — these are the characteristics which have made Senator NICKS strong with the people and with his associates.

MICHAEL NORTON.

Senator NORTON is the representative of the Fifth District, and in every particular is a self-made man. His career shows what a man with little or no advantages can accomplish, with energy and determination.

Mr. NORTON was born in Ireland, on the 25th day of December, 1837. His parents came to this country when he was only about five months old, became residents of the city of New York, and lived there until their death. He is entirely self-educated, never having attended school over six months. His parents being in moderate circumstances, he was obliged at an early day to earn his own living. He has had a varied life, but yet active, and has seen the world in a variety of phases. Possessing a strong practical turn of mind and an excellent memory, life has been a school from which he has drawn far more knowledge than others would gain by close study. He commenced working out when but eight years old, his first situation being in a crockery factory, where he remained three years. At the age of eleven he went into the employ of SWIFT & Co., sugar refiners, where he remained five years. He then engaged on the ocean steamer Atlantic, of the Collins line, as a mess boy, and made six trips across the Atlantic in that capacity. At the expiration of his service on that vessel he learned the cooper's trade.

In 1861 he enlisted in the volunteer service and was elected Captain of Company D, of the 25th Regiment. He was mustered in the service in May of that year, thus being one of the earliest to respond to the call of the country. While in this service he received the news of the death of his father and the severe illness of his mother. This threw the care of his father's family upon his shoulders, and compelled him to resign his position in the army and return to New York, which he did in November of that year.

In 1862, he ran for Alderman in the Third Aldermanic District. There were four Democratic candidates running, and Mr. NORTON was second in the race, being defeated by JOHN T. HENRY. He was again a candidate in 1864, and elected; was re-elected in 1866, and still holds his position, his second term expiring on the 1st of January, 1869. Since he has been a member of that board, he has served on some of the most important committees, having held the position of Chairman of the Committee on Streets, of Lamps and Gas, and of the Joint Committee on Accounts. He has also been a member of the Committee on Finance, and Wharves and Piers.

In political affiliations, he is identified with Tammany Hall, and connected with both the ward and general committees of that organization, at the present time head-ing the delegation from the eighth ward in the General Committee. He is an active worker in his party, and generally acknowledged as one of the strongest men in the organization of that ward.

Mr. NORTON is a man of strong practical common sense, and knows how to make his knowledge of politics available. Few men of his education can compare with him in his control of men to carry his points. In securing his nomination for the position of Senator, he exhibited this talent to a degree seldom equaled, even by those who profess to be experienced political tacticians. He makes no pretentions to speech-making, and is a man of few words. His district comprises the Eighth, Ninth, Fifteenth and Sixteenth wards of New York, a district in which the Republicans have more strength than any other in the city. He ran on the Tammany nomination, with CHARLES BLAUVELT, as the Mozart candidate, and two Republican candidates against him. The result at the time of his nomination was considered doubtful, but he came out of the conflict with seven hundred and thirty-three more votes than received by all his competitors combined.

In personal appearance, he is a man above the medium size, stout, muscular and powerfully built, with smoothly shaven face, brown hair and florid complexion.

JOHN O'DONNELL.

Senator O'Donnell is a native of Fort Ann, Washington county, New York, where he was born in 1827. His father was born in Ireland and his mother in America. In early life he removed to Lyme, Jefferson county, and in 1849, settled in Lowville, Lewis county, where he now resides. Here he commenced trade, as a general merchant; and, by earnest and careful attention to business, gradually extended his means, and acquired the confidence and respect of his fellow citizens. He subsequently purchased largely of real estate, in the most central and eligible points for business in the village, and erected large and commodious blocks of buildings, extending along both streets, which have added greatly to the business facilities of the place. Within a year or two, he has withdrawn from trade, as a successful merchant. Senator O'Donnell is known at home, as a man of great energy and perseverance, and seldom undertakes an enterprise without carrying it through.

In 1864, he was on the Republican State Committee, and was a delegate to the Baltimore Convention, which renominated President Lincoln. In the same year he was elected to the Assembly from Lewis county. In that body, he served as Chairman of the Committee on the Internal Affairs of Towns and Counties, and was noted for the diligent attention he bestowed upon the interests of his constituents, and upon all measures for the public welfare. He obtained, in various appropriations for Lewis county, for building a bridge, lock and dam, on Black river, and for the improvement of Beaver river, over fifty thousand dollars; also, secured the passage of an act removing the Court House from Martinsburgh to Lowville; and was the author of an act of great importance to the dairy interests of the State:—" To protect butter and cheese manufactories."

In 1865, he was elected Senator for the Eighteenth District (Lewis and Jefferson), in the place of Hon. JAMES A. BELL against ANDREW CORNWALL, the Democratic candidate. He was Chairman of the Senatorial Committee upon Internal Affairs of Towns and Counties, and a member of the Committee upon Insurance, and upon Public Expenditures. Mr. O'DONNELL reported the New York Excise Bill, and was active in securing its passage through the Senate; he was the author of the bill to protect " Primary Meetings, Caucuses and Conventions of Political Parties; " also of the bill to divide the safety fund of $80,000, remaining in the Bank Department, among the bill-holders of the Lewis County, Yates county, and Reciprocity Banks, resulting in a payment of nearly fifty per cent to the billholders. During the campaign of 1866, he was very active, and spoke some forty times, at political meetings, held by appointment of the State Committee. During the session of 1867, Senator O'DONNELL introduced a measure distinguished for its originality and for its success in the Legislature. It was known as the " O'DONNELL Railroad Bill." It provided in the place of State aid to individual roads, a general plan by which the State should aid any steam railroad in the State — out of the county and city of New York — that should build and complete in good running order, twenty miles of road, where a parallel road is not already built, or in process of building, within an average distance of ten miles thereof; and that the Treasurer of the State upon the certificate of the State Engineer that the conditions had been complied with, upon the warrant of the Comptroller, should pay to the said road five thousand dollars per mile, for every twenty miles of road so constructed. It was with difficulty that a report, even for *consideration*, could be obtained from the railroad committee in the Senate. At the first appearance of the bill in committee of the whole but two Senators were in favor of it, but upon discussion it was regarded more favorably, and after repeated and exhaustive examination in debate upon the floor of the Senate it passed by a large vote. Afterwards it passed the Assembly, but was vetoed by Governor FENTON. The success of this measure was justly regarded by the friends of the Senator, as flattering to his perseverance, and they are sanguine that it will yet become a part of the fundamental law of the State.

The bills to extend the provisions of the Metropolitan excise law over the State, and the bill to suppress obscene literature, to prohibit the employment of railroad conductors and other employés who use intoxicating liquors, as a beverage, were passed by him in the Senate, but failed in the Assembly. The Senator is the recognized champion of the temperance interest in the Legislature, and never fails to respond when that interest is before the Senate.

Senator O'DONNELL was re-elected to the Senate at the last election over LEWIS H. BROWN by 1,647 majority. He is Chairman of the Commitee on Finance, or the Premier of the Senate, a position unanimously conceded to him by his associates, and by the party, as a reward for his fidelity to the interests of the State, and for his unbending integrity and honesty. He is also a member of the Committees on Printing, Privileges and Elections, and Public Health.

The Senator is devoting his entire time this session to the revision of the Assessment Law, and if we may judge from his success in the past, this great subject will be thoroughly mastered, and the State will have an assessment law that will deal justly with its citizens, in place of the miserable laws that now disgrace the State.

As a public speaker, Senator O'DONNELL is energetic, fluent and argumentative, seldom failing to fix the attention of a political opponent, and always leaving the impression, that he is correct and conscientious in his views.

ABIAH W. PALMER.

There are some natures which have a magnetic power by which they attract to themselves the sympathies of acquaintances, irrespective of political tenets and social creeds. Whether they are favored with wealth or doomed to poverty, it seems to matter little, so far as the number of their friends is concerned. They go through life, making this man happy by a smile, that one joyful by a kindly word or act, and when they pass out from the world, there is many a mourner for them who does not wear the insignia of sorrow, and yet who secretly murmurs a benediction over their graves, and consecrates a grateful memory to their good deeds. We are uttering no empty plaudit, as hundreds can attest, when we say that Senator PALMER belongs to this class of men.

His father ABIAH PALMER, was a Captain in the army during the war of 1812. He was a man of wealth and influence, and was highly appreciated by a large circle of friends.

ABIAH W. PALMER, the gentleman whose name heads this article, was born on the 25th day of January, 1835, in the town of Amenia, Dutchess county, N. Y., on the old homestead, which has for many years been in the possession of the PALMER family, and on which Mr. PALMER now resides. Both of his parents died when he was still in his early childhood. He pursued his studies at the Amenia Seminary, and afterwards, at the Oneida Conference Seminary, in Cazenovia, with a view to a complete collegiate course. At nineteen, he entered the Sophomore class, at Union College; but in 1856 he was compelled by ill health to relinquish his studies, and to seek remedies at the Clifton Springs Water Cure, in which institution he remained during several months. Having been convinced that he needed a different kind of treatment, he made arrangements for a protracted visit to Europe. Accordingly, in 1857, he went to that country, where he not only visited the cities of Great Britain and the Continent, but also availed himself of opportunities for acquiring a knowledge of modern languages.

In 1859, Mr. PALMER returned from Europe, and resumed the management of his estate, in Amenia, paying particular attention to mining for iron ore, a large bed of that metal being on his lands. In the fall of that year, he was nominated for member of the Assembly, by the Republican party, and elected by a large majority, though the District had, hitherto, been closely contested by both parties. It will be perceived that Mr. PALMER entered upon his political career, when he was but little over twenty-four years old. Up to that period, his time had been spent either in school or abroad; but we are not to suppose that he had formed no decided opinions relative to public affairs; on the contrary, he had been among the foremost to indorse the enduring principles of universal freedom, which were confirmed in his mind by the contrast which was presented to his observation, while in Europe. Therefore, though among the younger members of the Assembly, he held an honorable and prominent place, in his official capacity; and was respected because he had integrity sufficient to enable him to resist the overtures of corrupt schemers. The following year, he was unanimously renominated for the same office; but, in consequence of ill health, he was compelled to decline the nomination. He thereupon withdrew from politics, and gave his attention to business and the restoration of his health.

In 1865, he again accepted the nomination for the Assembly, and was elected by the largest majority ever given by his district. His talents were recognized, and he was appointed as a member of the Committees of Ways and Means, and Revision and Rules. While serving on the former Committee, his attention was called to the necessity of making provisions for the better accommodation of the insane. He succeeded in effecting the enactment of a law authorizing the Governor to appoint Commissioners to select a site for a new asylum for the insane. The following summer, Mr. PALMER was appointed by Governor Fenton, as Chairman of that Board. He devoted nearly the whole of his attention, during the ensuing season, to the selection of a proper site, and strenuously urged upon the inhabitants, at different points, along the Hudson River, to make proposals for having the institution located in their localities. The city of Poughkeepsie offered the most liberal and desirable inducements for the purpose in question; and consequently the Commissioners decided to establish the asylum at that place. Thereupon, a splendid farm of two hundred acres, affording one of the most beautiful sites on the Hudson, was purchased, costing the city of Poughkeepsie and the remainder of Dutchess county $85,000.

During that year Mr. PALMER was again renominated, but his delicate state of health compelled him to decline the candidacy. During the session of the Legislature of 1866, he presented the report of the Commissioners relative to their action, and procured the passage of an act accepting the site, on the part of the State, and also an act for the establishment and organization of the Hudson River State Hospital for the Insane; and secured an appropriation of $100,000, with which to commence work upon the building. Under this act he was appointed one of the Managers, on behalf of the State, for the consummation of the plans; and was subsequently elected President of the Board of Managers. This honor was justly deserved, for Mr. PALMER had initiated and done much towards perfecting one of the most benevolent and humane charities dispensed by the State of New York. In fact, the accomplishment of this beneficent purpose was the master-good which he desired to have conferred upon suffering humanity; and he entered into the work, actuated by sympathy for the unfortunate and by motives of an exalted charity. The time will come when many, having emerged from the terrors of disordered minds, will have cause to be grateful for the impulses which prompted Mr. PALMER in his devotion to this project.

In 1867, Mr. PALMER was unanimously nominated as the Republican candidate for State Senator for the Eleventh District, composed of Dutchess and Columbia counties. The result shows his great popularity; for although his district gave the Democratic State ticket, nearly two hundred majority, yet Mr. PALMER was elected by nearly seven hundred majority. In the Senate, he is Chairman of the Committee on Banks (Senator PALMER is now a bank president) and Charitable and Religious Societies, and is a member of the Committees on Municipal Affairs and Agriculture.

Senator PALMER's mien is that of a true American gentleman. His features are clearly defined, and indicate the benevolence of his nature; and his voice, almost always modulated to gentleness, is magnetic. He is esteemed by his colleagues in the Senate, as one of the most sterling men in the Legislature; and it is with much pleasure that we improve this opportunity for paying tribute to a man whom we have learned to admire.

ABRAHAM X. PARKER.

Senator PARKER was born in the year 1831, in Addison county, Vermont. Although his career has been brief, it has demonstrated that he is possessed of commanding qualities, and is destined to take front rank with New York's most honored and admired sons. The branch of the family from which he descended settled originally, before the Revolution, near Boston. He was educated in the St. Lawrence Academy, at Potsdam, and subsequently studied law for a year with Hon. HENRY L. KNOWLES, of that place. In 1854, he attended the lectures at the Albany Law School, and was then admitted as Attorney. He subsequently practiced for six months in the office of Hon. ELI COOK and FREEMAN J. FITHIAN, then in the full tide of a large practice, at Buffalo, and was, for a considerable time, in the office of JAMES NOXON, at Syracuse.

Mr. PARKER opened an office in Potsdam, in 1856, where he has since continued in the practice of his profession. He is regarded as an eminently safe counsellor, and is an exceedingly effective practitioner at the bar. He enjoys the extensive practice such talents are sure to command. From the time of his location in Potsdam to the present, each year, including that of 1856, has found Mr. PARKER on the stump, a fearless yet discreet champion of the principles of the Republican party. He has never been anything else but a Republican.

Mr. PARKER was, for many years, Chief Engineer of the fire department of Potsdam, and a trustee of St. Lawrence Academy. He is President of the village, and has held the position several preceding years. He is a member of the local board of managers of the State Normal School, located at Potsdam. He was a Justice of the Peace from 1857 to 1861, when he resigned. In all these positions he has commended himself to his fellow-citizens by his able and faithful discharge of the trusts reposed in him.

He was member of the Assembly in 1863, and, although a new member, was at once given the Chairmanship of a very important committee, that of Claims, and he fulfilled the delicate and responsible duties of the arduous position with signal credit. The following year he was re-elected, and was appointed Chairman of the Committee on Commerce and Navigation, a position requiring a high order of talent, and the strictest integrity, and it found in Mr. PARKER a man every way adapted to the place. He entered a special protest against renomination in 1865, but his constituents so highly appreciated his earnest and successful efforts in their behalf, as well as the advanced position he held in the Assembly as a general legislator, and ready and effective debater, that he was renominated by acclamation. He was, however, compelled peremptorily to decline, by reason of business engagements. He was appointed Postmaster of Potsdam in the spring of 1865, and in the fall of 1866 was removed, for opposing the HOFFMAN and PRUYN ticket. He was unanimously nominated to his present position, and was elected by over six thousand majority. He holds the honorable positions of Chairman of the Committees on Insurance and Public Health, and is a member of the Committees on Railroads and Public Expenditures. He is one of the most reliable and useful members of the Senate, and is a man of acknowledged power and ability. During the canvass, the New York World well said of him, that he "was considered one of the most straightforward members during the sessions of 1863-4. He is a zealous Republican, but free from bigotry. He was a candidate for Clerk of Assembly in 1867, and received a large vote in the Republican caucus. He is an able, industrious and incorruptible Senator." This tribute from a political opponent is worth more than any commendation of ours.

JAMES F. PIERCE.

The Second Senatorial District is this year represented by a Democrat, in the person of JAMES F. PIERCE. He was born in Madrid, St. Lawrence county, on the 8th day of April, 1830, and is therefore about thirty-eight years of age. His parents were natives of New England. His father was a physician and a graduate of Dartmouth College, New Hampshire.

Mr. PIERCE at an early age prepared to enter college, taking the preliminary steps for a collegiate course in the St. Lawrence Academy; but his health failing him he was compelled to abandon all ideas of a collegiate education. This proved a great drawback to his advancement and ambition. A few years of self-denial and careful attention to his health, enabled him to so far regain it that he entered upon the study of law in the office of Judge HENRY L. KNOWLES, of Potsdam. He remained there pursuing his studies about fifteen months, when circumstances opened to him a wider field, and he was able to secure for himself better advantages, by going to the city of Troy, and entering the law office of Hon. JOB PIERSON and WM. A. BEACH, where his law studies were completed.

He was admitted to the bar at Albany, in the year 1851. when only twenty-one years of age.

After his admission it was discovered that a pulmonary difficulty was making serious inroads upon his health, and there being a family predisposition in this direction, after consultation with, and under the advice of some of our most eminent physicians, he sought the mild and genial climate of St. Augustine, Florida, where he remained three years. Sea bathing, with the balmy air of that locality, and such remedial agents as were prescribed by his physicians, had the desired effect, and he was restored to his usual health. While at St. Augustine, Mr. PIERCE occupied an office with the Hon. ISAAC H. BRONSON, now deceased, then United States Judge for the Eastern District of Florida, whose friendship he retained up to the period of his death. Among the visitors to that section was Governor MARCY, whose acquaintance Mr. PIERCE formed, which grew into intimate personal relations. During the campaign which resulted in the election of FRANKLIN PIERCE as President, he took an active part on the stump and otherwise, and was a frequent contributor to the "Ancient City," the only Democratic paper published at St. Augustine.

On his return from Florida, he again resumed the practice of his profession, and in 1856 took up his residence at Canton, St. Lawrence county, the home of SILAS WRIGHT.

At the hazard of paying Mr. PIERCE an equivocal compliment, it may be said of him that he is by instinct a politician; he early formed a taste for politics, and the excitement incident to political life has always had a charm for him. For years he was the regular delegate to the Democratic State Convention from his district, and in this way became intimately acquainted with the representative men of the party in the State, whose confidence he enjoys.

At the commencement of the war, Mr. PIERCE believing that the Union ought to be preserved, took an active part in raising troops, speaking in almost every town in his county, and taking hold with a zeal unequaled by few men in that locality. Mr. PIERCE, however, remained faithful and unswerving in his adherence to his party and its principles, to which he has ever been warmly and devotedly attached. In 1862, the party being in a hopeless minority, a Union ticket was formed, Mr. PIERCE being placed on it as a candidate for County Clerk, on account of the work which he had performed, his activity in raising troops, and the interest which he took in the cause of the Union. A strong effort was made to defeat him, but he came out of the contest successfully, his majority being about one thousand. His appearance at the Democratic State Convention while holding that position, was hailed with a perfect ovation. The idea of a Democrat being elected to a county office in St. Lawrence county, was looked upon as a remarkable event, and the person so elected a curiosity.

In 1865, Mr. PIERCE removed to the city of New York, and there engaged in the practice of his profession. Soon after this he was employed as counsel to the Merchants' Union Express Company, which position he still holds. In the fall of 1866, he took up his residence in Brooklyn, and in the fall of 1867, was nominated by the Democrats of the Second Senatorial District, a district which has heretofore been represented by a Republican; and although comparatively a stranger in the district, he was elected by nearly four thousand majority. At the commencement of the present session, he was placed by the Lieutenant-Governor on the Committees on Commerce and Navigation, and Retrenchment.

In person, he is above the medium height, slim built, straight and upright figure, large, full bluish gray eyes, dark brown hair, and wears a moustache. He still bears the appearance of his former lung difficulties, and cannot be said to be a person of robust health. He is a person of cultivated manners, a clear head, fine social qualities, warm and sincere in his attachments, calculated to make friends wherever he goes, and to become popular in the Senate. There was no person nominated for the Senate last fall who received so universal commendation from the press of all parties, as did Mr. PIERCE. The Republicans from his native county in several instances volunteered their services in his behalf, a fact that shows his personal popularity among those who knew him the best.

CHARLES STANFORD.

Senator STANFORD was born on the 26th day of April, 1819, in the town of Watervliet, Albany county, New York. His father, JOSIAH STANFORD, a native of New England, early settled in that town. During his long life he was distinguished for his integrity, energy of character, and intelligence. He was both a farmer and contractor. He died in 1862, widely known and lamented. His mother, whose maiden name was ELIZABETH PHILLIPS, was a native of Vermont, and is still living, at the age of seventy-seven, and has a remarkably strong and vigorous mind. Of six sons, five are still living, three in California, one in Australia, and one the subject of this sketch. After receiving a common school education, young STANFORD further prosecuted his studies at the Prattstown

Academy, in Steuben county, and the Clinton Liberal Institute, in Oneida county. Leaving school, the future Senator devoted his time to the assistance of his father upon the farm, and in the prosecution of his various contracts. In 1844 he took a large contract upon his own responsibility, in the city of Albany, to grade the ravine then known as the Hudson street hollow. This enterprise proving a success, was followed by contracts upon the Pittsfield and North Adams, and the Hudson River Railroads. While engaged upon the Hudson River Railroad an incident occurred, bringing out the characteristics of the man and the qualities which have given him success in the world. Owing to sharp competition, the contracts were all taken low. After a partial performance, nearly all the other contractors abandoned their contracts and the railroad company informed Mr. STANFORD that he would be permitted to abandon his. His reply was, "I take no contracts to throw up;" and he finished his work, making a fair profit where the others predicted a loss.

In 1850, he went to California, then just opening its gates of golden promise to the world. His brothers either accompanied or soon followed him. In connection with, we believe, three of them, he founded a commercial house, which soon rose to be one of the largest and wealthiest upon the Pacific coast. The firm of STANFORD BROTHERS, then first organized, still exists, the Senator remaining at its head. Neither disastrous fires, nor financial panics, have disturbed its solidity, though a loser by both. It has established branches in different parts of California. In 1859, in connection with two of his brothers, he established a large commercial house in Melbourne, Australia, and soon after, branches in Sidney and New Zealand. The trade of these several houses is very large. One of his brothers, the Hon. LELAND STANFORD, was elected Governor of the State of California, in 1861, and held the office for two years. He is the President of the Central Pacific Railroad, now being rapidly constructed, and soon about to form the extreme western link of the great chain of railroads across the continent.

In 1854, the interests of his firm requiring that one of its members should reside near New York city, Mr. STANFORD returned to the State of New York, and, in 1861, took up his residence in Schenectady county, purchasing a large farm in the town of Niskayuna, where he has since resided. In 1863, he was elected by the Republican party to represent his county in the Assembly. He was a member of the Committees on Public Lands and Public Printing. He was again elected in 1864, and was made Chairman of the responsible Committee on Railroads. He was chosen a delegate to the Baltimore Convention in 1864, and voted for the renomination of President LINCOLN. In the fall of 1865, he was prevailed upon to accept the Republican nomination for Senator of the Fourteenth District. This district was composed of Schenectady, Schoharie and Delaware counties, and, according to the previous elections, was largely Democratic. He was elected, however, by a majority of 1,614. This result was as gratifying to the friends of Mr. STANFORD as it was unexpected to his opponents. During this campaign, he established the Schenectady Daily Union; he still remains its proprietor. It is one of the handsomest daily papers in the State, is conducted with enterprise and talent, having done much to change the county of Schenectady from one of doubtful politics to a Republican stronghold.

Mr. STANFORD rendered invaluable service to the State, in 1867, in his capacity as Chairman of the Senate Committee of Investigation into the Management of the Canals of the State. The effective labors of that Committee are well known and need but a reference from us. To the bold, fearless and rigid scrutiny of Senator STANFORD is the public indebted for the exposure of the nefarious frauds which have been perpetrated on the Canals of the State. He was nominated as an Independant Republican, for re-election, in a district considerably altered from the one in which he was originally elected as Senator the preceding term. The regular nomination was given to the Senator who had represented the greater portion of the district the previous session. Many of Mr. STANFORD's friends, who had admired his upright course, deemed it due him that he should be returned, and due to the State that he should be placed where he could complete the work he had so successfully begun. He was therefore nominated and elected, receiving a liberal Democratic support. He is a strong Republican.

Mr. STANFORD is now in the prime of life. He is a man of robust and portly frame, fine presence, and an easy dignity of manner. In the Senate he is a working, rather than a talking member. He is Chairman of the Committee on Canals, second on Commerce and Navigation, and a member of the Committee on Insurance and Retrenchment. In the preceding Senate he was a member of the Committees on Commerce and Navigation, Agriculture, and the Erection and Division of Towns and Counties, being Chairman of the latter Committee. It need hardly be said that he is a man of strong common sense, great energy of character, firmness of purpose, and untiring industry. With him obstacles are the things to be surmounted, not hindrances to advancement. A conviction that a measure is right, secures for it his support; and though the measure may, for the moment, be unpopular, his support of it is none the less zealous;

he is willing to wait for justice. To his other qualities he adds an integrity that is unquestioned, and a private character above reproach. The schemes of corruption which are but too frequently the objects of legislative favor, find in Mr. STANFORD neither advocate nor friend, as he has convincingly proven in his action in regard to canal frauds. Too rich to desire a bribe, and too honest to take one, he is a good type of the public servant, whom the State can illy spare.

FRANCIS S. THAYER.

This gentleman, who represents the Twelfth District in the State Senate, comes of the old Massachusetts Puritan stock. His father came from the Bay State to Vermont, and in Dummerstown, Windham county, in the Green Mountain State, the subject of this sketch was born on the 11th of September, 1822. He is one of a family of eleven brothers and sisters. He lived in that county until he was nineteen years old, enjoying the ordinary advantages of education then usually falling to the lot of sons of that State. Here was ripened a rugged constitution, and those habits of industry, thrift and good morals were formed which laid the foundation for future strength of character and usefulness. At eighteen years of age he was elected captain of a military company, and held that position until he left the State. Up to nineteen years of age he had worked on a farm, and for a time was a clerk in a country store. In the summer of 1841 he came to Hoosick Falls, Rensselaer county, New York, where his father had removed. He remained a few weeks here, and then went to Cambridge Academy, in the adjoining county of Washington, where he received instruction for four months, and acquired a fair education in all the English branches.

In the winter of 1842, he taught school in the village of North Bennington, Vermont, and "boarded around" in the families of the scholars. In those days, no young man's education was considered "complete" without this experience. In the spring of 1842, Mr. THAYER came to Troy, and was employed as a clerk in the flour store of HOWLAND & BILLS, the first year receiving only one hundred dollars and board. But he soon mastered the business, and his aptitude, discretion, foresight, judgment and business qualifications were of so high an order that he was admitted a partner in the firm at the end of five years. Mr. THAYER has remained in the flour and milling business ever since, being extensively and heavily engaged in the manufacture of flour, and has acquired, as the result of good judgment and proper attention to business, a handsome competency. His firm has from the first been one of the largest concerns in his line of business in the city of Troy. The brands of flour from his mills are widely known in the markets of the country as among the best known as Troy flour.

Politically, Mr. THAYER was a Whig from first manhood until the old Whig party had "outlived its usefulness" and was mainly absorbed into the Republican organization. His first vote was cast for HENRY CLAY, of whom he was a staunch supporter, in 1844. Since the formation of the Republican party, he has been one of its most ardent and unflinching members. Mr. THAYER has been several times a delegate to State and local conventions, but beyond this, he has steadily declined political honors, until his acceptance of the nomination for Senator in the fall of 1867, when he was elected by 1,600 majority, running 532 votes ahead of his ticket in his own county.

Mr. THAYER is a warm friend of the Canals of the State, and takes especial interest in the welfare of the Champlain canal. His marked integrity, sound judgment, practical knowledge, and unwavering support of whatever cause he espouses, will render his services of the most valuable character in defending, protecting and fostering in the Senate, not only the Canal interests of his constituents, but also all others, whether of a local or general character, which may be affected by State legislation. Self-reliant, discreet, clear-headed, and with an unerring judgment, and a wide practical knowledge of public interests and public wants, he will prove a most valuable member of the Senate, no less than a prominent and influential associate in the leading counsels of the Republican party of the State.

Senator THAYER is Chairman of Committees on Manufactures and Public Expenditures, and a member of the Committees on Canals and Public Buildings.

WILLIAM M. TWEED.

Were we called upon to select from among the many able and distinguished men in the Senate the most remarkable man of them all, we should, unhesitatingly, name WILLIAM M. TWEED. Not that he would be picked out as such by a stranger, visiting the Senate Chamber. There are others who would undoubtedly be awarded the meed of superiority, as they would certainly be entitled to it, in regard to a number of the qualities that enter into the character of an able, eloquent, laborious and influential Senator. Nevertheless, the capacities of Mr. TWEED's mind are so peculiar and strong, and his achievements so marked and unusual, that we are justified in setting him down as the most remarkable man in the Senate.

Mr. TWEED was born in New York city April 3d, 1823. Both his father and mother were of Scotch descent. The former was born in New York city and the latter on Long Island. He commenced preparation for active life by studying law, and graduated at the Law School of the New York University. He was for a number of years extensively engaged in the manufacture of chairs, but is now practicing law.

Mr. TWEED's first official position, was that of Alderman of the Seventh Ward, New York city, which he held in 1852 and 1853. The following year he was nominated and elected to the Thirty-third Congress, and held a seat in that body in 1855 and 1856. He was School Commissioner of the Seventh Ward in 1856 and 1857, evincing a warm interest in the cause of education, and excellent judgment, and was very successful in the management of schools under his charge. He has been a Supervisor of the city of New York since 1856, and has been Chairman of the Board. In all these positions, Mr. TWEED has shown a keen insight into the motives of men, ready tact in moulding them to his purposes, and singular power as an organizer and director of legislative bodies. He has been Deputy Street Commissioner of New York city since 1861, and gives to the position untiring industry, wise direction and stirring energy. He was elected to the present Senate by a majority of about twelve thousand, where he maintains fully his reputation as a superior parliamentary leader. As a member of the Committee on Finance, his experienced counsels are invaluable.

But it is not with Mr. TWEED, principally or chiefly as a successful officer, that we have to do. He stands unsurpassed as a political organizer. He has held, since 1861, the Chairmanship of the Tammany Hall General Committee, an organization than which there exists none more powerful, compact and overshadowing. Its sway cannot be successfully resisted in the city of New York, either in the Democratic party or out of it, and it wields a powerful influence in State and National politics. Its plans are admirably laid and thoroughly executed. Mr. TWEED is the executive head of this organization. We need bring no other fact than this to fully justify our opening remark. The man who can maintain himself at the head of Tammany Hall, as its acknowledged leader, must be a remarkable man. A casual observer would fail to perceive in Mr. TWEED the elements of his success. His rotund corpulent form, quiet movements, and not extraordinary countenance, give no evidence of superior talent. But behind that unimpressive exterior there is both an engine and an engineer of motive and guiding powers unsurpassed. It may be difficult to designate the true secret of

Mr. TWEED's great success as an organizing politician. His intellect is quick and active; his perceptive faculties are very keen; he has rare discrimination in the choice of his agencies, and is ever true to his engagements and loyal to his friends. He is magnanimous to a fault, where magnanimity is appreciated, and unrelenting to those who insist on his hostility. He seeks the advancement of young men, and chooses wise and experienced counsellors as his intimates; his temperament is of the nervous, sanguine order, which knows no faltering nor doubt, and he is sagacious, cool and determined.

These are some of the characteristics which place Mr. TWEED in the front rank as a remarkably effective organizer. We believe we will not be regarded as over-estimating the man by those who know him best.

JAMES B. VAN PETTEN.

Senator VAN PETTEN was born June 19th, 1827, in Sterling, Cayuga county, New York, and graduated at the Wesleyan University, in the class of 1850. Before the war he was well known as the very successful Principal of Fairfield Seminary, one of the oldest and most popular institutions of the State. Though a literary man and practical educator, he was always public spirited and much interested in national affairs. During the administration of POLK and PIERCE he belonged to the Democratic party, but broke from it on account of its pro-slavery tendencies, and supported JOHN C. FREMONT for President. Since that time he has been identified with the Republican party.

In the Spring of 1861 he resigned his position as Principal of Fairfield Seminary, and went to the field as Chaplain of the Thirty-fourth New York Volunteers. In this capacity he not only gained the reputation of a faithful chaplain, but evinced a decided military spirit, and in his brigade and division was known as the "fighting parson." He remained with the Thirty-fourth New York Volunteers until the Fall of 1862, and was with it at Fair Oaks and in all the marching and fighting on the Peninsula until the Second Bull Run. He then accepted the position of Lieutenant-Colonel of the One Hundred and Sixtieth New York Volunteers, and went with his regiment on the "Banks Expedition," to the Department of the Gulf. In three weeks from the time he entered the department, the Colonel of the regiment went on detached service, and he was left the permanent commander of that brave and distinguished regiment for two years. He participated with it in every expedition and important battle in the Department of the Gulf, and was often noticed in the public prints and commended in orders, for superior gallantry and merit. He distinguished himself in the Cotten and Bislen affairs; in the assault on Port Hudson on the memorable 27th of May and the bloody 14th of June, 1863; and again, on the Red River Expedition, in the severe engagements of "Sabine Cross-roads," "Pleasant Grove," "Mansusa," and "Carre River." In the summer of 1864, he shared in the perils and achievements of the most brilliant campaign of the war, that of Sheridan in the Shenandoah Valley. At the battle of Winchester, on the 19th of September, he was severely wounded, early in the day, but with characteristic fortitude and resolution, remained on the field until the battle was won. This he did against the advice of his generals and to the admiration of the brigade. For this he received the warmest commendation of Generals McMILLEN, EMORY and SHERIDAN, and was recommended for the commission of Brigadier General. In the Fall of 1864, while home on account of his wounds, he received a staff appointment from Governor FENTON, which he did not accept, as he preferred to remain in active service until the war was over, and took the colonelcy of the One Hundred and Ninety-third New York Volunteers and returned to the field. With this regiment he joined the army of the Shenandoah, commanded by Brevet Major-General TORBERT. From this he was transferred to the Department of West Virginia, commanded by Major-General EMORY, and assigned to the command of the District of Cumberland, with headquarters at Cumberland, Maryland. Subsequently he was assigned to the command of the District of Harper's Ferry, West Virginia. His services were recognized at Washington; and in March, 1865, he was commissioned Brigadier-General by brevet, for gallant and meritorious service. During the Summer and Fall of 1865 he was in the Department of West Virginia, and in command of the District of Cumberland. He remained in the military service until February 10th, 1866, and then returned to the position he occupied before the war, as principal of Fairfield Seminary.

He has the reputation of an accomplished scholar and eloquent speaker. Though a clergyman and educator by profession, he early acquired a critical knowledge of the fundamental principles of law, and is well qualified for the position he now occupies. Senator VAN PETTEN is Chairman of the Committee on Militia and on Internal Affairs of Towns and Counties, and is a member of the Committees on Literature and Engrossed Bills.

STEPHEN K. WILLIAMS.

Senator WILLIAMS was born in Bennington, Vermont, May 9th, 1819. His father, RICHARD P. WILLIAMS, M. D., emigrated to what is now the village of Newark, then new and unsettled, in Wayne county, New York, when the subject of our sketch was four years of age.

Mr. WILLIAMS early evinced that aptness and proficiency in his studies, which have been so characteristic of him throughout his after life. During his boyhood he was studious and reserved, reading much, particularly history and biography, being far in advance of most boys of his age in his studies. For this, he was indebted much to the kind attentions of his father, who taught him during his evenings. Owing to his thorough preparation for a collegiate course, and evident maturity of qualification, the faculty of Union College in his case varied the rule requiring the applicant for admission to be sixteen years old, and, at the early age of fifteen, admitted him to the Sophomore Class, with which he steadily advanced until he graduated with marked distinction, in the year 1837.

After a few months travel in the Eastern and Southern States, having chosen the profession of the law, he commenced the study of it in the office of Judge SHERWOOD, at Newark, Wayne county, and finally completed his preparatory reading in the office of the Hon. GEORGE H. MIDDLETON, late of Syracuse, and was admitted to practice in the year 1842. He at once entered into copartnership with Judge MIDDLETON; and his success as a practitioner, was marked and continuous. In some respects his first business connection was a fortunate one. Judge MIDDLE-

TON, was a man of much more than ordinary caliber; he was a thorough scholar, possessing a fine judicial mind, and an able and effective advocate. But the multifarious and confining details of the office business were particularly distasteful to him, and to these, from necessity as well as from choice, Mr. WILLIAMS applied himself with tireless energy. With such zeal and earnestness did he prosecute his labor, that, for weeks together, all through his professional life, his lamp might be seen burning almost into the small hours, night after night, thus laying the foundation of the success which has since crowned his professional labors. A few years was sufficient to make him known as one of the leading lawyers of his district.

As a student, he was laborious, indefatigable; as a lawyer, scrupulously faithful to the interests of his clients, and untiring in the advocacy of their claims; and despising the mere trickery by which too many of the profession are willing to gain temporary forensic triumphs, he acquired, with the bench, a high reputation for candor and frankness as well as legal attainments; and with the Bar, the character of a fair, courteous and gentlemanly practitioner, whose professional reputation was a guaranty against chicanery.

Mr. WILLIAMS has always been an earnest and a consistent politician, believing in human progress and the doctrine of the equal rights of all, and has made it the object of some of his leading efforts, to advocate the extension of equal rights to all races and conditions of men.

He has always devoted himself so closely to his profession as to prevent all thought of political preferment — having held but one public office, that of District Attorney of his county — until 1863, when he was elected Senator of the Twenty-fifth District; to which office he was re-elected, in the fall of 1865, by a majority of over four thousand, and more than two hundred in advance of his ticket, and was again elected, in 1867, by a flattering vote. During these terms he has held important positions on committees, such as Railroads, Judiciary, State Prisons, Retrenchment, &c., and takes a prominent part in all the proceedings of the Senate. Within a few years he has several times been proposed for Congress from his district, but the claims of locality taking precedence, the nomination went to Cayuga county.

In 1865, Mr. WILLIAMS was a delegate to the Baltimore National Convention, which renominated ABRAHAM LINCOLN for the Presidency. He aided in the admission of the Louisiana delegates into that convention, whom he regarded as entitled to representation there, as they had formed a loyal constitution and a loyal government which was then in the hands of loyal men. In regard to his action on that occasion, the New Orleans True Delta, then a loyal paper, and published by Hon. WILLIAM R. FISH, said:

"It is well known to most of our readers, that when the Louisiana delegation presented themselves as members of the Baltimore Convention, in April last, there was considerable opposition to their admission. It is not generally known, however, how that opposition was overcome, at least, on the part of the New York delegates. Mr. WILLIAMS, a member from that State, enjoying the confidence of Mr. PRESTON KING, the Chairman of the Committee on Credentials, and the respect and good will of all the other members who knew him, used his influence, both publicly and privately, in behalf of the admission of our delegates; and it is not too much to attribute their admission, in a great measure, to his exertions. This circumstance forms a connecting link between the New York State Senator and the citizens of Louisiana."

He has always been an earnest and effective friend of the canals of this State, and has endeavored, several times, to abolish the system of repairs by contract; but the strong influences, interested in preserving the present system, have thus far prevented the accomplishment of its repeal.

In the Senate, Mr. WILLIAMS has been a firm friend of the soldier. In 1864 he introduced a bill "for the relief of the families of volunteers in actual service in the army and navy of the United States;" supported warmly and efficiently the Constitutional amendment, giving them the right to vote while in the field; dedicated his services, for several months each year, during the war, to the promotion of the interests of volunteers, and gave his active support to bills raising bounties for soldiers.

Senator WILLIAMS is a ready and accomplished debater, speaking seldom on unimportant questions, but on issues of importance, always taking a prominent part.

JAMES TERWILLIGER,

CLERK OF THE SENATE.

Mr. TERWILLIGER is a native of New Scotland, Albany county, New York, where he was born January 30th, 1825. He is of Holland and Scotch lineage. In the year 1836, he removed to the town of De Witt, Onondaga county; and, up to the age of eighteen, his time was spent in working on the farm, and obtaining the meager education imparted by the district schools. He early manifested a great love for books and newspapers. He seized everything of the kind which came in his way, and devoured the contents with avidity. His tastes were more particularly in sympathy with works of a political nature, and biographies of statesmen; and thus his thoughts were turned to the workings of political machinery. In the mean time, until he was twenty-six years old, he labored on his father's farm, familiarizing himself with all of the weary routine of agricultural toil. In 1851, a new chapter was opened in his life. Laying aside the implements of manual work, he invested his capital in journalism, and became one of the proprietors of the Syracuse Daily Journal. His connection with that newspaper continued until 1855, when he was appointed Deputy Clerk of the Assembly, by R. U. SHERMAN, then Clerk of the House. In 1856, he received the appointment of Journal Clerk of the Senate, and held that appointment for four years, at the end of which time he was elected Clerk of the Senate. Mr. TERWILLIGER has since been four times elected without opposition. In addition to this post of honor and responsibility, he has held others of similar importance.

In fact, the past eighteen or twenty years of his life have been more or less employed in arranging the details of either county or State campaigns, and in supervising the order of legislative business. Mr. TERWILLIGER was chosen Clerk of the Board of Supervisors of Onondaga county, in 1849; and, from the organization of the Republican party in 1856, to the year 1860, he was Secretary of the Onondaga County Republican Committee, when he was elected Secretary of the Republican State Committee. He conducted the memorable presidential campaign of that year with masterly tact and acceptance, and originated the plan of sending speakers, by the State Committee, into different sections, a practice now so generally adopted. Mr. TERWILLIGER has been Secretary or Acting Secretary of the Republican Union State Committee ever since, except the years 1862, '64 and '67. In the canvass of 1864, he was Acting Secretary of the National Union Executive Committee, and additionally aided the State Committee very materially.

When the lamented PRESTON KING was appointed Collector of the Port of New York, the position of Private and Confidential Secretary to the Collector was offered to Mr. TERWILLIGER, without any solicitation or previous knowledge of the matter, on his part. Induced by friendship for Mr. KING, he accepted the place, and held it until the appointment of the present Collector, when he resigned.

Mr. TERWILLIGER's familiarity with all the ramifications of political forces; his very large acquaintance with the leaders of parties in this State and the country at large; his ready comprehension of the right thing in the right place, render his services almost invaluable. As Clerk of the Senate, he is a master. All of the duties attending that post are as familiar to him, as are the successions of propositions of Euclid, to a professor in college; and his marked executive abilities, his steady application to the rapid dispatch of business, and his almost uninterrupted attendance upon the sessions of the Senate, greatly enhance the value of his services.

There is no bluster in his composition. The calm dignity of the perfect gentleman always rests upon him, and the smile of good nature is rarely missed from his face. Mr. TERWILLIGER is held in high estimation by both parties. At the close of each term, elegant testimonials have been presented to him by the Senators, as an expression of their appreciation of his ability and kindness.

MEMBERS OF THE ASSEMBLY.

WILLIAM HITCHMAN,

SPEAKER OF THE ASSEMBLY.

The Speaker of the House is one of that class of men, now very common, who have pressed their own way to the front, over many and serious obstacles. Indeed, of nearly all our public men can the American people with excusable pride boastingly say, they carved their own way to fortune and to fame. It is the genius of our institutions that young men, born with noble impulses and honorable ambitions, as they press energetically on to the goal of their hopes, find the way opening clearer and brighter before them. It is the first hills that need bravery and toil in the surmounting — ever after, the race is only limited by the endurance. The Speaker is of those who find no limit to their determinations, having before them only steady, persistent, earnest struggling, and a preparation and cultivation for its rewards.

William Hitchman is a native of New York city, having been born in Pearl street, near New street, November 18, 1830. His father, at that time, kept a livery stable in the last named street; but being unsuccessful there, he soon after removed to Yorkville. Willie Hitchman was a favorite pupil in the public school in Eighty-sixth street, where he received his early education. His conduct record was always of the highest, and the head of the class the usual reward of his natural intelligence and application to study. The old gentleman, with an amount of sound common sense rarely to be found, determined that his son should have a trade. The teacher, Mr. THOMAS SPOFFORD—afterwards Alderman and member of Assembly—remonstrated earnestly, that the lad's superior mental powers fitted him for a profession, and begged that one be chosen for him. The father's answer deserves to be written in gold and set in a framework of diamonds, to be placed in the home of every father and every son in the land: "LET HIM GET A TRADE TO EARN HIS BREAD, AND THEN THE PROFESSION AFTERWARD, IF HE CHOOSES." And the trade was learned. WILLIE seemed to have a taste for carriage painting, and he was apprenticed to JAMES FLYNN, whose shop was at that time in Eighty-sixth street, near Third avenue. He entered upon the calling with industry, and mastered all the mysteries and intricacies of the craft, in a comparatively short time. Young HITCHMAN possessed the very common attachment to "the machine," and served a full term as member of Engine forty-five, filling the position of Secretary most of the time.

His apprenticeship being ended, he entered the carriage manufactory of ISAAC LOCKWOOD, at the North End, where he worked some time, but the avocation not agreeing with his health, he determined on a change. He secured a position in the old Municipal Police Department of New York city. He was almost immediately promoted to a Sergeantcy, and held the office of Lieutenant of the Nineteenth Ward Police at the time of the institution of the Metropolitan Police system. He then, while the litigation between the two Departments was pending, entered the office of DENNIS MCCARTHY, United States Weigher, as clerk, and conducted the business for a year in a masterly manner. Thus far we find Mr. HITCHMAN filling with fidelity the various subordinate trusts committed to him. We now come to the turning point in his career. We find, as in all cases of the advance of young men, that the opportunity which made elevation possible to Mr. HITCHMAN was of the most ordinary kind, and that it was merely his own energy, industry and perception that secured advancement. In 1859, he was appointed engrossing clerk of the Board of Aldermen of New York city, and held the position over eight years, discharging the duty with ability and usefulness. That was his opportunity. Young men are found on every hand with opportunities equally or more conducive to success. The chance it gave was simply the opportunity for self-improvement; and, surely, many have that. His desk was located in the City Library. While his time was well occupied in his public duties, he yet had leisure hours, and those hours were devoted to laying the foundation for higher positions. Manuals of Parliamentary practice, debates in Congress, political, statistical, historical and scientific works, were not only read but studied. Thus he stored his mind with valuable material, while day by day he made his mental acquirements the more valuable, by a constantly augmenting practical experience with the world.

Mr. HITCHMAN was elected a member of the Board of School Trustees of the Nineteenth Ward in 1860, and was re-elected. At the close of his second term, he was chosen School Commissioner, and held the office during the term, which expired shortly after the opening of the Assembly. He was a wise and discriminating officer, and won the affections of both scholars and teachers. Mr. HITCHMAN'S

Democracy is of the kind that favored the vigorous crushing of rebellion, and the speedy reunion of the country, under but one, and that the good old flag. He has been a valuable member of Tammany Hall General Committee since 1861, and its efficient Secretary since 1863. He was elected a Trustee of the Fire Department in 1864, and still retains the position. He was chosen member of the Constitutional Convention in the spring of 1867, and served in that body on several important committees. His wise appreciation of correct fundamental principles, keen perceptions and cultivated judgment, won for him many friends in that body.

Mr. HITCHMAN's nomination to the Assembly attests his popularity. He had no thought toward nor aspiration for the office, but each of the two wards in his district had their favorite candidate, and the struggle for success became so earnest that it was impossible for either to break the tie in the Convention. In this critical period, and within but a few days of the election, Mr. HITCHMAN's name was suggested as a compromise, and was received with warmth by both the candidates and their supporters. He finally, with reluctance, yielded to the logic of the position and the urgency of his friends, and accepted the nomination. The canvass was no easy one, but he was triumphantly elected. The Speakership was still less anticipated or sought. But his party being in the ascendancy, many leading minds turned to him as best fitted, by accomplishments and position, to fill the post. In the canvass he had to contend with the prestige of the legislative experience of Mr. JACOBS, the strength of Mr. FLAGG in the interior, and the powerful influences operating in favor of both. He succeeded, after an interesting struggle, in caucus. His only drawback to the highest and most immediate success as a presiding officer, was his lack of experience in the Assembly. But he brought to the discharge of the duties a well trained intellect, a cool and quick mind, and a firm and unyielding resolution. His success has been remarkable. Prompt, decided and impartial, even his strongest opponents can find nothing in him worthy of censure. His mistakes, even at the outset, were few and unimportant, and his determined effort to become efficient in the routine duties of the Chair, and a master of the rules by which it is governed, was crowned with the highest success. His unaffected but cordial courtesy, bland manners, and firm but pleasant administration, have made for him friends of the whole membership of the House. His voice is fluent, pleasant and correct. In the designation of his appointees, and selection of his committees he was very successful. He is a man about the ordinary size, well built, but neither stout nor tall, of long features, fair complexion, mild eye, and bold development of the head. In public life he is charitable and elevated in tone, while in his domestic relations he is affectionate and kind. At home, beloved; abroad, respected and honored, the career of life but just opens before him. It can be nothing else than a prosperous and happy one.

ALFRED THEODORE ACKERT.

Mr. ACKERT is one of the youngest members of the Assembly. He is a lawyer of much promise, and more than ordinary ability. By his own perseverance and energy he has acquired an excellent education. He is descended from German and Dutch ancestry, who settled at Rhinebeck, Dutchess county, some time before the American Revolution, at which place he was born April 15th, 1840. Until seventeen years of age, he was employed upon his father's farm, attending common school at intervals. He then pursued a thorough course of studies, first at the Amenia Seminary, Dutchess county, New York, and afterward at the Fort Edward, New York, Collegiate Institute, always receiving the highest honors. In 1861, he commenced reading law in the office of H. M. TAYLOR, at Rhinebeck, and soon after came to Albany to attend lectures at its celebrated Law University, from which institution he graduated honorably in 1863, receiving the highest commendations from the professors. While in Albany he was in the office of Messrs. CAGGER & PORTER.

Mr. ACKERT commenced the practice of his profession in the city of New York in the fall of 1863, with the firm of WETMORE & BOWNE, maintaining his residence at Rhinebeck.

He received the unanimous nomination by acclamation for member of Assembly from the Second District of Dutchess county, at the Democratic Assembly Convention last fall, and was elected by a majority of 183 over Hon. MARK D. WILBER, the Republican candidate, who for three years had represented the district in the Legislature, and who expected to be triumphantly re-elected. His district comprises the city of Poughkeepsie, and seven country towns. His vote in his own town was very flattering, carrying it by 45 majority, a gain of 171 over the previous year.

Mr. ACKERT has an unblemished character and reputation. He is a worthy and deserving young man, and reflects credit upon the district which sent him to the Assembly, the first and only office he ever held.

He is a prominent and active legislator, perfectly independent, and sustains with energy every measure he believes to be right. He is no mere partisan, although a firm adherent to the principles of his party. He seldom occupies the time of the house with speech-making, but when important measures are under consideration presents his views in a terse and vigorous way, with a clear, ringing voice, and always commands the attention of the members. He is a member of the Judiciary Committee, Chairman of Committee on Grievances, and a member of Committee on Indian Affairs.

AUGUSTUS G. S. ALLIS.

Mr. ALLIS, who represents the First Assembly District of Onondaga county, was born in Cazenovia, Madison County, January 5, 1831. His father, ELISHA ALLIS, was a native of Whately, Mass., and his mother is a direct descendant of the STANLEYS, of Hartford, Conn. He was christened by his grandfather, JAMES STANLEY, against whom, he says, he has always borne a slight grudge for the burden of his name, AUGUSTUS GRIDLEY STANLEY ALLIS. At an early age he manifested an aptness for study, and when able to attend school regularly ranked among the first in his classes. Owing to unfortunate speculations, his father lost largely, and at the age of fifteen he was thrown entirely upon his own resources. His first earnings for two years were voluntarily devoted toward paying off his father's indebtedness, thus relieving him from much annoyance and embarrassment. He then resolved to obtain a good education. He taught his first school at the early age of seventeen, and used the earnings in attending the State Normal School. His means being necessarily limited, he was obliged to practice the most rigid economy. He was prepared to graduate with the highest honors of the school in 1851, but desiring to review some of his studies, he, with two others, declined the diplomas and returned the succeeding term, when he organized the Experimental School and received the most flattering testimonials from the Superintendent of the Department. He refused several advantageous offers to teach, being intent on study, but finally yielded to the urgent personal appeal of Prof. PHELPS, received his diploma and accepted a situation at

Brockport, N. Y., where he taught two years. He then came to Albany, and, under a private instructor, pursued the study of the languages. After thus spending some months here, two vacancies occurred in the city schools, and he went before the examining committee of the Board of Education. The examinations were conducted by Commissioners COLE, CARPENTER and McELROY, and were protracted and thorough. There were many applicants from all parts of the State, including several noted teachers, and Mr. ALLIS was selected for the school on Washington avenue. His success was marked. After the close of the first term, there were more applicants for seats than there were places for them. At the end of the year he resigned to enter college, pursuant to a former resolve. The Board of Education offered a liberal advance of salary, and patrons proffered from their private purse, but he adhered to his resolution. The remarks of the Albany press, at the time, were most flattering, and the proceedings of the Board highly complimentary. He has conducted successful Teacher's Institutes in several of the large cities in the interior of the State. He attended New York Central College for a time, and entered Union College regularly in 1855. After being there a short time circumstances of a private nature, creditable to his head and heart, led him to take a voyage to Europe. He returned with an additional fund of knowledge, his own health benefited, and that of his wife completely restored. On his return, he entered upon the study of the law in the office of JEROME FULLER, at Brockport, and December 7th, 1856, was admitted to the bar. The following spring he was chosen Police Justice of the place, and held the office until he was induced to accept the position of Principal of the High School at Joliet, Ill., where he remained two years. In 1860 he returned East, in consequence of the health of his aged parents, and opened a claim office in Syracuse, in connection with Major PARK WHEELER, now Treasurer of Onondaga county. He was elected Justice of the Peace in 1864, entering upon his duties in January, 1865, and still continues in their discharge. He is also partner in the wholesale house of WHEELER, ALLIS & Co.

The persistent energy, indomitable perseverance and strict integrity of Mr. ALLIS have given him the confidence of the community in which he resides, and enabled him to discharge his professional and other duties with marked success and honor. His varied experience, genial manner, and firm principle, make him a valuable member of the House. In the Assembly, he is a member of the Judiciary Committee and of the sub-Committee of the Whole.

ALEXANDER H. ANDREWS.

Mr. A. H. ANDREWS is the second son of JOHN B. ANDREWS, a pioneer, who emigrated from Vermont and settled in Massena, St. Lawrence county, in 1810, engaging in the mercantile business. He performed a prominent part in the settlement and progress of the town, holding the offices of Supervisor, Town Clerk, and Justice of the Peace. His family consists of five sons and one daughter, all of whom are now living in their native town. He died at the age of sixty-seven. All of that name in this country, trace their origin to two brothers who emigrated from England about 1640, one of whom settled in Connecticut and the other in Massachusetts. The family to which the present member belongs is descended from the one that settled in Connecticut.

ALEXANDER H., the second son, was born in Massena, April 10, 1819. He attended the common school of the village until he was thirteen years of age, when he entered the academy at Fort Covington, Franklin county, where he remained a year, and he was also a year at the St. Lawrence University. His education, therefore, in the English academic studies, was as good as could be obtained at that time. When not at school he was employed in his father's store, and had no acquaintance with any other pursuit.

On attaining his majority, he engaged in mercantile business in Massena, with his elder brother. At the same time he was appointed Postmaster under HARRISON's administration, to succeed his father, and held the office until removed by President POLK. About this time, the village was stirred by a spirit of military enthusiasm, a uniformed militia company was organized and Mr. ANDREWS elected to the command. He had no taste for mercantile life, and his success not having been what his youthful anticipations had pictured, he determined, at the age of thirty, to engage in agricultural pursuits, and in this his prosperity has been far more gratifying than he had anticipated. He was Census Marshal in 1855 and in 1865, and was special agent under the Provost Marshal in 1863-4. In politics, Mr. ANDREWS was formerly a Whig, and an ardent admirer of HENRY CLAY. In 1855, he was a delegate to the County Convention that organized the Republican party in St. Lawrence county. He is, and ever has been, thoroughly radical in his views, leaning strongly to the extreme measures of the Old Commoner, Thad. Stevens.

Mr. ANDREWS was elected to the Assembly from the Third District of St. Lawrence county, by a majority of 2,338. In his legislative duties he is quiet and unassuming, straightforward in all he says and does, and is a man of sound judgment and great solidity of character.

WILLIAM S. ANDREWS.

The subject of this sketch is one of the youngest, and decidedly the youngest looking man in the Assembly, although his career has been as varied and full of adventure as that of many an older man. He was born in Houston, Texas, July 8th, 1841, his parents being from New England; and is a son of S. P. ANDREWS, the scientific and philosophical writer and linguist, author of Discoveries in Chinese, and other works. At a very early age he came North, and has since resided in the cities of New York and Brooklyn the greater portion of the time.

Mr. ANDREWS at an early age developed a taste for the dramatic art, and in the winter of 1860 and '61, we find him occupying a prominent position as an actor at Niblo's Garden, in New York, he being then eighteen years of age.

Immediately on the receipt of the intelligence of the bombardment of Fort Sumter, he enlisted in the volunteer force as a private; and in June, of 1861, while in the field, was commissioned as a Second Lieutenant in the Ninth New York (Hawkins' Zouaves). He participated in the battle of Big Bethel, known as the first battle of the war, and was in the first boat which landed at Hatteras Inlet, in August of 1861, under BUTLER. Shortly afterwards he was attached to the staff of Brigadier General THOMAS WILLIAMS, commanding District of North Carolina, in the capacity of topographical engineer, where he acquired a familiarity with the inhabitants and topography of the coast of North Carolina, which enabled him to render signal service in the BURNSIDE Expedition.

On the arrival of General BURNSIDE at Hatteras in the winter of 1862, Mr. ANDREWS was transferred to his staff as a special aid. Some sixty pilots being required for the expedition, Mr. ANDREWS was intrusted with the duty of procuring them; in the performance of which duty he was obliged to penetrate many miles into the enemy's country.

Mr. ANDREWS was now placed by General BURNSIDE in charge of the secret service. He succeeded in obtaining correct information as to the number and position of guns, number of troops, location of batteries, &c., within the enemy's lines on Roanoke Island.

On the 7th of February, 1862, the day of the landing of our troops on Roanoke Island, he went in a small boat to the shore, and, under a sharp fire of musketry, selected a landing place for the troops, and found a channel-way for the transports to the shore. Returning to the fleet, he was ordered to pilot the troops to the shore, which difficult duty he successfully performed.*

Mr. ANDREWS then entered the Signal Corps of the United States Army, in which corps he was a First Lieutenant until near the close of the war, when, in consequence of ill health, he left the service. While in the Signal Corps he participated in most of the engagements under BURNSIDE and POPE, in North Carolina and Virginia, and under GILMORE and TERRY in South Carolina, where he remained until his withdrawal from the army.

While stationed on board gunboats in the York River, as a signal officer, he perfected an invention for signaling from within the turrets of "Monitor" vessels; and he was sent to South Carolina to apply his invention to the

---

*See reports of Major-Generals A. E. BURNSIDE and JOHN G. FOSTER of the Battle of Roanoke Island, and operations leading thereto.

Monitors then off Charleston (before the bombardment of Fort Sumter). The invention, though perfectly successful, was only used once or twice, as there was a prejudice against the presence of army officers in the fleet, and no time was allowed for the proper instruction of naval officers in its use.

On leaving the army, Mr. ANDREWS returned to the stage, and after traveling for a time East and West, he was for two years the leading comedian of the Winter Garden Theatre, in New York, where he appeared in all of EDWIN BOOTH's plays. He met with a success which, had he remained in it, would have carried him to the top of his profession. His personations of the Grave Digger in Hamlet, Launcelot Gobbo in The Merchant of Venice, Lord Dundreary, and many other parts, will not be soon forgotten by New York play-goers. As an actor, he was chiefly remarkable for his versatility and power of delineating character, he being equally excellent as the polished gentleman or the uncouth clown.

Having accepted an appointment as Deputy Collector of Internal Revenue in the city of Brooklyn, he determined to quit the stage, and made his farewell appearance on the occasion of a complimentary benefit, tendered by the Mayor and other distinguished citizens of New York.

He was a Deputy Collector under three Collectors, and when T. C. CALLICOT was suspended from office Mr. ANDREWS was appointed Acting Collector in his place, which position he held until after his election to the Assembly.

In politics Mr. ANDREWS has heretofore been a Republican, although moderate in his views, and opposed to the policy of the party in this State as regards their legislation on local affairs, and the passage of sumptuary laws. He received a nomination for the Assembly as a "Soldiers' and Sailors'" candidate, without regard to party, and was indorsed by the Democrats. He ran ahead of his ticket and was elected by a large majority, in a district heretofore largely Republican.

He went into the Democratic caucus, and has, on all State questions, voted uniformly with that party. He is a valued member of the Committee on Railroads and Federal Relations. Mr. ANDREWS is a ready debater, presenting his points compactly, forcibly and eloquently. He is unobtrusive in manner, congenial and pleasant. He is of a sandy complexion, fair features, and handsome expression. Tasty in his attire, and unaffected in style, he is one of the most promising young men in the House. His social habits are correct, and his public life unspotted.

RAYMOND P. BABCOCK.

Mr. BABCOCK is a quiet and observing member of the House, who has lived to a good and green old age, and rejoices in being respected and honored by the sterling old county of Cortland. He was born April 19, 1800, in Hopkinton, Rhode Island, the little State in which American liberty was cradled, and shows his attachment to the free principles of ROGER WILLIAMS by a strong devotion to the cardinal features of the Republican party. His educational advantages, so far as schooling is concerned, were limited to the common schools, but he has had the broader education of a close contact with the world, in an active life. He is a successful farmer, of the town of Scott, Cortland county. His neighbors and friends have borne frequent witness to the sterling probity of his character, by frequent elections to the offices of Justice of the Peace and Supervisor. In these days of degenerate offspring, it is refreshing to witness one of his years able to attend to the arduous labors incident to the faithful discharge of the duties of member of Assembly. His last days give promise of being his best days, in that they are so pregnant with the evidence of the attachment and confidence of his constituents.

LYMAN BALCOM.

Mr. BALCOM was born on the 19th of November, 1800, in the town of Preston, Chenango county. He worked with his father, SAMUEL BALCOM, farming and lumbering on the Susquehanna river, until April 1820, when he bought his time from him at $100. On the 12th of July following he married CLARISSA HALLENBECK. Both were poor, and all her worldly goods was a bed. He had $50 in cash, which he had saved from the odd pennies he had picked up. On holidays his father would give the boys the day, and twenty-five cents with which to observe it. LYMAN then laid the foundation of his present competency by saving the silver, and when he had from $3 to $5 would put it on interest. This is the way the $50 had been made up. He at once, on marriage, ran in debt $3,600 for real estate, and engaged in farming and lumbering. He visited Baltimore with lumber each year until January 6, 1826, when he sold out, paid up all his debts, and had $5,000 left. So much for patient industry and prudent management, both on the part of the frugal and active wife, as well as the laborious and energetic husband. He then moved from Greene to Oxford, where he continued in the same avocation until April, 1835, when he removed to Steuben county. In the fall of 1836, a little more than ten years since the first balancing of books, he sold out, settled up, and had $22,000 left. He continued farming and lumbering until 1855, since which he has confined himself to farming and dealing in real estate. He has three sons and four daughters, all of whom are well married and comfortably settled.

Mr. BALCOM voted the "Bucktail" ticket from 1821 to 1826, then the Jackson ticket until 1830, then the Whig ticket until 1854, and since then has been a firm Republican. He has held various town offices, has been Vice-President of the Steuben County Agricultural Society eight years, and its President four years. He was appointed by Governor Seward and confirmed by the Senate, County Judge of Steuben county in January, 1840, and held the office five years.

It is a curious fact, that Mr. BALCOM's opponent in the late canvass, was his own brother, who is the only Democrat in the family. He achieved considerable notoriety by introducing into the Assembly resolutions in favor of a "greenback theory" of National finances, and sustained them in a strong speech. He is a member of the Committees on Indian Affairs and Two-thirds and Three-fifths Bills.

Mr. BALCOM's personal habits are the most exemplary. He neither uses tobacco nor drinks liquor, and is one of the most genial and pleasant of men. He has the old Roman integrity and the rugged, far-seeing intellect of the successful yeoman. He has several brothers, all of whom are possessed of marked talents. Among them is RANSOM BALCOM, a Justice of the Supreme Court.

GEORGE J. BAMLER.

Mr. BAMLER is the representative from the first district of Erie county, and was elected to the present Assembly on the Democratic ticket, by a majority of six hundred and fifty-six over JOHN HOY, Republican.

Mr. BAMLER is a native of Bavaria, in which country he was born April 21, 1835. When eight years old his family emigrated to this country, and settled in Buffalo, where he has ever since resided, and is now engaged in mercantile business in that city. He is known as an active and influential Democratic politician in his locality, and exercises great influence among his German friends. In 1863, he was elected a member of the Common Council of Buffalo, and re-elected in 1865. In the Assembly he is a member of the Committees on Cities, and Trade and Manufactures, and is a faithful and intelligent member.

MATTHEW P. BEMUS.

Mr. BEMUS is descended from a family of some note in colonial New York. His father, Captain CHARLES BEMUS, commanded a company during the War of 1812; and Mr. WILLIAM BEMUS, his grandfather, was a prominent citizen of the county of Rensselaer, and an early settler of Chautauqua county. He married Miss MARY PRENDERGAST, so that the subject of this sketch is a lineal descendant of one of the most reputable families of Western New York.

MATTHEW P. BEMUS was born in the town of Ellery on the 3d of January, 1818. He received a common school education, displaying extraordinary tact, shrewdness and proficiency. On arriving at maturity, he engaged in mercantile business, which he prosecuted for ten years.

He early took an active interest in politics, and was a zealous Whig, first taking the field in favor of the election of General WILLIAM HENRY HARRISON for President, and WILLIAM H. SEWARD for Governor. In 1840 he received the appointment of County Treasurer, and held the office for six years. He was then nominated for County Clerk, and elected. At this time he was regarded as one of the most promising and energetic young men in the county.

About this time he made purchase of a tract of land in the town of Chautauqua, 1,400 acres in area, and engaged in agriculture. For ten years ensuing, he pretty much withdrew from prominence in political matters, to give his attention to private business. But he could not remain inert, and finally engaged upon an extended field of operations, embracing local improvements both at home and elsewhere. Several of the most prominent measures which were acted upon by the Legislature of 1860, and subsequently, received their impress from his active efforts; and, upon the breaking out of the rebellion, he entered more actively than ever into the political and other movements required for supporting the national administration.

Three years since he became the Inspector of the Buffalo, Corry and Pittsburgh Railroad. This road extends from Brockton to Corry, and is designed to afford another route for coal and other products of Western Pennsylvania to Buffalo. The future prosperity of Chautauqua county is closely associated with this enterprise, which Mr. BEMUS is so conspicuously prosecuting. It is hardly necessary to add that such energy and public spirit have won favor and general popularity among his fellow-citizens. In the spring of 1867, he was elected Supervisor of the town of Chautauqua, there being no opposing candidate. In the ensuing autumn, he became the Republican candidate for member of Assembly. Extraneous circumstances gave rise to a violent opposition to his election, and an independent Republican candidate was placed in the field. Mr. BEMUS, however, received a majority of 376. This spring he was unanimously re-elected Supervisor of Chautauqua. His identification with the material interests of the county, his great energy and perseverance, and his personal suavity of manner, account for his influence and popularity. He possesses rare power of calculating chances, and so is seldom disappointed. His life has been a continued succession of struggles, and generally of successes.

CHAUNCEY C. BENNETT.

Mr. BENNETT, the member from Broome county, is thirty-eight years of age. He was born in the town of Lincklaen, Chenango county, N. Y., August 23d, 1829. His ancestors were New England people. WOLCOTT BENNETT, his grandfather, a native of Connecticut, served as a commissioned officer in the Revolutionary army, under General WASHINGTON.

Mr. BENNETT has received an academic education, but is essentially a self-made man. He has always been an attentive reader of law, and for several years held the office of Justice of the Peace in Chenango county and in Broome county. He was elected Justice in his native town when he was twenty-three years of age, and was a number of times re-chosen. It is extremely creditable to his judgment that in a large business, during which he decided about four hundred cases, there was but one case of probably fifty that were appealed in which his decision was not sustained. He was also Supervisor of Lincklaen.

In 1859, Mr. BENNETT removed to the town of Triangle, in Broome connty, where he now resides. In Triangle he was elected and re-elected Justice of the Peace, and in 1865, 1866 and 1867, was chosen Supervisor. He was a very active supporter of the late war, and used his time and means freely.

Mr. BENNETT is a farmer, and makes his business as such a sort of profession. A large part of his time at home is devoted to his ample library, and to various publications of the day. His probity, ability and geniality have secured to him the confidence and esteem of the people of his district in a marked degree. Quickness of discernment, readiness of action and undoubted integrity are among his most decided characteristics.

In politics, Mr. BENNETT has been a Republican since the Republican Party was organized, and he is "strong in the faith." His majority as representative was about 1,100. He is a member of the Committee on the Affairs of Villages.

WILLIAM C. BENTLEY.

WM. C. BENTLEY, Member from the Second District of Otsego county, is 58 years of age. He was born in the city of Albany in the year 1810. His ancestors came from England about the year 1750, and settled in Rhode Island, Providence Plantations. His father, Captain RANDALL S. BENTLEY, was long a citizen of Albany. WILLIAM received a good education. He chose the profession of law and removed to Butternuts, Otsego county, where he engaged in the practice of his profession, and has resided there for over thirty-five years. He has held various offices in the town where he resides, and has always been an earnest and consistent advocate of Democratic principles. In 1867 he accepted the nomination of the Democracy for Member of Assembly for the Second District of Otsego, and was elected by a small majority over his opponent, Mr. HENRY R. WASHBURN, being the first Democrat returned from that district for fifteen years. He is Chairman of the Committee of Claims, and member of the Committees on Ways and Means, and Sub-Committee of the Whole.

Mr. BENTLEY is a man of solid parts. His judgment is sound, his mind clear and discerning, his integrity unyielding, and he is a gentleman of the old school, courteous and kind. He has been a Democratic wheel horse in his town for years, and is well versed in general politics.

WILLIAM G. BERGEN.

Mr. BERGEN was born in Ireland, February 17th, 1829. His parents emigrated to America in the year 1830, settling in the city of New York, where they still reside. Mr. BERGEN was early sent to a private school, in which he pursued his studies until, the age of fourteen years, when he obtained employment in the office of the Courier and Enquirer newspaper. He served in the capacity of office boy in the editorial department of this establishment, until, desiring to learn the printer's art, he became an apprentice to the business. In consequence of ill health, he was obliged to abandon the craft for one more laborious, and to him more healthful. He finally learned the trade of a mason, which he now follows.

Mr. BERGEN is quiet and retiring in his manners, fond of study, but withal a pleasant and agreeable gentleman, having a large circle of earnest friends, amongst whom he is very popular. He has been a life-long, earnest Democrat. He has never sought any prominence as an active worker for his party, and has never held any political office whatever, before being elected to his present position. He represents the Ninth Assembly District, comprising the Ninth and part of the Sixteenth Wards of the city of New York, in which he received a decided majority.

Mr. BERGEN is a member of the Committees on Public Printing and Charitable and Religious Societies.

LAFAYETTE J. BIGELOW.

Mr. BIGELOW was born in the town of Ellisburgh, Jefferson county, New York, on the 13th of May, 1835. His parents came from Vermont, and his father, JOTHAM BIGELOW, was a farmer in independent circumstances, who always took a lively interest in public affairs, held the office of Supervisor of his town for several years, and in 1835 and '36, was a member of Assembly. LAFAYETTE, his youngest son, was sent to Union Academy, at quite an early age. At this excellent institution he was prepared for college, and entered the Sophomore class of Union College in the fall of 1854. While there he was studious and stood about average in general scholarship. He was elected President of the Adelphic Society of that institution, and once read a poem before it. He was always fond of general reading, and was more given to perusing the English classics than in digging after the Greek roots, or divining the subtle mysteries of the higher mathematics. In composition, declamation and extemporaneous speaking, he took rank among the first while at school.

At the end of the Junior year, feeling anxious to begin active life, and having already decided on his profession, he left Union College and entered the University of Albany, Department of Law, in the fall of 1855. He graduated at this institution in the spring of 1857, receiving the degree of LL.B., and while there he took the silver medal as the prize for the second best original essay on the subject of "Eminent Domain."

In May, 1857, he removed to Watertown, and commenced the practice of law in company with BRADLEY WINSLOW, Esq., a young gentleman who had just been admitted to the Bar. In 1861, he was appointed District Attorney, to take the place of his law partner who had been elected to the office, but who entered the volunteer service early in that year, and served in the Union army with distinction, rising successively from Lieutenant to Colonel. In the spring of 1865, while in command of his regiment, he was shot through the abdomen, and did not recover until months after. Mr. BIGELOW served out his official term as District Attorney, and gave his partner, in the field, $600 out of the $800 salary of the office.

In the fall of 1862, he was nominated almost by acclamation for District Attorney, and was elected by a large majority. For three years longer, he discharged the duties of the office with entire satisfaction to the county, and had the reputation of being a very faithful and successful public prosecutor. In the fall of 1863, following an inclination which he had long felt for the editorial profession, he bought an interest in the Daily and Weekly Reformer, published at Watertown, and one of the largest and most influential Union journals of Northern New York.

Mr. BIGELOW has, for a young man, a high reputation as a campaign speaker and literary lecturer. In the campaign of 1864, he took a prominent part, and spoke in Brooklyn and different parts of the State. In politics, he has always been a Republican, and has never acted with any other party. During the rebellion, he made many Union Speeches; was a member of the War Committee in his county, and rendered effective service in raising recruits.

Mr. BIGELOW'S tastes are really literary, rather than political, and is a graceful and vigorous writer. He has lectured before some of the first Lyceums in this State, and his name is frequently seen in some of our popular periodicals. At the commencement of Union College, in 1866, he received the honorary degree of A. M., as a recognition of his literary character. He has always taken an interest in educational matters; is a trustee of St. Lawrence University, and of two Academies. In the winter of 1865 and '66, he held the office of Assistant Clerk of the Assembly.

In the fall of 1866, Mr. BIGELOW was nominated for Assembly, receiving twenty-nine of the thirty votes in the convention on a first ballot. He was elected by a majority of one thousand six hundred and seventy-eight.

He was made Chairman of the Committee on Printing, and accorded a position on Colleges, Academies and Common Schools, of which he was an active member. He supported earnestly the bill to establish free schools, and opposed most bills making any appropriation not necessary for the support of the government. His constituents approved his course; he was renominated by acclamation and re-elected by a large majority. This session he was accorded a place on the Committee on Public Education, and has been conspicuous in supporting measures of retrenchment and reform in all departments of public expenditure, and especially in checking the extravagance in the printing of useless documents. He is an excellent debater and one of the most intellectual members of the House.

NEHEMIAH C. BRADSTREET.

Nehemiah Cleaveland Bradstreet and Nathaniel Foster Bradstreet, *twin* sons of Samuel and Mehitabel Bradstreet, were born in Danvers, Essex county, Massachusetts, April 25, 1821. Their mother's nativity was Boxford, Massachusetts. She was an elder sister to the late General Jacob Gould, of Rochester, and was born March 19th, 1791, and is now residing in that city. Their father, Samuel Bradstreet, was born in Topsfield, Massachusetts, August 26th, 1789, and was a lineal descendant of the venerable Simon Bradstreet, one of the Colonial Governors of Massachusetts. He was a farmer, and was born upon and occupied, during most of his life, the hereditary estate of his noble ancestor, which was situate on the banks of the Ipswich river, remarkable for its beautiful meanderings and diversified scenery. Topsfield made no boast of its educational edifices, but within those musty walls were puritanical discipline and earnest study. At the age of fourteen, with Greenleaf's National Arithmetic and Brown's Grammar at heart, the rustic could enter the Academy; two years in which completed the scholastic days. Such were the advantages of Mr. Bradstreet's education. The family removed to the vicinity of Rochester, New York, in the year 1838.

The subject of this sketch was at once invited to a clerkship in the shoe and leather house of his uncle, General Gould, and at the expiration of three years was admitted as a co-partner, continuing such until 1863, when he retired from mercantile life and has since devoted his attention to the management of his farm.

Young BRADSTREET had scarcely made his bow as a citizen of Rochester when he was served with a "notice" to "appear armed and equipped as the law directs" for military duty and inspection. Having responded to the call according to "military tactics," he resolved to merge "parliamentary tactics" in the amusement, and at the ensuing election of officers for the company, he showed his skill by a triumphant election as captain, receiving his commission, and in due time an honorable discharge. He also served five years in the fire department, and now holds his exempt fireman's certificate.

Mr. BRADSTREET undoubtedly received his penchant for public affairs from his associations with General GOULD, who, as is well known, did not allow his interest to flag either in local or general politics. He had been early taught that JEFFERSON was the father of Democracy, and had learned that in 1769, when first chosen a Representative to the Legislature of Virginia, he proposed a bill for the permission of the "Emancipation of Slaves," and it is not, therefore, singular that in 1848, just in the flush of manhood, he should have been found listening to the eloquence of CHARLES FRANCIS ADAMS, at a Free Soil Convention, or have been captivated by the bewitching oratory of JOHN VAN BUREN.

We may, perhaps, date Mr. B.'s interest and influence in politics from the memorable period just alluded to — though choosing the work of a private in the ranks.

Mr. BRADSTREET was, however, called out as a candidate for Supervisor in 1857, and was duly elected to that office. At the charter elections of 1859, 1861 and 1864, Mr. B. was the Democratic nominee for Alderman, and was in each case triumphantly elected over the strongest opponents that could be pitted against him.

Upon entering the Common Council, of which he was a member for nearly six years, he at once familiarized himself with the charter and with parliamentary rules, and gave his fullest energies to the honor of the Board and to the promotion of the best interests of the city. His actions and votes were always based upon the principle of "the greatest good to the greatest number." In the Spring of 1863, when the spirit of national politics was somewhat acrid, the Republicans of Rochester, believing themselves invincible at the ballot box, placed in nomination for the mayoralty the Hon. SAMUEL WILDER, a gentleman embodying the Radical ideas intended to be endorsed at the polls. The Democracy determined to meet their opponents with manliness and zeal, and selecting Mr. BRADSTREET as the standard bearer of Conservatism. After one of the most exciting contests ever witnessed at the charter election, he was chosen Mayor by 512 majority over Mr. WILDER.

An incident occurred in this canvass which probably inured somewhat to the success of Mr. BRADSTREET. His twin brother, who bears an almost exact likeness to him, and who is fond of a good joke, being frequently accosted as the supposed candidate for the mayoralty, would improve a good opportunity in the course of conversation to suggest that faithful service for *him* (his brother), would be remembered, if any position should be sought, in case of success. The consequence was, that Mr. BRADSTREET, not being apprised of what had occurred, was considerably confused after his election at the numerous *reminders*, when, in fact, he had made no promises at all. The sequel was, however, soon found, and the joke was considered so good that no ill-feeling was engendered.

Mr. BRADSTREET heartily espoused the National cause in the late war, and showed his sympathy with the soldiers in a practical way, by assisting to relieve their families.

He gave his constant attention to the distribution of the funds provided for relief. In procuring volunteers to fill the quotas, he was particularly active, and assisted those who avowed their readiness to go to the field. As Mayor, Rochester probably never had a more industrious chief magistrate than Mr. BRADSTREET.

Mr. BRADSTREET declined being a candidate for re-election in 1864, but in 1865 was put in nomination again for Mayor without opposition. Disaffection had arisen in the party, and he was defeated by a few votes. He soon after removed to his farm, some six miles from the city. Returning to town again with his family some time during the past summer, he was again called upon to enter the political arena.

The Republican party had placed in nomination for the Assembly Hon. HENRY CRIBBEN, the member from Rochester last year, who was supposed to be invincible from his connection with the Eight Hour Movement, and from the fact of his belonging to sundry organizations of working men, composed mainly of Democrats. Mr. BRADSTREET took the field, as the Democratic nominee, only three days before election, and yet so well were his former services to the party and city remembered, that against tremendous odds he was elected over Mr. CRIBBEN by 57 majority.

Mr. BRADSTREET is Chairman of the Committee on Canals, and has introduced and carried through the House several very important measures for the maintenance of those great commercial highways. He is a high toned gentleman; a man of marked abilities, and is one of the leading minds of the Assembly. He is courteous and elevated in demeanor, self-possessed and firm in action; respectful and kind in his personal intercourse; thorough and able in the discharge of his duties, and respected and beloved by all.

WILLIAM BRISTOL.

Mr. BRISTOL, the member from Wyoming, was born at Gainesville, in that county, May 7th, 1821, and has resided there ever since. His father was a native of this State, and a fine type of the resolute and hardy pioneers who planted in Western New York, the germ of that intelligence, industry, wealth and patriotism which now characterize that section of the State. He was a Member of the Assembly of 1823. His mother, a woman of strong character and sterling virtues, was a worthy daughter of Massachusetts. His grandfather was a Revolutionary hero, and his father, a soldier in the war of 1812. Like many others of our successful men, Mr. BRISTOL received in a common school the basis of his education. Personally directing the management of his extensive farm, he has occupied himself principally as a wool dealer. His large business operations have been generally successful, and he possesses an ample fortune, which is as generously used as it was honorably won. Mr. BRISTOL's wide-awake and intelligent interest in political affairs, began before he could vote. He was originally a Democrat; in 1848, became an active and influential Barn-Burner, and in the Syracuse Barn-Burner Convention of 1856, which indorsed FREMONT, he was one of the few representatives of his section of the State. Since that time, he has been an enthusiastic Republican. He was Presidential Elector for the Twenty-ninth District in 1864, and was one of the Secretaries of the College. He was unanimously chosen Supervisor of his town in the years 1863–66, and served as Chairman of the Board for two years.

In 1862, when President LINCOLN issued his call for 600,000 Volunteers, Governor MORGAN appointed Mr. BRISTOL one of the War Committee for the Thirtieth District. At this time he was at Rochester, deeply engaged in business. He immediately returned home. On Sunday, notice was read from the pulpit of one of the churches, inviting all who desired to aid in crushing the Rebellion to meet in his orchard. The Thursday following, largely through his indefatigable energy, a full company, made up of some of the finest young men that left the State at their country's call, was enrolled, ready for duty. It was the first company on the muster-roll of the famous First New York Dragoons. Three years afterward, when "all that were left of them" returned from following the fiery SHERIDAN, out of money and anxious to go to their friends previous to being paid off, Mr. BRISTOL interested himself in getting them released from their miserable quarters near Rochester, and advanced them money from his private purse to carry them to their waiting homes. In the same pleasant grove, where, three years before, these brave boys had enlisted, a grand pic-nic was gotten up to welcome their return. Over four thousand persons were present, and it was one of the most notable rural gatherings ever held in that section. By the unanimous wish of his fellow-citizens, the whole matter of volunteering, bounties, &c., was left to his discretion, and so well was the duty done that the repeated calls were always honored, and the town owes not a dollar for bounties. The same good management was manifested in the conduct of the county's volunteering and finances, by the Committee of Supervisors, of which he was Chairman, and the county paid its last bond, in 1866. Aside from private bounties paid to volunteers from his town, their families received many substantial tokens of his remembrance. The soldier and the soldier's family had no truer friend than he.

Mr. BRISTOL is now in his second term as member, having been twice elected by flattering majorities, serving each year on the Committee on Cities, and also the present year on the Sub-Committee of the Whole. Personally he is a gentleman of fine appearance, open and courteous manners, and most generous impulses — a man of ability, experience in the world, and strong common sense — having a large acquaintance among the public men of the State, and the good will and confidence of his constituents. The position which he holds is very responsible. He has discharged its duties with faithfulness to his constituents, honor to the State, and credit to himself. His reputation is unsullied. He is one of the most energetic and successful workers and organizers in the House.

AUGUSTUS A. BRUSH.

Mr. Brush's ancestors came to this country from England, and settled on Long Island. They were very conspicuously identified with the early history of this nation. His grandfather served, during the revolution, as an officer of various ranks, from Captain up to General, and his bravery gave him the respect of his fellow officers.

Mr. Brush left school, at the age of twenty, and entered upon a mercantile life, in the town of East Fishkill, New York, to which he had removed from New Fairfield, Connecticut. He still conducts the business of a general country store, in that place. He was elected School Commissioner in 1860, and re-elected in 1863. The watchful manner in which he took care of the school interests in his district, afforded great gratification to the inhabitants. His irreproachable character, and searching insight into human nature, were two very important qualifications for a man in his official position. In his intercourse with his fellow-citizens, he always extended a courteous greeting to all, whether in exalted or humble station, and thus won their high regard, which they plainly exhibited by electing him to a still more exalted office, in the Legislature, and by re-electing him to a second term. He is an effective worker in politics. Possessing a noble heart, he gives willingly and liberally, whenever charity appeals to him for assistance; and, with a firm purpose to avoid that which might compromise his honor, he combines the qualities of a good public officer and reliable friend.

He is a member of the Committees on Public Health and Medical Colleges and Societies, and held the same positions last year, with that on State Charitable Institutions. In the transaction of legislative business, he assumes no showy demeanor for the sake of effect; but talks and acts with a motive to make himself useful.

SAMUEL W. BUEL.

Mr. Buell was born in Broadalbin, Fulton county, N. Y., on the 16th day of March, 1830. His ancestors were from the State of Connecticut. His early educational advantages were such only as the common schools of his native town afforded. His father was a farmer, and he resided with him and followed that occupation till he was eighteen years of age, when his father permitted him to enter upon the active business of life on his own account, and receive the proceeds thereof for his own benefit. He then engaged in the lumbering business, and has ever since followed it, carrying it on as successfully as he could have hoped to do. His present residence is in the town of Benson, in the county of Hamilton.

He has always acted with the Democratic party. During the late war he was styled a War Democrat, and exerted all his influence, which was very considerable, for preserving the Union and maintaining the Constitution. Though possessed of considerable political influence, he never sought and would not consent to hold an office until the fall of 1866, when he was persuaded to accept the nomination for School Commissioner of Hamilton county, and was elected by a large majority. He still holds the office, discharging its duties with general acceptance.

In the fall of 1867, without his knowledge or consent, and while he was absent from the county, he was nominated by the Democratic party for Member of Assembly, and very reluctantly consented to become a candidate. At the election he received the largest majority ever given in Hamilton county for any candidate, and a majority of fifty-six in Fulton county, which the preceding year had given the Republican candidate for Member of Assembly a majority of over nine hundred. We could give no better evidence than this of the confidence reposed in his integrity and ability, and of his personal popularity. He is an energetic, hard working and successful member, and is Chairman of the responsible Committee on Public Printing. He is also a member of the Sub-committee of the Whole.

EDWARD I. BURHANS.

Mr. Burhans is one of that class of men who, by steady application, make no little progress in the work as well as the honors of life. Such men may not make so brilliant displays as others do, but persevering honest purpose brings them a certain reward, which is frequently more preferable, when a whole life-time is being summed up, than that which is measured out to many who started in life with pecuniary advantages in their favor.

Mr. Burhans was born in the town of Roxbury, N. Y., March 25th, 1804. His parents were among the first settlers of the town, having moved thither from Ulster county. His father was of Holland ancestry and his mother of French Huguenot extraction. When he was five years old his mother died; but the loss which he had to sustain thereby was partially made up by the kindness of his grand parents, with whom he lived for a few years. Until he was nine years old, he did not speak English at all, having been taught to talk Dutch up to that period. At about that time, however, a new field was opened to him, in the way of school-life. But the opportunities were very circumscribed, and lasted only until he was twelve; after that, he was obliged to get his education at home. Possessing keen intellectual faculties, and being especially inclined to mathematics, he soon mastered the common English branches sufficiently to be able to take up surveying in its practical details when he was fifteen; and at sixteen, he taught school during a winter term. At the age of twenty-one Mr. Burhans entered the mercantile business without any capital, and has continued therein until the present time. In the meantime, he has carried on farming, and bought and sold real estate to considerable extent. He has been, and now is, a thorough worker, rising early and toiling late. When nineteen years old he first tasted the successes of politics by being elected Inspector of Common Schools, and three years after he was made Justice of the Peace, and acted in that capacity for sixteen years. He was also Post Master from 1837 to 1850, and Supervisor for several terms. During the year 1844 he was elected to the Assembly; and was a member of the State Senate during 1858–59. Such were his honesty of principles and practical knowledge of legal matters, that he was appointed County Judge in 1845, his term being terminated January 1st, 1847, by the requirements and action of the new Constitution.

Mr. BURHANS was a candidate for delegate to the Constitutional Convention in the Spring of 1867, but was defeated. He was elected to his present office in the Assembly by forty majority. He is Chairman of the Committee on the Erection and Division of Towns and Counties and a member of the Committee on Federal Relations. Though he does not consider himself a strict party man, his views not agreeing in full with those of either party, yet he voted for JACKSON, CASS, PIERCE, BUCHANAN and McCLELLAN, all of which is enough to confirm him as a Democrat through everlasting ages.

Mr. BURHANS has largely and frequently contributed to the wants of schools and churches; and his liberality in aiding young men in acquiring an education and in entering business, has made many a heart grateful for his kindness. His experience in legislative matters, coupled with his superior judgment, make him a useful and valuable member.

DENNIS BURNS.

Mr. BURNS is the representative from the Second District of New York. He was born in Ireland in the year 1827, and came to New York when ten years of age, and has ever since resided in that city. He learned the trade of a stone-cutter, but some years since was compelled to relinquish it, on account of his health, and now holds a position in the County Clerk's office. In 1867, he was elected to the Assembly on the Democratic ticket (Tammany), and was chosen by a plurality of 1,101 votes over JAMES DONOVAN, Union Democrat. This is the first elective position he ever held, and previous to last fall was never a candidate for any office. He is a member of two important committees, Banks and Claims.

Mr. BURNS is kind hearted, sociable, enjoys a good joke, and has the faculty of making plenty of friends. He is an energetic member, and scrutinizes closely every measure which comes up for consideration.

PATRICK BURNS.

Mr. BURNS, one of the Representatives from Kings county, is a native of the county of Monaghan, Ireland, and was born January 1st, 1833. His parents emigrated to this country about twenty-four years ago and settled in Brooklyn, in the Second and Fifth Wards of which they have resided ever since. Mr. BURNS was early apprenticed to a shipjoiner, and became an adept in the business of ship-building, at which he worked for about seven years; the most of the time being in the employ of the Government at the Brooklyn Navy Yard. He early attached himself to the Democratic party, in whose ranks he was an active worker. At the age of twenty-one he was elected a member of the Democratic General Committee; and, in 1862, was chosen to represent the Fifth Ward in the Board of Supervisors, serving during his term as Chairman of the Alms House Committee, and Committees on Grades, Relief of Families of Volunteers, Courts, County Jail, and Bounties. As a member of the latter Committee, he was assigned to the receiving ship North Carolina, where he paid the bounties to the volunteers accredited to Kings county. The duties of this position were very arduous, but Mr. BURNS acquitted himself with credit, and won the praise of his associates and the public. Just before the close of his term as Supervisor, in 1864, he was unanimously nominated as the candidate of his party for the Assembly, and was elected by over five hundred majority, notwithstanding an Independent Democrat took the field against him. In the Assembly of 1865, he served on the Committee on Salt, but its duties not taking much of his time, he devoted himself to the affairs of his city, and became a useful member. Mr. Burns made quite a reputation in an effort to have all the streets of Brooklyn opened to the public, but failed, owing to the desperate efforts of property owners, who insist upon holding the thoroughfares in which they live, as private property, subject to no local control. In 1865, Mr. BURNS started an extensive kindling-wood factory, which proved a pecuniary success. At the present time he carries on an extensive distillery. In the Fall of 1866, he was again nominated for the Assembly, to which he was chosen by a majority of nearly two thousand, and was re-elected last year by a largely increased vote. Mr. BURNS is a gentleman of generous impulses, enlarged experience and good judgment. He is quite an effective debater and an active working member of the House. He is a member of the Committees on Commerce and Navigation, and Expenditures of Executive Department.

JONAS K. BUTTON.

Jonas K. Button, member of Assembly from the First District of Cattaraugus county, was born in the town of Machias, Cattaraugus county, N. Y., May 3d, 1821.

His parents were of Welsh extraction, and emigrated from Vermont to Cattaraugus county in the year 1816.

To a common school education, in his case, was super-added the mental discipline acquired by an active business life, and a careful study of human nature. He is by profession a farmer, and until recently has dealt extensively in cattle.

Mr. Button is emphatically a self-made man. He began life for himself at the age of eighteen, since which time, by force of his own energy, he has accumulated a handsome property, and is one of the largest land-holders in his native county. His residence, built after a design of his own, is one of the finest in Western New York.

Mr. Button enjoyed in a high degree the friendship of the late Hon. Peter Ten Broeck during his life time; the last named gentleman reposing such unbounded confidence in his integrity that, at his death, he appointed him sole executor of his will, and President of the Board of Trustees of the Ten Broeck Free Academy, an institution the construction and endowment of which Mr. Ten Broeck handsomely provided for in his last will and testament.

In 1843, Mr. Button was elected School Inspector in the town of Machias, and continued to hold the office until its abolishment. In 1847, he removed to Franklinville, where he has since resided.

As regards politics, Mr. BUTTON is a staunch Democrat; nevertheless, in a county strongly Republican, whenever he has allowed himself to become a candidate for office, he has uniformly run ahead of his ticket. In 1853, '54, he was elected Supervisor of the town of Franklinville, and was re-elected in 1857. In the fall of the same year, he was nominated for member of Assembly, Hon. HENRY VAN AERNAM, the successful candidate, beating him by about two hundred votes. In 1862, he was nominated again for the same office, and was defeated by Hon. A. L. ALLEN, the Republican candidate. In 1864, Mr. BUTTON's friends nominated him for Member of Congress from the Thirty-first Congressional District. He was defeated, however, by the Republican candidate, Hon. HENRY VAN AERNAM, the present incumbent. In 1867 he was again nominated for Member of Assembly, defeating the Republican candidate, Hon. GIDEON SEARLE, by 772 votes, in a district which gave the Republican State ticket a majority of nearly 650. He is a member of the Canal Committee, and also that on Roads and Bridges.

In private life, Mr. BUTTON is eminently social. His large-heartedness, combined with honorable dealing, has won for him a large circle of friends. In the Assembly he is closely attentive to his legislative duties, and is highly esteemed.

ALANSON B. CADY.

The representative of the second district of Oneida, is a native of the county of Herkimer, where, in Newport, he was born on the 15th of November, 1810. His father was a native of Rhode Island, and his mother of Vermont. He had, however, seen but five years, when his parents removed to Waterville, Oneida county, where, from that day, Mr. Cady has made it his home. In the common school and academy of his adopted village, Mr. Cady received as good an education as was in those comparatively primitive days, accorded to American youth. At the age of seventeen Mr. Cady commenced life for himself, as an apprenticed builder. Industry was rewarded by success, and after years of faithful application to business, by a natural sequence, we find Mr. Cady, from a boy with no other capital than a strong hand and an honest heart, risen to a man of influence and competence. Mr. Cady has in his house a fine library, purchased with money earned when he was an apprentice boy, "after hours," that is, after the conclusion of the regular duties of the day.

Politically, Mr. Cady was formerly a Whig, but was the first man in his town to join the Republican party. Though not taking a very active part in politics, he has still been frequently a delegate to the State Conventions of his party, and in 1860 was an alternate delegate to the Chicago Convention, which nominated Abraham Lincoln for the Presidency. When Joshua A. Spencer ran as an independent candidate against O. B. Matteson, Republican, in the Oneida District, for Congress, Mr. Cady felt it his duty to espouse the cause of Mr. SPENCER. Through his influence, Mr. SPENCER received nearly one hundred votes in the town of Sangerfield.

This is Mr. CADY's first political office. As a Member of Assembly he is conscientious and industrious, and represents faithfully and intelligently the interests both of his constituents and the State. Mr. CADY, in " ye olden time," was connected with the military of the State, and in 1832-3 was Colonel of the 45th Regiment State Militia.

In appearance, Mr. CADY is the physical FALSTAFF of the Legislature, bringing down more pounds avoirdupois than any of his colleagues. In manner, uniformly courteous, affable, and considerate of the feelings of all with whom he mingles, Mr. CADY is as good a specimen of the gentleman of the old school as is often found.

WINFIELD S. CAMERON.

Mr. CAMERON is a descendant of a Scottish family or clan that has occupied no small part in the history of that country. He possesses in an eminent degree the peculiar traits which distinguish his countrymen, and his success in life, achieved against the most unfavorable circumstances, has called into action the excellent qualities for which his race is remarkable.

Mr. CAMERON was born June 5th, 1838, in the town of Ellicott, Chautauqua county, New York. His father, JOHN A. CAMERON, died when he was four years of age. From the age of twelve until seventeen, he spent the summers in working for wages as a farm laborer, and the winters in attending school. During the winters of the two succeeding years, he attended the Academy at Jamestown, New York. The following four years were spent in farm labor, and in rafting lumber down the Alleghany and Ohio rivers to Cincinnati and other places; and the three succeeding years were spent by him in alternately teaching a district school, and in attending the Academy at Randolph, New York. In 1862, he entered the office of ALEXANDER SHELDON, of Randolph, as a student at law. While prosecuting the study of law at this place, the second call of President LINCOLN for more troops was issued. After a severe mental struggle, he enlisted as a private in Company H, of the 154th Regiment New York Volunteers. He was first promoted to the office of Sergeant, then to that of Second-Lieutenant, and finally to that of First-Lieutenant. He was wounded in the thigh at the battle of Chancellorsville. While lying on the ground after being wounded, he was captured by stragglers following the rebel army, and robbed of his watch and his money. He was held as a prisoner about two weeks, when he was released on parol, and was brought into the Union lines. His wound healed, and at the expiration of six months he was regularly exchanged, and rejoined his regiment, which, in the meantime, had been transferred to the Army of the West. He took part in the battle of Lookout Mountain and the Knoxville campaign. The following year he was made Captain of the Color Company of his Regiment. With this company he was engaged in the battle of Rocky Faced Ridge, in Georgia. His company, on going into the fight, numbered twenty-four men. He came out with only seven. On the same day his brother JOHN, a member of the 9th New York Cavalry, was instantly killed by a Minnie ball, at the battle of the Wilderness. His mother, on learning this sad event, urged him to leave the service. He obtained a leave of absence, in order to visit his mother, but on arriving at home, learned the painful fact that she was dead. His grief at his double loss only made him more anxious to rejoin his regiment, which he did without delay. Some time afterward he was placed on the staff of General P. H. JONES, commanding the Second Brigade of General GEARY's Division, Twentieth Army Corps. He was afterward detached to serve as Assistant Inspector-General on the Staff of General A. S. WILLIAMS, commanding the Twentieth Army Corps, in which capacity he served until the close of the war.

On being mustered out of the service, Mr. CAMERON returned to Jamestown, New York, and resumed the study of law, and prosecuted the same at that place until the latter part of 1865, when he entered the Albany Law

School. In May following he was admitted to the Bar, and soon after opened an office and commenced practice at Jamestown, New York.

In recognition of his patriotic services, Mr. CAMERON was made a Major, by brevet, by President JOHNSON, for "gallant conduct during the campaign of Georgia and the Carolinas," his appointment to date from March 11th, 1865. He was also breveted Lieutenant-Colonel by Governor FENTON, for gallant conduct at the battle of Lookout Mountain. So honorable and patriotic a record naturally enough attracted the attention of his party, and he was, with the greatest unanimity, made a candidate for Member of Assembly for the Second District of Chautauqua county, and was elected by 1,527 majority. He is a member of the Committee on Commerce and Navigation. He is a gentleman of fine appearance, agreeable manners, and a warm friend. Although a good talker, he is remarkably quiet in the House, seldom taking part in debate.

TIMOTHY J. CAMPBELL.

Mr. CAMPBELL, who represents the Sixth District of the county of New York, is one of the young men of the Assembly, having been elected to his present position at the age of twenty-seven. Born of Scotch-Irish ancestry, in the County of Cavan, Ireland, in January, 1840, he was brought by his parents to the city of New York when a child of five years. At the proper age, young CAMPBELL was placed in the public schools of his adopted city, and continued therein until he was twelve years old. Impelled by a laudable ambition to be independent of the support of his parents, who were in humble circumstances, he left school at that early age, and connected himself with an institution not less worthy of being ranked as an educator—the printing press. Thus early thrown upon his own resources, whatever success in life he has since attained is due to his own exertion. Meanwhile, the labors of the day at the press being ended, young CAMPBELL, desirous to make up for the deficiency of early training at the public schools, added to his practical business education a further book knowledge gained by attending evening schools. He also joined a debating club, and by participating in its weekly disputations he familiarized himself with the prominent political and social topics of the day, and there doubtless laid the foundation of his future success. In the meantime he rose through the various gradations of a printing office from "fly boy" at the press, up to general office manager, serving at times in job offices and again in various newspaper offices, including the Herald, Express and Times.

During a portion of the year 1860, while the dark and threatening war clouds were rolling up, obscuring our political horizon, we find Mr. CAMPBELL living in Augusta, Georgia, and connected with the office of the Dispatch, there published. He soon, however, returned to New York, where, with the exception of the few months spent in the south, he has always resided since coming to America. For the past three years, ignoring types and cases, Mr. CAMPBELL has been a clerk in the office of the County Clerk of New York. Though never till now having held official position, Mr. CAMPBELL has yet for some years been active in local municipal politics, and is now a member of the General Committee of Tammany Hall. As a member of the Fire Department in the good old days of the "volunteer" system, he had his share of "perilous adventure and hairbreadth 'scapes." Though serving his first term, the Speaker recognized the ability of Mr. CAMPBELL by placing him at the head of the Committee on Roads and Bridges, and also making him a member of the Committee on Internal Affairs of Towns and Counties. Socially, Mr. CAMPBELL is one of the most genial of men, uniting with the firmness, pertinacity and frankness of the Scotch, the characteristic humor, hearty friendship and unswerving fidelity of the Irish. Possessed of such a happily compounded nature, it is not surprising that his friends are many, and grappled with "hooks of steel."

WILLIAM H. CHAPMAN.

Mr. CHAPMAN is one of the clear-headed and intelligent members of the House. He shows a ready appreciation of the duties of the office, and with the requisite experience will make a valuable member. He was born in New Hartford, Oneida county, November 13, 1820. His parents both emigrated from England in 1810, and in 1811 his father purchased a hotel in New Hartford, which is still standing and is now owned by his son, the present member, who is also responsible for its management, although he himself resides on a farm, which, in the order of its arrangements and beauty of the buildings, is an ornament to the village. His father died when the son was but three years of age, leaving his mother in moderate circumstances, needing the labor of all her children to aid in the maintenance of the family. WILLIAM's education was therefore confined to the common school, and he was able to attend but three months in the year. He lived in the hotel purchased by his father until he was 29 years of age, when he built his present handsome residence. He has always taken an active interest in politics, being a strict adherent to the principles of the Democratic Party, but he has never before held office. In 1854 he was the Democratic candidate for Member of Assembly from the First District of Oneida, but the district being strongly Whig he was defeated, although he ran 250 ahead of his ticket. He represents the First District of Oneida County, and was elected by a majority of 94. He is Chairman of the Committee on Indian Affairs.

JOHN C. CHISM.

Mr. CHISM, who represents the first district of Albany county, is a gentleman of warm social qualities, energetic in business, clear discernment, penetrating observation and untiring industry. He was born in Schenectady county, January 18, 1822, and graduated from the Schenectady Lyceum. He resides in the town of Guilderland, Albany county. He is an attorney-at-law, by profession, and acts as Insurance agent and auctioneer. He prosecutes a successful business. His fellow-citizens have evinced their appreciation of his abilities, and their confidence in his integrity, by keeping him in the office of Justice of the Peace for twelve years. That he has been faithful to the trusts reposed in him, is evinced by his continuance in that office, and his election to the one he now holds. Mr. CHISM is fast acquiring that familiarity with the routine and intricacies of legislation, necessary to the wise and proper discharge of the duties resting upon him. Quick, persevering and apt, he bids fair, with the requisite experience to make a successful legislator.

GEORGE CLARK.

Mr. CLARK represents Schuyler county. His family is of English extraction. His parents removed from Orange county in this State to Tyrone, Steuben county, in the year 1800, at which place he was born June 25th, 1820. He passed the first twenty years of his life in the manner usual to farmers' sons of that day, that is most of the time at work in the fields, with a little of book education at common school thrown in at intervals. The pursuit of agriculture was rather against his inclination, and hence, at the age of twenty-one, he gratified the constructive propensities of his disposition by learning the trade of a carpenter. This occupation he pursued for eleven years, when his plans for the future again were changed, and he entered upon a mercantile career, in which he is still engaged. He is also largely interested in the lumbering business in the State of Michigan.

Mr. CLARK, on becoming a voter, acted with the Whig party, and afterward with many of his Whig brethren entered the Republican ranks. He was a great admirer of HENRY CLAY. He was elected town clerk in 1848, and was re-elected to that office for four consecutive years. In 1854 he was elected to the office of Supervisor, and was re-elected to that office every year for the six succeeding years. In 1859 he accepted a nomination as an Independent or People's candidate for member of Assembly, against the regular Republican candidate, and came within a few votes of an election. In 1862 he was appointed by Governor MORGAN, Enrolling Officer for his town. He was elected to the position he now holds, by a majority of 336 over ANDREW N. ACKERLY, the Democratic candidate.

Mr. CLARK enjoys to a high degree, the confidence and esteem of his neighbors. He gave great satisfaction, and established a fine reputation for official integrity and executive ability, in the discharge of his duties as Supervisor. In his present position he is very faithful in his attention to legislative matters, and anxious to give his vote on every measure so as to secure the greatest good to the greatest number. He has power, but he exercises it in a quiet, persuasive way. He has pleasing manners and strong social feelings, and easily makes friends.

WILLIAM S. CLARK.

Mr. CLARK's grand-parents, who were born in Dutchess county, New York, settled in Coeymans, Albany county, during the year 1773. His paternal grandfather being unable to endure the privations of pioneer life, died at the age of thirty-two; his maternal grandfather, REUBEN STANTON, was among those who, by their vigor and hardihood, contributed much to clear up the wildnerness in Coeymans, in the days when homes were never safe, in consequence of the depredations of marauders from the army in the war preceding the Revolution. He was, for some years, a licentiate in the Baptist Church, and was regularly ordained by that denomination, in 1793, continuing to preach until he was disqualified by age. Mr. CLARK's parents settled on a farm in Carlisle, Schoharie county, in 1813, where his father died in 1849. His mother is still living; and, though eighty years old, she is healthful and active, with faculties unimpaired, and with her dark brown hair scarcely marked with a thread of silver.

Mr. CLARK was favored with good educational opportunities, having attended some of the academies of Schoharie and Madison counties. He was a teacher during several winters, and then chose law as a profession; he graduated from the Albany Law School in the spring of 1858, and returned to Sloansville, where he now resides. Since then, however, he has gratified his desire for travel very largely, and has also been identified with all movements of public interest in his locality, yet devoting himself to the practice of his profession.

Mr. CLARK was elected Town Superintendent of Common Schools, in the year 1850, and was Commissioner of Excise during the years 1862, '63 and '64.

He was nominated by acclamation by the Democrats, and elected without opposition to the Assembly of 1867, and was renominated and returned to the present Legislature by a majority of 1,778, leading his ticket just a hundred. During the war, his talents and influence were exerted to sustain the government, by addressing war and bounty meetings, and encouraging volunteering, both in his own and the surrounding counties. He has always been a Democrat, and various political articles from his pen, which have appeared through the public press—among them his discussions of the proposed Constitutional Convention in 1858, and of the Constitutional modifications suggested in the Convention of 1867—display a repleteness of ideas and a vigor of analysis above the ordinary cast of mind.

Mr. CLARK has a finely cultivated literary taste, and exhibits in his composition a certain *vim* and dash which excite and insure one's admiration. His "Memoir of CHARLES HOWARD PHELPS," which was written for the Trustees of Dudley Observatory, and subsequently published by them, is a chaste and beautiful tribute to the memory of one whose whole soul was inspired with the grandeur of Astronomy, and whose life trembled at the impressions of those master thoughts which seem to transfigure the whole being.

The position taken by Mr. CLARK in the Legislature of 1867, was recognized by his appointment, by Speaker PITTS, as a member of the Joint Committee to investigate the management of the canals. His ability and legislative experience made him quite a prominent candidate for Speaker of the present House, for which position he received favorable commendations from the press, but in deference to the unanimity of the New York delegation, and in recognition of the claim of the New York Democracy, Mr. CLARK withdrew from the canvass prior to the caucus.

As we should expect from such antecedents, Mr. CLARK's conception of legislative duties is not confined to mere local interests, but embraces in its scope legislation of a general character, and the comprehensiveness both of his views and his familiarity with the requirements of the people, is indicated by the bills introduced by him in relation to the registry, assessment, and highway laws of the State. In debate, he is ready, forcible, logical, and at times eloquent, always having the attention of the House; and by his suavity of manner and geniality of nature, has secured, not only the good will but the personal regard of all his associates in the Assembly.

In his position of Chairman of the Committee on the Internal Affairs of Towns and Counties, he has been indefatigable in his labors to facilitate the progress of the measures submitted to the scrutiny of the Committee. He serves also on the Committee on Charitable and Religious Societies, and on Local General Orders. Mr. CLARK is in the prime of life, enjoys a good joke or a keen sarcasm with the same zest that an epicure relishes his salads and "green seal;" and we doubt not that his versatile intelligence and recognized ability will secure for him higher positions and larger trusts; and however high the position the future may assign him, he will discharge its duties with fidelity unquestioned and honor untarnished.

WILLIAM F. COOK.

Mr. COOK was born at Kingsbury, Washington county, N. Y., October 8, 1810. His parents on both sides were from Connecticut; their ancestors were from England. He received a common school education. His parents died when he was about fourteen years of age, but he continued to reside on his father's farm, with an elder brother, until he was thirty-five. He held various town offices while a resident of Kingsbury, and in 1846 removed to Whitehall and engaged as foreman in a steam planing mill and lumber yard. He remained in that place about seven years, and in 1853 removed to Champlain, Clinton county, where he engaged in the lumber and planing mill business as one of the firm of HOYT, COOK & Co. (now W. F. COOK & Co.), where he has since resided.

Mr. COOK always acted with the Whigs until the organization of the Republican party. He was not engaged in the military service during the rebellion, but gave evidence of his loyalty to the Union by consenting that his only son, who was then just ready to enter college, should go and battle against armed treason. His son enlisted as a private, and soon after was made a corporal, in the Thirty-fourth Regiment New York Volunteers. Soon after reaching Washington, he was detailed for service in the Signal Corps, and was attached to General BANKS' Division. He was engaged at the battles of Winchester and Cedar Mountain, and was with General BANKS' command in the retreat from the Shenandoah Valley, and was in the second Bull Run campaign. Soon after he was sent to Sugar Loaf Mountain to watch the movements of the rebel army across the Potomac, and sent the first despatches to Washington of LEE's army crossing the river. Previous to the battle of Antietam, he, with another officer, captured a bearer of despatches from DAVIS to LEE, who was under the escort of two rebel soldiers, when they were surprised and surrounded by a detachtachment of STUART's cavalry, and captured, together with their prisoners and despatches, and sent to Libby Prison. After a month of suffering, he was exchanged, and again entering the service, remained his full time, and was honorably discharged. In June, 1862, he was recommended for promotion by his superior officers, and it was approved by General BANKS, but the recommendation failed to be acted upon, either by Governors MORGAN or SEYMOUR. His services have been recognized, however, by a First-Lieutenant's commission by brevet, from Governor FENTON.

Mr. COOK is one of the first business men of Clinton county. He holds the esteem and confidence of his fellow-citizens in a marked degree, as is shown by the fact that in the late canvass, when so many Republican districts went Democratic, he was elected by a large majority, to succeed a Democrat. He is a man every way worthy of this high mark of regard. Of mature judgment, integrity of purpose, and clear discernment, he brings to the halls of legislation qualities more important than that of mere ability to speak with credit. He is unostentatious, but as valuable as he is retiring.

ANDREW CORNWALL.

It is many years since Jefferson county has had a Democratic representative in the Legislature. For a long period in the annals of politics it could be depended upon for rousing majorities for the Whig and Republican candidates. Last year the Second Assembly District was represented by Hon. ALBERT SHAW, Republican, who was elected to the Assembly by a majority of eleven hundred and fifty-four. He was a candidate for re-election last Fall, but the large majority given him the previous year was overcome by Mr. CORNWALL, who was chosen by a majority of four hundred and five. Local causes, undoubtedly, contributed to a considerable extent to this result; but it is proper to say that the flattering vote given to the present member was in a great measure due to his personal popularity.

Mr. CORNWALL was born at Pultneyville, Wayne county, New York, in 1814, and on the 25th of March last celebrated his 54th birth-day. His parents were natives of Old Chatham (now Portland), Connecticut, who removed to Wayne county about the year 1800. After attending school until thirteen years of age, he entered a country store as clerk. In 1844, he removed to Alexandria Bay, Jefferson county, his present residence, and opened a store, and has continued in mercantile business there for the past twenty-one years. From his youth Mr. CORNWALL has taken a lively interest in politics, always acting with the Democratic party. For eleven successive years he has been Supervisor of the town of Alexandria. In 1865, he was the Democratic candidate for Senator for the Eighteenth District, against Hon. JOHN O'DONNELL, but the district being largely Republican, he was of course defeated.

During the Rebellion he was one of the War Committee of his county, and as Supervisor of his town, filled all the quotas for volunteers promptly, and with less local bounty than was required for any other town in the county, that furnished as many men.

Mr. CORNWALL is possessed of sound common sense, is prudent and thoughtful, and always watchful of the interests of his constituents. His address is pleasant and his manner courteous. In the Assembly he makes no pretension to oratorical display, and seldom takes up time in debate. He is a member of the Committees on Ways and Means, Manufacture of Salt, and Sub-committee of the Whole.

NATHANIEL DAILY.

Mr. DAILY is a staunch member of the Republican party. His political antecedents, prior to 1856, were Democratic; in fact, he held the office of Justice of the Peace by favor of the Democrats as early as the year 1847, and has continued to hold it for the last twenty years. Like thousands of others, however, who are not completely "wedded to their idols," he energetically entered into the movements which resulted in the formation of the Republican party. From that time to the present, Mr. DAILY has been found on the pioneer lines of political advancement. He unhesitatingly indorses the measures adopted by Congress to restore the South to the rights and privileges of the government; and believes that those measures are sufficiently lenient to meet the demands of mercy, and the approval of every loyal heart.

Mr. DAILY was born in Hampton, Washington county, N. Y., October 3, 1813. His father followed farming as an occupation. But during the conflict between this country and Great Britain, in 1812, he gave up his agricultural calling and entered the army, returning to his former pursuits at the termination of the war. His son NATHANIEL, the subject of this article, received as good an education as was afforded by the common schools of that time. Having mingled the toil of the farm with the toil of the school room during his youth, he also became a farmer. But he likewise possessed business sagacity, and, as a consequence, speculated from time to time in cattle, sheep and wool, until, at last, no small amount of his means and attention was turned in that direction.

During the recent war at the South, when homes were being made dark by the devastations of battles which laid low the pride of many a northern household, Mr. DAILY was elected Chairman of the Town War Committee appointed to raise men and means for the relief of an endangered government. In 1862, he was elected Justice of Sessions, and re-elected in 1863. He was elected to the present Legislature by 152 majority. He serves on the Committee on Public Lands.

Mr. DAILY is a good legislator, possessing a strong mind and good judgment, qualities which peculiarly fit him for the position he occupies.

JOHN MARTIN DAVIS.

Mr. DAVIS was born August 9th, 1826, in the town of Lima, Livingston county. His grand-father, EZRA DAVIS, was of Welsh extraction, but a native of the State of Connecticut. He was one of the early volunteers in the great struggle for the independence of the colonies; and during that long and eventful period of our National history, was in the ranks of the army, doing much credit to himself, and valuable service to his country.

His father MARTIN DAVIS, born in Columbia county, State of New York, was one of the pioneers in the early settlement of what was then, and is still known as the Genesee country, and was identified with the early history, the rapid growth, and final prosperity of that rich and productive region. He, too, like his father EZRA, as a citizen soldier, performed military service for his country, being engaged along the Canada lines in the war of 1812;

but subsequently becoming a member of the religious Society of Friends — a body opposed in theory and in principle to the art of war — he declined to receive from the general government the bounty afterwards provided by Congress for the soldiers of the war of 1812. Ignoring to a great extent the exciting subject of politics, he devoted his time during the remainder of his life to agriculture and the careful training of his somewhat large family of children, of which the subject of this sketch is the eighth.

Mr. DAVIS received as his principal legacy from his father's estate a fair common school education and the precepts of a parent alive to the best interests of his children. He has served by appointment and election, as superintendent of common schools in the town of Mendon, Monroe county, where he now resides. Also, by appointment and election, as a Justice of the Peace for the same time; represented the town in the board of Supervisors of Monroe county in the year 1861, was re-elected in 1862, and also in 1867. He was a candidate for member of Assembly from the first Assembly district of Monroe county in 1866, but received the minority vote by fifteen ballots, occasioned undoubtedly by a difficulty in the Republican party growing out of the election of a member of Congress in the Twenty-eighth Congressional district of New York, of which the first Assembly district of Monroe forms a part. In the fall of 1867, he was again nominated, and was elected.

Mr. DAVIS is a man of sterling worth. His judgment is ripe and discerning; his principles pure and inflexible; his action generally judicious and taken with energy. He is ever at the post of duty, and fearless in meeting all its demands. He has secured the confidence and respect of his associates in the House, and makes a valuable working member.

LEWIS P. DAYTON.

Dr. Dayton is a native of the county which he in part represents. He comes of the staunch stock of the Puritans, being descended in a direct line from John Dayton, who was one of the little band that came over in the Mayflower. From that remote ancestor are descended all those bearing that name living in America. The parents of Dr. Dayton removed from Connecticut to Erie county, New York, in 1814. At that day Western New York was comparatively a wilderness, and bold indeed was the pioneer who could venture to establish his home in its midst. Buffalo was then an insignificant village, recently reduced to ashes by British incendiaries, and Black Rock loomed up as the principal town of that county, and, indeed, of that section of the State. For years afterward it was questionable which of these villages would eventually be the city, which nature seemed to have marked out to lie at the foot of Lake Erie.

In that county, in the felicitously named town of Eden, on the 10th day of October, 1820, the future physician, whose life we now outline, first saw the light. He learned the rudimentary branches at the little school house near his country home, and then was sent at different periods to Aurora and Springville Academies for a more advanced educational training. Having resolved to become a disciple of Esculapius, Mr. Dayton went to the Geneva Medical College, from which, in due time, he received his professional degree. Settling in the village of Black Rock, since swallowed up by the ambitious city of Buffalo, our now Dr. Dayton entered upon the practice of his profession, which has since grown to be very large. In 1852, Dr. DAYTON, who had always taken a deep interest in the cause of education, was elected Superintendent of Schools in his adopted village. Subsequently, Black Rock having become the twelfth Ward of Buffalo, Dr. DAYTON was elected Alderman. In 1855, and again in 1859, he was President of the Buffalo Common Council. In 1864, he was elected County Clerk of Erie county, running considerably ahead of his ticket, as he invariably does. This office he held until the first of January, 1868. Last fall in a district which gave the Republican general ticket nearly 300 majority, and which in 1866 sent a Republican Assemblyman, Dr. DAYTON, though a Democrat as he has always been, received a majority of 42 over his competitor.

In making up the committees of the Assembly, the Speaker placed Dr. DAYTON on Canals and on Public Health. At the Democractic joint caucus to nominate a Metropolitan Police Commissioner, Dr. DAYTON was called to preside.

The Doctor is not a "talking member," yet there are few men in the Assembly who exert greater influence, or attend more closely to their official duties. Of strict integrity, and possessing no little experience in public affairs, Dr. DAYTON is a man whose public career does honor to himself, and who, by his sacrifice of private interest to look after the public good, is entitled to the gratitude of all friends of honest and intelligent legislation.

JOHN DECKER.

Mr. DECKER is perhaps more widely known in the city of New York than any of her representatives. He was born in the Third Ward in February, 1823; and, when old enough, was sent by his parents to the public school in Fulton street. At the age of fifteen he shipped as cook on board of a vessel employed in the coasting trade. But though of an adventurous turn, he did not relish this mode of life, and accordingly returned home the next year, where he remained till he became of age. In 1844 he joined the Volunteer Fire Department of the city of New York, and belonged to Engine 14. In 1848 he was elected Assistant Foreman, and re-elected in 1849. The next year he became Foreman, but declined a second election. In 1853 he was chosen Assistant Engineer, and was re-elected in 1856 and 1859. At this period he was perhaps the most popular man in the Fire Department. He was elected Chief Engineer in 1861 and again in 1863. Two years afterward the Metropolitan Fire Department was established by the Legislature, and Mr. DECKER was thus removed from office. He made his residence at Port Richmond, on Staten Island, and has been ever since engaged in real estate business. In the Fall of 1867 he was nominated by the Democrats to represent Richmond county in the Assembly, and received 2,336 votes, a majority of 1,096. He is a member of the committee on State Prisons, and Sub-Committee of the Whole, and is a hard-working and popular representative.

Mr. DECKER took an active part in the organization of the 1st and 2nd Regiments of Fire Zouaves, and was elected Colonel of the Second. He held the position while the incipient steps were taken, and then resigned. He was often at the seat of war, attending to the wants of his former associates, particularly after they had been engaged in battle. In this way, as well as by his unfailing courtesy and obliging temper, he became regarded as the father and counsellor of the firemen and their friends.

HIRAM EATON.

Mr. EATON's ancestors were natives of New England. He was born in Manlius, Onondaga county, New York, June 20, 1808, and is, therefore, nearly sixty years old, though he has the appearance of being much younger.

For several years he was engaged in the transportation business on the Erie canal, but since 1853, has been engaged in banking, and is, at the present time, Cashier of the Fayetteville National Bank. He was formerly a Whig, but since the Republican party has been in existence, has uniformly supported its principles and candidates. He was elected to the Assembly by a majority of 316, and serves on the Committee on Salt.

BENJAMIN FARLEY.

Mr. FARLEY is one of that class of intelligent farmers who constitute the happiest and most useful of our citizens. He was born in Salem, Massachusetts, October 4, 1810, of parents, whose ancestors came from England. In 1815 his parents settled in the town of Pompey, Onondaga county. After remaining at this latter place some time they removed to Leroy, Genesee county. Here the subject of this sketch attained his majority, gaining that strength of body which a life upon a farm tends to impart, and that vigor of mind which may be obtained from a good common school education, and the great lessons to be learned from the broad pages of the book of nature. Becoming a voter he allied himself with the Whig party. In 1842, he moved into Niagara county, going bravely to work upon a portion of land which was then a wilderness. He was soon called upon to fill various town offices, and in 1857 he was elected by the Republican party to the office of Sheriff, and in the discharge of the duties of that office gave universal satisfaction. In 1865, he filled the office of Supervisor of his town. During the rebellion he was very active and efficient in raising money and securing men to fill the several quotas of his town. In 1867 he was elected to the present Assembly, from the Second District of Niagara county.

Mr. FARLEY takes great interest in agricultural affairs, and in aiding to bring the truths of science to bear upon the tillage of the soil. He has served as President of the Agricultural Society of his town and also of that of his county.

RICHARD FLACH.

Mr. FLACH, who represents the Second District of Erie county in the Assembly, is a native of Saxony, and is thirty-five years old. He immigrated with his parents to this country, and settled in Buffalo when he was about fourteen years of age. He received a good education at a Seminary in Saxony, and in private schools in Buffalo. He has always resided in Buffalo since coming to this country, except for two years, which he spent in traveling through the Southern States. He is a merchant.

Mr. FLACH is a Democrat. In 1860, he was chosen Supervisor, and from 1862 to 1866 was an Alderman. In 1863, he held a position as Lieutenant in the 65th Regiment New York State Militia, and served in the Pennsylvania campaign, under orders from Governor SEYMOUR. He is now Colonel of the regiment, and is interested in everything that tends to promote the welfare of the Home Guard of the State. He was elected to the Assembly by a majority of four hundred and ninety-six over our old friend, GEORGE W. BULL.

Mr. FLACH is chairman of the Committee on Militia, and a member of the Committee on Aliens, and is prompt and faithful in the discharge of his Legislative duties.

JOHN LAMSON FLAGG.

Mr. FLAGG was born in Nashua, New Hampshire, September 11th, 1836. His boyhood, up to the age of twelve, was spent in the place of his nativity. In 1848, his parents removed with him to Troy, New York, where he has ever since resided. Being desirous of obtaining a good classical education, he prepared for college in the schools of Troy, and, in 1853, entered Harvard. While at that institution, he ranked well as a student, and was highly esteemed for his gentlemanly qualities. He graduated in 1857. Soon afterwards, as a first step toward the study of the profession of the law, Mr. FLAGG entered the law office of the late Hon. DAVID L. SEYMOUR, who was then in business with Hon. GEORGE VAN SANTVOORD, both of whom had a wide reputation for their vigorous legal acumen. Meanwhile, he attended lectures at the Albany Law School. In the month of December, 1858, the degree of LL.B. was conferred upon him, by that institution; and he was thereupon admitted to the Bar. A short time subsequent, a partnership was formed between himself and the late Hon. JOB PIERSON, a lawyer of repute. This partnership was terminated by the death of Mr. PIERSON, in 1861. Shortly after that occurrence, Mr. FLAGG formed a partnership with JACOB GEBHARD RUNKLE, of Schoharie county, under the name of RUNKLE & FLAGG, which still exists. At about this time he received the degree of A. M. at Harvard; and in 1867, the honorary degree of A. M. from Union. At the bar, he is recognized as a lawyer of sound judgment and many acquirements; and is remarkable for his equanimity of temper, even when points go against his cause.

But, in addition to his knowledge of the law, he has taken pains to cultivate a fine literary taste. He early identified himself with the Young Men's Association of Troy, an organization well known in literary circles as being one of the most active and flourishing in the Union. The Debating Society connected therewith first elected him as its President. Subsequently he was elected Corresponding Secretary of the Association proper, and, in that capacity, he arranged a course of lectures. The Association afterwards still further honored him by electing him President.

Mr. FLAGG has always been a Democrat. Under the auspices of the Democracy, he was elected member of the Board of Education in March, 1860, and served two years, representing the Third Ward of his city. He proved to be an efficient officer, having the true educational interests of the people at heart, by introducing many reformatory measures into the schools. He was among the leading members of the Board.

In March, 1862, he was elected Police Justice of Troy, by a large majority, in which capacity he served for three years. As Police Justice he acquired a reputation for vigorously enforcing the laws against persons who were clearly guilty; and toward the close of his term, many a villainous fellow who had broken the laws, knew that he would have a good measure of justice meted out to him by Justice FLAGG. Such measures were indeed essential to the good of Society, for crime seemed rampant in that locality.

In the spring of 1866, the office of Mayor of the city of Troy was conferred upon him by a majority of 350 against his opponent, though his predecessor was of the opposite political faith, and the city was in the hands of the Republicans.

During the year of his mayoralty, the Common Council over which he presided, was politically a tie, there being eleven members of each party; and a sharp contest was kept up for the control of the local legislation. On those occasions, he displayed an intimate knowledge of parliamentary rules, and good executive ability. This state of affairs concerning the Common Council, of course became very unpleasant, therefore, during the session of the Legislature, in 1867, a bill was introduced to take away the right of the mayor to vote. The passage of such a law would have broken the tie in the Common Council of Troy. The proposed measure caused no small excitement in that city, and had the effect to produce an elaborate presentation of the subject before the Committee on Cities, by which the bill was favorably reported to the Assembly; but it never became a law.

At the city election, in March, Mr. FLAGG was re-elected mayor by five hundred majority; and, inasmuch as his party also secured a majority in the Common Council, he has probably had a pleasanter official year than before.

Last Fall he was elected to the Assembly by a majority of ten hundred and forty, although his predecessor, who was a Republican, had received a majority of eight hundred and fourteen.

On the organization of the present Legislature, his name was prominently used as candidate for Speaker. Mr. HITCHMAN, however, was the choice of the majority; and consequently, Mr. FLAGG was rightfully made Chairman of the Committee of Ways and Means, the most important position below the Speakership. He is likewise a member of the Committee on Federal Relations. In his labors in committees, he is patient and industrious, and manifests a good broad judgment. In the Assembly, he shows a fair and courteous spirit in debate, and makes friends in both parties.

He is a director of the Troy City National Bank, and is also an officer of the Troy & Lansingburgh Horse Railroad Company, and President of the Rensselaer Park Association. His father, JOHN FLAGG, Esq., has for years held a position of wealth and influence in Troy; and to-day is counted among the leading citizens of that city. In 1860, Mr. FLAGG, the subject of this article, married Miss ELLEN H. BROWN, of Providence, Rhode Island, a lady of superior accomplishments, possessing excellent taste in literature and art. Her name is known to the public as that of a poetess; and her pleasant social attainments are appreciated by a wide circle of friends.

FREDERICK H. FLAGGE.

Mr. FLAGGE was born in Hanover, Germany, December 12th, 1829. He belongs to a respectable family, and received an excellent education in the public schools, becoming proficient in German literature, and learning both the French and English languages. On coming to manhood he emigrated to this country and took up his residence in the city of New York. He engaged in mercantile business and has been for many years an extensive dealer in groceries. More recently he has carried on business in the 22d Ward, although he formerly resided in the Eighth. As was very natural, he always bore his part in Ward politics, and held, for a time, a place on the Tammany Hall General Committee. A year ago he was dropped off by the managers of the party, and was placed in nomination by the Mozart Democrats for the Assembly in the 17th District, against Colonel JOEL W. MASON, Republican. The result was his election by the handsome plurality of 436 votes.

Mr. FLAGGE is a quiet man, minding his own business, kind-hearted and always ready to do a good turn for a friend. He is a little inclined to impatience, however, when business becomes prosy; evidently believing that a legislator should be wide awake and active, neither fooling away time nor spending it stupidly.

ALEXANDER FREAR.

In the seventeenth century, three brothers, Huguenots, bearing the name of FREAR, obtained from the United States of Holland a grant of lands on the Hudson River, now embraced in the counties of Ulster and Dutchess. Their descendants are still numerous in that region, and are generally thrifty, prosperous citizens. Several of them have been characterized by their deep interest in politics. When the Republicans of this State were divided between the supporters of General DANIEL D. TOMPKINS and the friends of DEWITT CLINTON, partisan feeling ran very high. Mr. JAMES B. FREAR, of Poughkeepsie, a man of active mind and character, was foremost among the "Bucktails," and retained the ascendency in the party in Dutchess county till the period of his death, in 1833. He was the father of the present member from New York.

ALEXANDER FREAR was born at Poughkeepsie, on the 18th day of August, 1820. He received a common school education, and also attended the academy in his native town. He began at an early age to display an aptness for business. At fourteen he was a clerk in a store in Poughkeepsie, and three years later went to New York "to seek his fortune." When only nineteen, he became a partner in the house of SHELDON & COMPANY, in Pearl street. He remained there till 1848, when he established the importing house of ALEXANDER FREAR & COMPANY, in New York, with branches in Chicago and Galena. This firm carried on a heavy business with great success, till the financial revulsion of 1857. The effects of this crisis were even more disastrous at the West than in New York, and the establishment was compelled to close up its affairs.

Mr. FREAR now entered more deeply into politics, and was elected to the Board of Councilmen from the Seventh Senatorial District. The next year he was chosen Alderman for the Eleventh District, consisting of the Twentieth Ward of the city of New York. In his official duties he displayed energy as indefatigable as that which had characterized him as a man of business.

When the rebellion broke out he was among the foremost in sustaining the Government, and employed his official as well as personal influence to secure the adoption of measures for furnishing men and money for the service of the country. His zeal in the matter disturbed for a time his political relations, and he took the lead in organizing a Union Association in the twentieth ward, in the autumn of 1861, comprising Democrats and Republicans, and electing its candidates for the Assembly and other offices.

In 1865, Mr. FREAR was the Tammany candidate for the Assembly, and was elected by a plurality of about eight hundred votes over OLIVER CHARLICK, the Mozart candidate, who had also a Republican nomination. In 1866 he was re-elected, receiving 2,671 votes, a plurality of over one thousand. Last fall he was again elected by a plurality of 434; the Democratic vote being divided between five candidates. By virtue of his position and his known sagacity, he is recognized as a leader of the House. He is always on hand, wary and indefatigable, and directs the principal movements of his political associates. Though never distinguished as a debater, he is one of the most effective and successful men that ever engaged in public business, and he always has enough on hand to occupy his attention. To superintend the details of party management, bring up the wayward and lagging, and see that everything receives attention in its turn, are duties constantly devolving upon him and thoroughly discharged. Yet he generally makes friends, and has always been as popular with his political adversaries as with his own associates. He is Chairman of the Committee on Cities — a very responsible position.

ROBERT FURMAN.

Mr. FURMAN, the member from Schenectady county, is a native of Oneida county, New York, and is now forty-two years of age. For twenty-five years past he has been a resident of the city of Schenectady, and is, therefore, as much identified with its business interests as though a native to the manor born.

Most of the time, during his residence in Schenectady, his attention has been given to the dry goods trade, though for several years past he has conducted cases before the courts of law; he having been admitted as an Attorney and Counsellor, besides permitted to practice in the United States Circuit Court.

Shortly after the enactment of the law constituting our present system of a State National Guard, he was commissioned, by Governor SEYMOUR, as Colonel of the 83d Regiment. The duties of the new position, conferred without solicitation and surprising the recipient, were of an order to make a civilian shrink from their acceptance, bestowed, as it was, during the progress of the late war, when military criticism ran high and charity for novices at military training was by no means a rule of guidance. Colonel FURMAN immediately took hold of his new duties with a will, and upon the first annual parade and inspection of the 83d Regiment, not merely surprised spectators and furloughed military men with the numerical strength and *esprit* of his Regiment, but received the commendation of the General commanding the Brigade. The 83d Regiment still preserves its military bearing, second to no other regiment in the State outside of New York city.

Colonel FURMAN has ever been identified with the politics of his adopted county. As a firm, consistent member of the Democratic party, he has been honored on more than one occasion with delegated positions of representative trust. His first office in the service of his county and State is that of Member of Assembly, now held. He was chosen, after a most animated canvass, by a majority of fifty votes; overcoming a majority of nearly five hundred votes obtained by his Republican predecessor. In the Assembly, Colonel FURMAN has been designated as Chairman of the Committee on Education. He also serves on the Committees on "Public Lands," and "Roads and Bridges."

That live enterprise of the age, the conception and completion of railroads, has ever met with a warm friend in the person of the member from Schenectady. No one in the city named was more instrumental in projecting and carrying out the noted Athens Railroad, or "cut off," as commonly termed. The preliminary survey line for that direct and demanded railway from Schenectady to Ogdensburgh — or rather from New York to the Canadas — known as the Northern Rairoad, which will come up for further action at the present legislative session, was only undertaken and accomplished through the strenuous efforts of Colonel FURMAN, in securing a small appropriation for purposes of the survey. The latter extending through a perfect wilderness of woods, seventy miles in extent, proved a most important and noticeable undertaking.

This sketch would not be complete without brief allusion to a handsome and commodious armory building now in process of construction, at Schenectady, and designed for the use of the Eighty-third Regiment State National Guards. The appropriation for the same was only secured by the personal efforts of the representative from Schenectady. The structure when complete will be an ornament to the city, and a standing monument to its projecting spirit. Enough has been written to show that, in all matters pertaining to the interests of Schenectady, and the material welfare of the Commonwealth, the present member, Colonel ROBERT FURMAN, is not wanting in attributes of energy and progressive improvement.

JOHN GALVIN.

The Emerald Isle, to whose sons, in so many ways, our country is indebted, and to which the Legislature of 1868 is indebted for not less than thirteen members, is also the fatherland of Mr. Galvin. He was born in Kings county, Ireland, in April, 1840. When six years old he was brought by his parents to America; they settling in the city of New York. His education was such as was afforded by the public schools of the Metropolis. Mr. GALVIN by occupation is a liquor dealer, on Grand street. He has always taken a deep interest in the political issues of the day; acting invariably with the Democratic party. In 1866 he was a nominee for the Assembly, but was defeated by one thousand majority. In 1867, in the same district, he was triumphantly elected, receiving the decidedly flattering majority of eighteen hundred votes. The present is the first political position he ever held. For several years however, he has been one of the General Committee of Tammany Hall, which has elevated so many others to political honors.

Mr. GALVIN, in the Assembly, is a member of two important Committees — Canals and Insurance. As becomes a member serving his first Legislative term, Mr. GALVIN has watched with scrutiny the course of Legislation, familiarizing himself with its multifarious and multitudinous duties, rather than taking an active participation therein. On one question, however — that of the repeal of the Metropolitan Excise Law — with which his opportunities rendered him especially familiar, Mr. GALVIN made a brief but telling speech in favor of the repeal of the present law, and of vesting the powers of the Board with the city authorities. Although dealing in liquors, he is himself strictly temperate in his habits, never having drank a glass of liquor or used tobacco in any shape.

SANFORD GIFFORD.

Mr. GIFFORD is serving his first term in the Legislature of the State; but notwithstanding this fact, he brings to his use no little experience as a business man, and no small amount of parliamentary knowledge, for his life has been an active one, both in public and private. He is prompt in his acts, brief in the expression of his opinions and devoid of ostentation. He was among the first who entered the Republican ranks, and has always continued to act in accordance with the principles advocated by that party. During the month of March, 1856, Mr. GIFFORD was elected Supervisor of the town of Ledyard, Cayuga county, and from that time to March, 1867, he held the same office for every successive term. During four years of that period he was Chairman of the Board, and for five years he was Chairman of the Committee on Equalization. Though his term of office as Supervisor expired in the Spring of 1867, yet the people were anxious to extend the field of his usefulness, and therefore nominated him for Member of the Assembly. His majority was very complimentary, being 1533. He is a member of the Committee on Trade and Manufactures.

Mr. GIFFORD was born in the town of Greenfield, Saratoga county, N. Y., but when he was five years old his parents removed with him to Ledyard, Cayuga county, where he has ever since continued to reside. Though Mr. GIFFORD is a farmer by occupation, yet he has good ideas of finance and trade. He is one of the Directors of the First National Bank of Aurora, and also is a member of the Executive Committee of the New York Central Insurance Company. These facts alone are sufficient to show in what high estimation he is held at home, and we presume that his record in the Assembly will favorably compare with that of his more circumscribed fields of action.

GEORGE M. GLEASON.

This gentleman, representing the First District of St. Lawrence county, was born in what was then called Poto Ferry, and which is now the town of Pitcairn, New York. He is thirty-eight years of age.

Mr. GLEASON enjoyed good educational privileges until eighteen years of age, and commenced life as a teacher, which occupation he followed for ten years. Since that time he has been engaged in farming. While attending with energy to his personal affairs, he has devoted no little of his time to matters affecting the interests of the locality in which he resides; and has five times been chosen Supervisor of the town of Pitcairn; has served five years as Justice of the Peace, and four years as Town Superintendent of public schools.

In September, 1861, Mr. GLEASON enlisted in the service of the United States, as a private in Company "D,"

60th Regiment, New York Volunteers. In October following, he was promoted to the rank of Second Lieutenant, in which capacity he served either with his company, then stationed at the Relay House, Maryland, guarding the Baltimore and Ohio Railroad, or in recruiting service at Ogdensburgh, until May, 1862, when his regiment was ordered to report to Gen. SIGEL at Harper's Ferry. Soon after their arrival he was appointed Assistant Quartermaster of the regiment, and accompanied it in its marches through the Shenandoah and Rappahannock valleys until August, when he was attacked with typhoid fever, in consequence of which he was reduced from one hundred and ninety pounds to one hundred and eight. The surgeon in charge informed him that there was no probability of his recovering his health while in active service, and he therefore tendered his resignation, accompanied by the surgeon's certificate of disability, which was accepted. In his emaciated condition he returned home.

About this time it was ascertained that, although one-half of those liable to military duty in his town had already enlisted, no credits to the town had been made; and after partially recovering his health, he visited Albany and Washington, and succeeded in having those who had entered the military service from that locality duly credited. He continued active in every movement set on foot with a view of reinforcing the army; aided the families of soldiers, and attended personally to the filling of the quotas of the town of Pitcairn; and also, under appointment from the Board of Supervisors, acted as one of the County Recruiting Agents for St. Lawrence county.

Mr. GLEASON first entered the Legislature in 1866; was re-elected to the Assembly of 1867 by an increased majority; was appointed one of the Committee on Claims, and was Chairman of the Committee on Indian Affairs.

He was returned to the present Assembly, having a larger majority than any other candidate upon the ticket. He enjoys the confidence and esteem of his constituents; is well informed in regard to the affairs of the State; is an undemonstrative but effective speaker, and having the advantage of experience, is one of the most useful of the members of the present Assembly.

ELIJAH M. K. GLENN.

Mr. GLENN was born of Scottish parentage, in Amsterdam, in this State, August 12th, 1807. His education in early life was limited. In his boyhood he learned the trade of a shoemaker, and continued to work at it for some years. When he arrived at manhood, in 1836, he identified himself with the anti-slavery movement. When a division in the ranks of the Abolitionists on the *right* and *duty* to vote under the Federal Constitution, took place, Mr. GLENN advocated the duty of voting. From 1838 to 1857, Mr. GLENN spent nearly fifteen years in lecturing on slavery, land reform and kindred topics. He held that all slave laws were void; that by the law of God and nature, the slave, as every man, was free, and that wicked men could not make valid laws to enslave him. Mr. GLENN advocated the doctrine that the Federal Government held the public lands in *trust for the landless;* that the Government had no right to sell in large parcels to speculators.

Mr. GLENN married at about twenty-one years of age. He has now living five sons and one daughter. His youngest child is nearly twenty-five years of age. He resided in Montgomery county during the first forty years of his life, and for the last twenty years in Macedon, Wayne county. He has held some trifling town offices in Florida and Macedon. He was a keeper in Sing Sing Prison from May, 1857, to September, 1859, and was Postmaster at Macedon from June, 1861, to March, 1866. For forty years he has been a strict temperance man, and believes in promoting the cause solely by moral suasion, and has no faith in prohibitory laws.

In 1828, he cast his *first* vote for JOHN Q. ADAMS for President. In 1840, he came to Albany to unite in the organization of the Liberty Party, and voted the Liberty ticket until the formation of the Republican Party; so in 1856 he went for "Free men and FREMONT." In 1860, he gave his preference to Mr. SEWARD as a candidate, but cheerfully acquiesced in the nomination of Mr. LINCOLN. In 1864, he did not think it wise to "swap horses in crossing the stream;"—he preferred LINCOLN to any or all others. From the nomination of Mr. LINCOLN, in 1860, to the day of his death, he had full and unwavering faith in his wisdom and integrity, and of course fully and cordially supported his administration and mourned his untimely death.

On the question of Reconstruction, as between President JOHNSON and Congress, he sides with Congress. He holds that "the loyal element, whether white or black, should form the nucleus or foundation around or upon which to construct, and that rebels and traitors can claim no voice in a government they have sought to destroy."

Mr. GLENN was elected to the Assembly from the First District of Cayuga county. He is a fine looking old gentleman, always in his seat during the sessions of the House, and closely watching its proceedings so that he may vote understandingly.

THEODORE GUIGOU.

Mr. GUIGOU is a native of Marseilles, France, where he was born January 8, 1817. With the exception of his son he is the only person by the name in the United States. He came with his father, AUGUSTUS GUIGOU, to this country in 1820. He received an excellent education, graduating from Columbia College in 1835.

Mr. GUIGOU resides at Shandaken, Ulster county, where he has been extensively engaged in the tanning business for many years. His integrity in business transactions, and his kindly and pleasant manner, have made him very popular, and he occupies a prominent and influential position among his neighbors. He has been Supervisor, and held many other local offices. He was elected to the Assembly on the Democratic ticket, by a majority of 533, over DAVID C. GRIFFIN, Republican. He is attentive and faithful to his duties in the Legislature, and his intelligence and superior judgment make him a valuable member. He was assigned by the Speaker to the Committees on Public Education and Agriculture.

JAMES M. HALSEY.

Mr. HALSEY represents Suffolk county, having been elected to the Assembly by the Democracy of that county by about 500 majority. He comes of excellent stock, his father being English and his mother Scotch in their origin. He was born in the town of Bridgehampton, Suffolk county, N. Y., May 22d, 1825. He enjoyed fair opportunities for obtaining a common school education, and made the most of them by diligent study. He has been engaged in farming during the greater portion of his life, but for the last six years, in addition to conducting the affairs of a fine farm, has been engaged in mercantile business. In all his undertakings he has been very succesful. Mr. HALSEY is and has been a firm supporter of the principles and candidates of the Democratic Party. He has held several town offices, and has served four years in the New York Custom House.

Mr. HALSEY is not a public speaker, and discharges his legislative duties by committee work and by means of conversation. He is a member of the Committee on State Charitable Institutions and also of the Committee on the Affairs of Villages. He is well qualified for either position, for while a friend to all real advancements and improvements, he is a rigid economist.

ANTHONY HARTMAN.

Mr. HARTMAN was born March 18th, 1835, in the city of New York. He is of German parentage, and received but a common school education. When about fifteen years of age he went to work in the tobacco manufacturing establishment of JOHN ANDERSON, in New York city, and left there about two years after, to enter the establishment of C. H. LILLIENTHAL, where he remained about seven years, when the establishment was destroyed by fire. While employed there, his right hand was caught in the machinery, by which he lost part of his thumb, and came near losing the hand.

He joined the Fire Department July 31st, 1856, as a member of Live Oak Engine Company, No. 44, in the old Volunteer Fire Department, and served his full term. In 1861, he assisted in raising a company in the Anderson Zouaves, afterwards known as the Sixty-second Regiment New York Volunteers. He was elected Second Lieutenant, and served nineteen weeks, when he left the service on account of losing a son, about three years old, by death. In the Fall of 1861, he took an active part in politics with his party (Democratic). On the 20th day of January, 1862, he was appointed to a clerkship in the Street Department, at a salary of one thousand dollars per annum, which was increased to fifteen hundred after he had been there a year.

In 1864 he joined one of the companies of the Eighty-fourth Regiment, National Guard, State of New York, as a private, and was only five weeks a member when he was promoted to a first lieutenancy. The regiment was called out to serve one hundred days, and he accompanied it, serving in Maryland and Virginia. After returning home he was again promoted, to a captaincy, but resigned in May last, on account of business engagements.

In the Fall of 1865 he was nominated and elected Councilman in New York by a large majority, notwithstanding there was great opposition to him. He was re-elected the following year for the term of one year, when the Legislature of 1867 extended the term another year. In 1867, he was elected to the Assembly from the Tenth District, New York city, on the Tammany Hall ticket, by twelve hundred and fifteen majority. The preceding year the Tammany Hall candidate had been defeated in the district by two hundred and ten votes. The district has a strong German population, and his constituents have great confidence in him. On the 15th of February, 1867, they presented him with a splendid gold watch. He is a man of ready parts, very popular in the House, and faithful in the discharge of his duties.

ABRAHAM E. HASBROUCK.

Mr. HASBROUCK represents the Second Assembly District of Ulster. He is a descendant of one of the original French Huguenots, who came to this country in 1680, and settled at Kingston, Ulster county, and afterwards became one of the proprietors, or "twelve men," to whom was granted the Paltz Patent. He was born July 7th, 1832. He received a good common school education, and passed one winter at Professor FAY's Academy at Poughkeepsie.

Mr. HASBROUCK has been for the past eighteen years largely engaged in the freighting business from New Paltz Landing to New York city, running the barge "Ulster County," one of the largest of its class on the Hudson river, and carrying to market the agricultural products of the fertile valley of the Walkill. In this capacity he gave general satisfaction to the farmers and business men of that locality.

Mr. HASBROUCK became interested in politics about the time of the organization of the American party, with which he identified himself, and became an active member. When that party ceased to exist he entered the ranks of the Democratic party, and has remained ever since one of its strongest supporters. He has held several town offices, and has often been pressed by his fellow townsmen to accept the nomination for the office of Supervisor, but would never consent to take it. In the fall of 1866, he was the candidate of the Democratic party for the office he now holds, but his district being strongly Republican and his opponent being a remarkably strong one — Hon. JACOB LE FEVER — he was defeated. At the late election he was again put in nomination, and was elected by a majority of 470, running about 200 ahead of his ticket.

Mr. HASBROUCK is a member of the Committee on Banks, Engrossed Bills, and Sub-Committee of the Whole, and is an active working member.

HARRIS B. HOWARD.

Mr. HOWARD is a native of Schodack, Rensselaer county, New York, where he was born April 27th, 1830. He is of English ancestry. During his childhood, his means for acquiring an education were limited, and he was obliged to accept those afforded by the common school. There is but little, in many of the district schools, to stimulate the minds of children to very lofty endeavors, as regards the acquirement of knowledge. And such was the experience of Mr. HOWARD. But when he grew older, and found that the world's horizon extended beyond his boyhood's home, he was eager to mingle in the general effort to win success. Possessing ready instincts, and a vast deal of self-reliance, he was able, after arriving at the age of maturity, to command the attention of his fellow-townsmen.

Mr. HOWARD is a merchant by occupation. He has followed that calling for a number of years. But he also has some proclivities for the law, as a profession; and though he has never made that a leading feature of his aims in life, yet he has practiced with average success in Justices' Courts. In the politics of his town, he has for several years taken no unimportant part; and while sharing in the work he has likewise participated in the honors; for he has held nearly every one of the town offices, and represented Schodack in the Board of Supervisors for three years. He has always been a Democrat, and as such has always strictly adhered to the principles of his party. He was elected to the Assembly, during the last campaign, by 680 majority; whereas his predecessor, a Republican, had a large vote in his favor.

Mr. HOWARD is Chairman of the Committee on State Charitable Institutions, and is a member of the Committee on the Division of Towns and Counties.

MYRON J. HUBBARD.

Mr. HUBBARD is a native of Westford, Otsego county, in which town he was born July 27, 1828. Both his grandfathers were soldiers of the Revolution, who came from Connecticut and settled in Otsego county while it was yet an almost unbroken wilderness. His father was a farmer and brought up his son to the same business. His education was obtained at the common school. He made better use of his advantages than many others who have had better facilities for acquiring a good education. When he was sixteen years old he commenced teaching school, and taught four winters, working on the farm during the summer. His occupation has always been that of a farmer, with the exception of two years when he was in the mercantile business, and four years when he was occupied in running a flouring and saw mill. He has always resided in the same town where he was born.

Mr. HUBBARD has always acted with the Democratic party, and by it has been elected to various town offices. He was Supervisor in 1854, Town Clerk in 1860, and Justice of the Peace in 1862. He was chosen to these positions notwithstanding the fact that prior to the Fall of 1862, the Democratic party was in a minority in his town. In 1862, the town, for the first time, gave a Democratic majority, and at that election he was elected Coroner of the county of Otsego. He was elected Railroad Commissioner in 1865, and held the office two years, and was re-elected Justice of the Peace in 1866, and is now serving his second term. He was elected member of Assembly last Fall, by a majority of sixty-two, in a very closely contested canvass. At the age of eighteen he enlisted in the State militia, and has been connected with it ever since, having held all the offices from Second Lieutenant up to Colonel. He is now Colonel of the Thirty-ninth Regiment New York State National Guard.

At the breaking out of the Rebellion, he, in connection with other citizens of the county, commenced recruiting volunteers, with the intention of raising a full regiment. Five hundred men were raised, and they were ordered into camp at Cherry Valley, Mr. HUBBARD acting as Lieutenant-Colonel. In June, 1862, he was ordered to Albany, where his command was consolidated with parts of other regiments and he returned home.

Mr. HUBBARD is an upright, fair and intelligent man, and a useful and energetic citizen. In the Assembly he serves his constituents diligently and faithfully. He is a member of the Committees on Banks, and Militia and Public Defense.

SAMUEL D. HUMPHREY.

Doctor SAMUEL D. HUMPHREY, Member of Assembly from the county of Putnam, is a fair exemplification of that persistence, endurance and ingenuity which have long been regarded as constituting the Yankee character. He was born in Hartland, Connecticut, April 4th, 1823. His parents died while he was young, so that at the age of twelve he was obliged to depend upon his own resources. He managed to secure an academic education at Wilbraham, Massachusetts. Chemistry had for him strong fascinations. In 1850 he established the Scientific Journal, which continues to bear his name, in the city of New York, and conducted it for nine years. At that time he made his residence at Morrisania in Westchester county. Resolving to adopt the profession of medicine, he attended the sessions of the New York Medical College in the winter of 1857-8. He had already made himself familiar with the practice; attended three terms, and finally graduated at the Bellevue Hospital Medical College in 1863. He removed shortly afterward to Patterson, Putnam county, his present residence, and entered upon a course of successful practice. As a medical practitioner he is eminently successful, quick, and very correct in judgment, kind and attentive to those who come under his charge; accomplishing a vast amount of labor, often riding sixty and eighty miles a day in his practice. Though not an active politician, the Democrats, having experienced repeated defeats, placed him in nomination for the Assembly. The result gratified their expectation. He was elected by a majority of 223 votes over Mr. MABIE, the Republican candidate.

He is Chairman of the Committee on Public Health, and Medical Colleges and Medical Societies; but he has made his mark principally by his zealous efforts in protecting the interests of the farmers along the line of the New York and Harlem Railroad, and to procure legislation for the reduction of the price for conveying milk on that road. Though dealing with a strong antagonist, he has shown himself an adversary of no mean ability, and a man to be dreaded by all monopolizing corporations, no matter of what magnitude they may be.

JAMES IRVING.

Mr. IRVING was born in the city of New York, on the 6th day of July, 1821. His father was a Protestant Irishman, and emigrated from Londonderry in 1808. His mother was a native of the United States. He was a bold lad, fond of adventure, but never neglectful of business. During his boyhood he attended several private schools, and was also a pupil in the public and higher schools for several seasons. He then went into the employment of the noted "CHRIS. GUIRE," in Washington Market, and remained with him ten years, sustaining a good reputation for industry and fidelity. He thus became familiar with the business in every department, and in 1847 engaged a market stand and began on his own account. His shrewdness in making purchases was unrivaled. He speedily became a leading man among the butchers of New York, buying and selling, on the average, one hundred head of cattle a week. He seldom varied five pounds from a correct estimate of the weight of an animal. His energy, good judgment and industry soon rendered him prosperous, and in ten years he had accumulated the handsome fortune of $400,000. He held large contracts for supplying the penitential and reformatory institutions on Ward's and Blackwell's Islands, and also for the army and navy. But the financial difficulties of 1857 seriously affected him, and half of his property was swallowed up by the disasters of that year. He continued in business, with varied success, till 1863, a period of sixteen years.

In 1847, Mr. IRVING was married to Miss HANNAH LEONARD, a sister of JAMES LEONARD, the well-known Inspector of the Metropolitan Police. Mrs. LEONARD, their mother, was a member of the Roman Catholic Church, a woman of superior mind, and of strictly conscientious principles, and carefully instructed her children in religious duties. Mrs. IRVING admirably displays the effect of her early culture, in her careful supervision of the conduct and education of her own children, six in number. In these matters she has the full concurrence of her husband, who professes no religious faith himself, but is liberal to all who do.

Mr. IRVING has taken an active part in politics for many years, belonging to the Tammany wing of the Democratic party. He was repeatedly in the field as a candidate without the regular nomination, and was always obliged to encounter a powerful combination of the factions opposed to him. It was always his boast, however, that he received a higher vote than the rival Democratic candidate. In 1865, he was a candidate for Alderman in the Fourteenth District, embracing the Eighteenth Ward, and received twice as great a number of votes as the regular

Democratic candidate, although defeated by Mr. JOSEPH B. VARNUM, Republican, by a small majority. The next year he was an independent candidate for the Assembly, against MICHAEL N. SALMON, Democratic Unionist, and HENRY BEENY, Republican, and was elected by a plurality of sixteen. In 1867, he was a candidate against HENRY RAWLEY, Republican, WILLIAM BEARD and MICHAEL S. LAMBERT, Democrats, and received a plurality of 279. He is one of the most faithful members of the Assembly, attending carefully to the business under consideration. He has also distinguished himself by a vigorous endeavor to procure the enactment of a bill regulating the sale of hay, to protect purchasers from imposition. The measure was defeated last winter, and he has renewed the struggle with better prospects of success. But, as a general rule, he remains quietly in his place, saying nothing, but always watching every measure that is proposed. He is a member of the Committees on Railroads, and Public Education.

JOHN C. JACOBS.

Mr. JACOBS is the acknowledged leader of the majority in the House. No member of that body has had so long and so varied an experience in parliamentary rules and usages and Legislative tactics as he. For many years he has been a constant attendant upon both branches of the Legislature in the capacity of special correspondent for some leading newspaper. This is also his second term as a member of the House. Added to this long and varied experience, is his effectiveness as a party manager and his readiness and ability in debate; his tireless activity and his dauntless courage in battling for his political principles. In short, there is that in his constitution and in his training which admirably fits him for the position of leadership which has been readily accorded him by his political brethren in the House. He was a prominent candidate for the Speakership, and would have filled that position well, but the Tammany men of New York city were opposed to him, and as they succeeded in securing a a majority of the country members he was defeated.

Mr. JACOBS was born December 16, 1838, in Lancaster county, Pa. The paternal ancestors of Mr. JACOBS, were of the old New England revolutionary stock, and several of them participated in the struggle for independence; the maternal side were of German origin, one of them having held a high position under FREDERICK THE GREAT, of Prussia.

When Mr. JACOBS was quite young, his parents removed to the city of Brooklyn, where, with the exception of a year, he has since resided. At an early age, he went to a select school, and was progressing rapidly, when his family removed to Philadelphia, which broke in upon his educational progress; and from his twelfth year, it may be said that his school house studies ended. Returning to Brooklyn he entered a lawyer's office, but growing dissatisfied with the day labor there laid out for him, sought and obtained a place in the large printing establishment of JOHN A. GRAY & Co., in New York. Here, as copy-holder, he became acquainted with many newspaper men of prominence — their journals being issued from the establishment — and soon cultivated a taste for the profession of a journalist. When eighteen years of age, he commenced newspaper life as a Reporter on the New York Express, and rapidly advanced, until he had charge of the political news columns. In 1860, he became the correspondent of the same paper, in Albany, remaining with it until 1865, when in the same capacity, he represented the New York World. In 1862, Mr. JACOBS volunteered to acompany McCLELLAN's army on its famous Peninsular campaign, as a correspondent, and, becoming attached to the 1st New York Volunteers, then in KEARNEY's Division, he had a chance to see, and participate in, some of the hardest fighting of the war. His account of the evacuation of Harrison's Landing, and the march to Yorktown, published in the Express, was extensively copied by the press, throughout the country.

Mr. JACOBS began his political life early. In the campaign of 1856, though but a boy, he was active in the opposition to FREMONT's election, and in 1860, was well known in Brooklyn as a leader among the young men who combined against the LINCOLN ticket. In 1863, he was nominated by the Democrats for Assembly, JOHN C. PERRY being the Republican candidate, THEOPHILUS C. CALLICOT and an independent Democrat, also running. This split defeated him. In 1865, he also ran, being again defeated by WILLIAM W. GOODRICH, after a contest of great severity. Mr. JACOBS' friends insisted that he should again run in 1866, and the Democratic convention nominated him by acclamation. The Republicans made every effort to defeat him, but this time he won by a majority of nearly nine hundred. In the last Assembly he was an active member, but devoted most of his time to local matters. He served on the Committees on Public Printing and Colleges, Academies and Schools. He was re-elected to the present House by a largely increased majority, and is a member of the Committee of Ways and Means, and Chairman of the Committee on Expenditures of the Executive Department.

Personally, Mr. JACOBS is a great favorite with all his acquaintances. Though an ardent and active partisan, pushing all party measures with vigor, there is yet a courteousness of manner, a fairness of dealing and a frankness of language in all his political endeavors, that does not fail to make even his opponents yield him a large share of admiration and respect. He is a man of large heart and warm sympathies, true to his friends and generous to his foes.

CHRISTOPHER JOHNSON.

Mr. Johnson, the representative of the Fifth Assembly District of New York city, was born in the First Ward of that city, on the 11th of February, 1836. His parents immigrated to this country from Ireland. They were of humble origin but poor, rendering it incumbent upon the son to begin early to earn the ordinary necessaries of life. But notwithstanding the limited opportunities for education, and the other disadvantages incident to his condition, his good judgment and native energy have united in securing for him a good measure of success in life.

At the early age of eight years he was apprenticed to a New Jersey farmer, with the time-honored privilege of going to school in winter, which was the only educational advantage, so far as schools are concerned, that he ever enjoyed. In 1847, he went to Goshen, Orange county, and remained there until November, 1849, immediately after the ravages of the epidemic of that year, when, tired of country life and desirous of seeing the city once more, he returned to New York. He did not remain there long, however, as the prostration of business which followed the epidemic compelled him to adopt the roving life of a seaman in the merchant service, and gave him the opportunity of seeing considerable of the world. In 1853 he shipped in the United States navy, and during the Crimean war was attached to the frigate Savannah. He was on the South American station during the excitement concerning the steamer America, in the harbor of Rio Janeiro. He returned to New York in November, 1856.

Mr. Johnson joined the Volunteer Fire Department of the city of New York in December, 1858, connecting himself with Engine Company No. 11. He had the honor of filling all the offices in the gift of the company, having been chosen Treasurer, Secretary, Assistant-Foreman and Foreman. He was unsuccessful in being re-elected to the latter office in 1862, his opponent being one of the recently chosen coroners of the city. In 1864, however, he beat the same opponent by a handsome majority, and was again re-elected in 1865. He served in that capacity until the Metropolitan Department was put into active operation in September of that year. His services in the Fire Department were valuable and efficient. He was clerk in the Board of Aldermen for the year 1865, and Assistant Clerk in the Street Department in 1867. He is a member of the Tammany Hall General Committee, and was the Tammany nominee for the Assembly, having three Democratic competitors and one Republican, and being elected by a plurality of 1,296 votes. He is a member of the Committee on Cities.

WILLIAM C. JONES.

Mr. JONES represents the Fifth District of Kings county, a district which in 1866 gave a Republican majority of 800, and in 1867 reversed it by giving Mr. JONES a majority of 500, a result attributable more perhaps to his personal popularity than sympathy with his political principles. He was born in New York city, October 19, 1822. His father was a native of Pennsylvania, and served in the war of 1812. His mother was a native of New York: both were of English ancestry. He received a good education, passed several years as clerk in a store, and then engaged in the granite business. Mr. JONES has been, for many years past, connected with the Brooklyn Navy Yard, and discharged his duties very efficiently, always having the confidence of the commanding officers. He is now a lessee of Government docks in Brooklyn. He was a member of the Assembly in 1860, serving on the Committee on Cities, and holds the same position now. During the rebellion, he was in the South Atlantic Blockading Squadron, serving on the staff of Fleet Engineer ROBERT DANBY, whose fleet consisted of one hundred vessels. Mr. JONES is what is properly termed a working member of the House. He is very attentive to the duties of the committee room, the place where legislation is really shaped. He is an intelligent and valuable member of the Committee on which he serves. He is pleasing in his personal manners, and makes many friends. His opinions are listened to with respect, and his counsels sought. He is of the class of men who practically impress much of their individuality on legislation.

FREDERICK JULIAND.

Mr. JULIAND was born in Greene, Chenango county, New York (his present residence), October 9th, 1806, being the youngest son of Captain JOSEPH JULIAND, a native of Lyons, France, who immigrated to this country during the stormy times of the French Revolution, and settled in Greene, in 1798 (a town purchased by the State from the Oneida and Tuscarora Indians, in 1785, and named in honor of General NATHANIEL GREENE). His was one of eight or ten French families who were the first white settlers of that vicinity. Among the incidents of their pioneer life they boast of a visit from the celebrated French Statesman TALLEYRAND.

The boyhood days of FREDERICK JULIAND were spent on his father's farm, he being the recipient of such privileges as the common schools of that day afforded. In his more advanced youth he received academic advantages at Oxford, in his own county, and at Utica.

Having served an apprenticeship as merchant's clerk, he embarked in the mercantile business, in his native town, which he successfully prosecuted for upward of twenty-five years, retiring from active pursuits, with a handsome competency, in 1860.

From his youth upward he has taken an interest in the political issues before the country. He was a staunch Whig in the days of that party, and at its dissolution became an equally ardent Republican, his opinions and advice having great weight in the locality where he was best known. He has twice been a member of the Union State Central Committee, and has held several offices of trust, in all of which he has served faithfully, and won a reputation for purity of purpose, dignity of character, ability and enterprise. He was Postmaster under HARRISON and TYLER; is one of the incorporators for locating the Soldiers' Home, and is one of the Trustees of the Inebriate Asylum, at Binghamton. He was a member of Assembly in 1856, serving upon the Committee on Banks, and was State Senator from the Twenty-third District, comprising the counties of Chenango, Madison and Cortland, in 1864 and '65, being chosen by a majority of 5,459. During this service, he was Chairman of the Committee on Public Printing, and a member of the Committees on Banks, Roads and Bridges, and Poor Laws. He earned considerable distinction as Senator, acquiring a name for exercising careful and comprehensive judgment, upon all matters of legislation, and for steadfastly advocating economy in conducting the affairs of the State. Standing in the foremost ranks of those whose honesty and firmness could be relied upon, his career as a Senator was without a blemish. Among the important questions settled by the Legislature while he was in the Senate, was that of the Chenango Canal extension. This measure was, through the immediate supervision and active exertions of Senator JULIAND, put into practical effect, and by virtue of the law passed, mainly by his influence, is now near its completion. The speech made by Mr. JULIAND, in its behalf before the Committee of the whole Senate, displayed careful research and wise judgment.

Mr. JULIAND was an effective supporter of the late war, contributing liberally from his time and means to sustain the Union. He was one of the Committee appointed by the Governor to raise recruits, and performed valuable service in that behalf. His liberality toward the families of absent soldiers, has made his name familiarly welcome at many a lonely fireside.

In the summer of 1864, the town of Greene had occasion to forward funds to an agent at Newbern, North Carolina, who was there endeavoring to enlist men to fill their quota. Much against his will Mr. JULIAND was induced to undertake the task. He started *via* Washington and Norfolk, taking the steamer Fawn at the latter place for Roanoke Island, *via* the Dismal Swamp Canal. When about 150 miles from Norfolk, the steamer was attacked by Guerrillas. Upward of a hundred shots were fired at the steamer, killing and wounding nine of the little party of only thirty. Mr. JULIAND and the remaining survivors were taken prisoners and robbed of all their baggage; the steamer was burned, and they were compelled to march, the whole night, thirty miles, to Elizabeth City, where, after being robbed of $6,000 (a portion of the funds he was transporting), he and Major JENNY of Syracuse, were paroled, through the interference of a friend, the remainder of the party being marched off to a vile Southern prison, where it has since been ascertained more than half of them died horrible deaths. Mr. JULIAND and his companions made their escape from rebel domain in a sail boat, after being without food or shelter for about two entire days.

His election to the Assembly of 1867 was a flattering expression of the esteem and regard in which he is held at home. The county by the late apportionment was reduced to one member, and there was considerable strife among prominent gentlemen for the position. Mr. JULIAND's name was not mentioned in that connection until the Convention which placed him in nomination had organized, and even then against his express desire. He received a unanimous nomination, and at the polls received

1,608 majority, the highest vote given to any candidate upon the ticket. He was nominated and re-elected last fall to the present Assembly. His experience makes him a valuable member.

PATRICK KEADY.

Mr. KEADY, the Member of Assembly from the Third District of Kings county, was born at Mount Equity, county of Roscommon, Ireland, on the 26th day of June, 1832. His parents soon after moved to Correen, an unpretending village about four miles distant from the town of Ballinasloe, where his father leased a small farm, which he worked for a few years, and then died. PATRICK had, at that time, just begun to go to school; but, being the oldest son, he was forced to stay at home and work the farm for the support of himself and his brothers and sisters. Finding farming unprofitable in his native country, he came to America, in 1851, in order to better his condition. Arriving here on the 17th day of March in that year, he lost no time in seeking employment, and was soon afterward bound as an apprentice to a prominent master painter, JOSIAH T. SMITH, of Brooklyn. Mr. KEADY could then scarcely write his own name in a legible manner, but, by his devotion to study in his leisure hours, he soon began to improve in the art of reading and writing. He rapidly acquired a knowledge of the country and was passionately fond of newspaper reading. Indeed, the price of newspapers, and his clothing and board bills, were, for a time, his only expense. By the advice of his employer, he practiced exact economy, and BENJAMIN FRANKLIN himself could not have been more scrupulous in this respect than he was for a time. In a few years he was able to aid his mother, two brothers and one sister, who were yet in Ireland, but who also came to this country shortly before Mr. KEADY's time for service had expired. Having served his apprenticeship according to agreement, he was paid full journeyman's wages by his employer, a compliment which falls to the lot of few apprentices, even in this country. Mr. KEADY continued to work at his trade in New York city, where he pursued it for upwards of fifteen years; he then found his health greatly impaired by his exhausting labors by day, and his studies by night. He at length concluded to find some other employment, and, having a taste for journalism, he at once commenced the study of shorthand writing. Having studied phonography for over a year, during which time he still worked at his trade, he sought and obtained a position as reporter on one of the New York daily papers. He has always been a Democrat in politics. In 1866 he was nominated for the Assembly, and was opposed during the campaign by the regular Republican candidate, and by a prominent Democrat also; but he defeated both by a plurality of over fifteen hundred votes. In 1867 he was re-elected by a majority which outnumbered both his opponents. The Republicans withdrew their candidate against him and, although he would not accept any formal endorsement at their hands, they voted for him almost to a man, thus leaving his two Democratic opponents to mourn their folly the day after election.

Mr. KEADY is still connected with the press, and will probably remain so for the remainder of his life. Whatever Mr. KEADY knows—and he is a gentleman of no little intelligence—is the result of close study under unfavorable circumstances. He still devotes his leisure hours to study, is temperate in his habits, and is refined in his deportment. He is an industrious member, a good debater, and takes an active part in all the proceedings of the House.

LAWRENCE D. KIERNAN.

Mr. KIERNAN was born February 12, 1844, about a mile from a small village known as Edgeworthstown, in the county Longford, Ireland. His parents were in moderate circumstances, his father being a farmer of limited means. After the death of both his parents, and about twelve years since, he immigrated to this country, and has since resided in New York city.

After attending the public school for a year, Mr. KIERNAN was admitted to the Free Academy. Here he distinguished himself by his application to and proficiency in his studies, and, on graduating with the highest honors in 1861, he received the first prize for public speaking. He at once entered on the study of the law, and in about six months was appointed a teacher in Grammar School eighteen, in which capacity he served with marked success and acceptability until his election to the Legislature. He continued the study of the law while employed as teacher, graduating from the Law Department of the New York University in 1865. During the Rebellion he was designated Private Secretary to the Irish Brigade, then commanded by General THOMAS FRANCIS MEAGHER, but never entered on the discharge of the duties of the office, owing to family embarrassments. He received the degree of Master of Arts from the New York College in 1864, and is now a member of the Alumni Committee on the relations of Alma Mater with kindred institutions. He was elected to the Assembly by a vote of 2,498 against 1,132 for Mr. FAY (Dem.), 431 for Mr. McDONOUGH (Dem.), and 1,435 for Mr. URMY (Rep.).

The record of Mr. KIERNAN's life, it will be thus seen, is but the recounting of a preparation for active life. He stands on the threshold of a career which bids fair to be bright and prosperous. His first introduction to political life in Albany was in the presentation of the name of WILLIAM HITCHMAN, as candidate for Speaker to the Democratic caucus. It was a brilliant effort, and contributed largely to the success of his nominee. Mr. KIERNAN's voice is clear, round and penetrating, and his enunciation accurate. He has a discriminating, logical, judicial mind, which will enable him to succeed as a counsellor, while his powers of oratory will make him a successful pleader. He finds an appropriate place in the Judiciary Committee room. In his modest anxiety to avoid that which has ruined many promising young men, too much speaking, Mr. KIERNAN seems to have commited the opposite error, for he rarely takes the floor. It is to be hoped that he will change his course somewhat in this regard, so as to give his powers their necessary development and discipline. If he maintains the well-balanced intellect he now possesses, and observes as closely and acts as intelligently through life, Mr. KIERNAN's career will be a proud one in the annals of our nation's history.

OLIVER H. P. KINNEY.

O. H. PERRY KINNEY was born in Sheshequin, Bradford county, Pennsylvania, on the 15th of December, 1819, and is consequently forty-eight years old. He traces his ancestry back to Vermont, thence to Scotland. His grandfather, JOSEPH KINNEY, was a soldier of the Revolution, and settled in the beautiful valley of Sheshequin, on the Susquehanna river, soon after the Wyoming massacre. His father, GEORGE KINNEY, was there born in 1790, and there reared to maturity a family of nine children, of whom PERRY was the sixth. The common district school became the fixed boundaries of the educational aspirations of the family. The eldest, JULIA H., (afterwards Mrs. SCOTT), became a poet of considerable celebrity, and contributed largely to the religious and literary periodicals of her day; among the latter being The New Yorker, then published by HORACE GREELEY. Since her death her writings have been collected and published.

PERRY (as he was always familiarly called), upon arriving at the age of twenty-one, broke through the barriers by which the family had long been hedged about, and by his own efforts succeeded in spending two quarters at an Academy in Towanda, the county seat, which little advantage he followed up by reading law with Hon. DAVID WILMOT, of "Wilmot Proviso" notoriety. He was admitted to the bar of Bradford county in 1844. He was candidate for District Attorney on the Whig ticket in 1847, and was defeated by but eighty-six votes in a canvass which showed a majority of five hundred against his party. He moved to Towanda in 1848, and entered into copartnership with E. W. BAIRD in the practice of law; but the next year he opened an office on his own account, and continued practice until the breaking out of the California gold excitement, when he sailed for the Golden State in September, 1851. He returned in July, 1853, with health so utterly broken as to forbid any serious labor, mental or physical, for several years.

In 1858 he was elected to the Lower House of the Pennsylvania Legislature by over 5,000 majority—a larger relative vote than any candidate ever received for any office in that county. In 1859 he was re-elected. During his first term he was on the Educational Committee, and his ardent labors in behalf of free common school education gave him the chairmanship of that important committee the next year. The second winter of his service he was made Chairman of a Select Committee to whom was referred innumerable petitions asking for a law to prevent blacks from coming into the State, or, in lieu thereof, a law to enslave them. Upon this, Mr. K. made an elaborate report setting forth the true relationship between man and man under our system of government, and evolving and defining those natural rights which pertain to all men, regardless of nationality. His report, though regarded as radical, and in advance of the day in which it was made, embodied the principles which have since obtained in the nation. He was appointed on the committees of two important cases of contested election, in one of which he was selected to write out the report. That report has become valuable as a precedent of important legal points settled.

In the fall of 1860, Mr. KINNEY purchased an interest in and became editor of the Waverly Advocate, published at Waverly, Tioga county, New York; and on the first of January following settled in that enterprising village. The Advocate, up to that time, had been a vacillating, unreliable, unimportant political paper; but he at once made it such an unswerving and undisguised exponent of Republicanism that its force and character were soon felt throughout the country. As an editor Mr. K. ranks as a clear, concise and forcible writer, making those principles which he conceives to be *right* the leading element of all his efforts, leaving policy as a matter of secondary and subordinate consideration. Earnestness and honesty of purpose have thus far characterized his editorial career; and as a wise and judicious manager of a political paper he stands deservedly high. For six years he was Assistant-Postmaster at Waverly, and had almost the entire control and responsibility of that office. That, together with the care of his paper, seriously impaired his health, and made a change desirable. He was elected in April, 1867, a delegate to the Constitutional Convention from the Twenty-fourth Senate district. In this convention he took no very active part, choosing to act in the capacity of a juror, and aim to give an honest and intelligent vote after hearing the facts, rather than venture into the deep water of constitutional debate. But his suggestions in committee and in convention were regarded as sound and eminently practical. He favored manhood suffrage, and opposed selecting the negro out as a target for politicians by separate submission. He was an ardent supporter of Woman Suffrage, and his speech on that subject was republished in many papers of the State and highly complimented for the spirit of humanity, and for its strong logical appeal in behalf of the mothers, wives and daughters of the Empire State. While a member of the Convention he was elected a member of the Assembly from Tioga county.

NICHOLAS B. LA BAU.

Mr. La Bau's *personelle* is really one of the finest in the Assembly. A person is attracted by his finely cut features which are decidedly classical, as well as by his polished manners and faultless exterior. He displays that carefulness in dress, which marks the gentleman of refinement, without creating an impression of superlative fastidiousness; and his rich voice, whether heard in debate or in conversation, is exceedingly pleasing.

He is a native of Trenton, New Jersey, at which place. he was born, July 29th, 1823. His maternal grandfather was born on the Island of Scio, of Greek parents, and came to this country while young, settling in Philadelphia He became one of the wealthiest merchants in that city. His paternal ancestry were Huguenots; they left France during the reign of Louis XIV, and settled in New Jersey.

Mr. La Bau is a graduate of Columbia College, New York. After leaving college, he studied law, and was admitted to practice at the Bar. He followed the legal profession until 1859, when, on account of ill health, he was compelled to relinquish his professional pursuits. In 1860, he had a severe and dangerous illness which confined him to his bed for six months; and he did not entirely recover from this attack, until January, 1863.

Up to the year 1859, he had identified himself with the first Division New York State Militia, and had served in almost every capacity—Aid to Brigadier-General, Brigade Judge Advocate, Captain New York City Guards; and when his health failed him, he was Lieutenant-Colonel of the 55th Regiment.

Mr. LA BAU was an ardent Union man, from the beginning of our national conflict, and, as soon as his health permitted, took an unmistakable position in favor of the Administration. He was, at that time, a resident of Richmond county, to which he had removed from New York, for the purpose of fully regaining his health. Richmond county was hopelessly Democratic: and its financial affairs were in the hands of a most corrupt ring. In 1863, the Board of Supervisors passed a resolution to raise, upon the bonds of the county, a sum sufficient to pay every drafted man's exemption fee; and they individually said: "Not a man shall go to the war from Richmond county." Such a flagrant determination to indirectly aid the active enemies at the South, was enough to make the blood boil in the veins of any true Union man! Mr. LA BAU took an earnest part in favor of the tax payers of the county, to break up the strongholds of corruption. He was the Union candidate for the Assembly, from Richmond county in 1863; but the Democratic tide was too strong against him, and his opponent was elected. In the spring of 1864, he canvassed the county against the corrupt Board of Supervisors, and in favor of the reformatory movement which he had inaugurated. His attempt was successful; for all of the Board, except one, were rejected; and honest, independent men were elected in their stead. In the autumn of the same year, he again ran for Member of Assembly, but he was beaten by the opposing candidate, nevertheless having run far ahead of his ticket.

In 1865, Mr. LA BAU's name was brought before the people of the First District as candidate for State Senator. After his nomination, the Democratic Committee split on the nominations of Mr. CHRISTIE and Mr. HAVENS, both factions claiming that their proceedings were regular.

Mr. LA BAU made a thorough canvass of the counties of Richmond and Suffolk, speaking to audiences nearly every night. Four days before the election, a reconciliation was effected between the two Democratic factions, and Mr. HAVENS withdrew in favor of Mr. CHRISTIE. Mr. LA BAU's chances for success were considered hopeless, as the district was Democratic by at least 1,800 majority. In fact, GEO. WILLIAM CURTIS had, in 1862, been defeated in running for Congress, by a majority of 1,308; and Mr. CHRISTIE, in 1863, had been elected to the Senate by 1,612, in his favor. Mr. LA BAU's friends, however, worked tenaciously, resolved not to give up the contest until the last moment. The result was his election by about seventy majority— a most satisfactory triumph, as it demonstrated his popularity among his constituents.

In the Senate of 1866-7, he was a member of the Committees on Judiciary, Engrossed Bills, and Roads and Bridges. He was a leading and influential Senator, and secured the passage of a number of important measures during the session.

Mr. LA BAU, having, during his Senatorial term, removed to Warren county, he yielded to the demands which the citizens of that county made upon his experience and superior qualifications, and accepted the nomination for the Assembly. He is a member of the Judiciary Committee.

As a debater, Mr. LA BAU is ready and perspicuous. His style of oratory is often florid, though not excessively so, and his points of advantage and defense are usually well selected. Ornate in rhetoric, and sagacious in argument, he is an opponent of gentlemanly bearing, and a colleague of fine culture.

JAMES D. LASHER.

One of the most attentive men to his duties in the House is JAMES D. LASHER, who represents the Second District of Oswego county. He is of German descent, and was born in 1814 in the town of Manlius, Onondaga county, New York. He was educated mostly in the common schools of his native place. He spent several years of his early life in New York city, and subsequently, some time in the South.

For many years he was a merchant tailor in the village of Fulton, but his health demanding the change, he retired upon a farm. He was also, at one time, quite extensively engaged in the lumbering business. During the past few years he has resumed his old avocation, and is now extensively engaged in the clothing business in Fulton.

Mr. LASHER very early took an active part in politics; always, until a recent period, being attached to the principles and fortunes of the Democratic party. In his own locality he has always been prominent in party matters. During his early residence in Fulton he was often elected Town Clerk, and frequently to offices under the village organization. After his removal to his farm he was elected Supervisor of the town of Granby, in 1849; and was again elected in 1850, and 1858, and again in 1864.

As a member of the "Local Legislature," Mr. LASHER always held a prominent position. He was a faithful and influential officer, and, in 1853, presided over the deliberations of the Board.

Mr. LASHER continued to act with the Democratic party until 1860. When the rebels fired upon Fort Sumter, and the secessionists plunged the country into a war, in the mad attempt to destroy the Union, he entered the ranks of the Republican party. Of the principles and measures of that party, he has since been a consistent and earnest supporter. During the war he was very active in the support of the government, and was very efficient in raising companies and filling the various quotas of soldiers asked of his own locality.

Mr. LASHER is a genial gentleman, of strong sound sense, and diligent and persevering in the support of any cause or measure which meets his approbation. As has been intimated above, he is attentive to his duties, and looks well to the interests of his constituents. He is a member of the Canal Committee.

THOMAS LAWRENCE.

Mr. LAWRENCE was born in the city of New York, May 16, 1819. He is a descendant of THOMAS LAWRENCE, one of the three LAWRENCE brothers who originally settled on Long Island, in 1644. His grandfather, THOMAS LAWRENCE, removed his family from New York city to Rockland county just previous to the Battle of Long Island, and they remained there until after peace was established, in 1786, when they removed to Mount Pleasant, Westchester county. He served in the Continental army under WASHINGTON, and at the close of the war held a Lieutenant's commission, with a brevet of Captain. WILLIAM LAWRENCE, the youngest son of THOMAS LAWRENCE, and the father of the subject of this notice, was born in New York city, February 4, 1776, and married, in 1795, THAMER FISHER, eldest daughter of

GILBERT FISHER, of Mount Pleasant. Mr. FISHER was known during the whole Revolutionary war as an active and zealous partisan Whig scout, serving under Major JONATHAN PAULDING. The FISHER family were among the earliest settlers of White Plains and vicinity. WILLIAM LAWRENCE removed to New York city immediately after his marriage, and started the first mill for grinding drugs in America, on the site of the present Essex Market, in that city. In the War of 1812, he volunteered for the defense of the city, and served until the danger was passed and the troops were disbanded.

In 1822, when THOMAS was but three years of age, his parents removed to Mount Pleasant, Westchester county, and his early education was consequently obtained in the district schools of the neighborhood, dividing his time as most boys did at that period who resided in agricultural districts, between working on the farm in summer and going to school in winter, until about the year 1833, when he entered the Mount Pleasant Academy at Sing Sing. He remained at this academy about two years, and then entered the law office of SMITH BARKER, in New York city, as a student at law. Too young at this time to appreciate the dry study of the law, he only remained one year, when he returned to the country and diversified his employment by working on his father's farm, attending school, teaching and surveying until 1842, when his health failing him, he removed to Adams county, Illinois, where he remained for over four years, following various pursuits and traveling over the greater part of the then inhabited West, even penetrating the Indian territory alone and on horseback.

He returned home with health completely restored, and again sought the law office of his old patron, SMITH BARKER, and, completing his studies, was admitted to the bar in February, 1851. He then took up his residence in the city of New York, following the practice of his profession, part of the time under his own name alone, and part of the time as one of the firm of Lockwood, Lawrence & Crosby, until 1858, when he removed to Nyack, Rockland county, his present place of residence. In 1859, he was elected District Attorney of that county, and served the term of three years, still, however, continuing his private practice in the city of New York, which he still follows.

His grandfathers, both on his father's and mother's side, were Jeffersonian Democrats. His father cast his first vote for Thomas Jefferson, and never varied in his support of Democratic principles, and Mr. Lawrence himself has always, from his first vote to his last, sustained the same political principles. By some considered ultra in his views, he cannot be accused of ever swerving. Taking his stand upon what he deemed the fundamental principles of our government, he resolutely opposed every measure of President Lincoln's administration for the subjection of the Southern States, and was one of the first, if not the first man, in this State who organized what was known as Peace Meetings during the war. Denounced by many, even of his former political friends, threatened with imprisonment and lynch law, he never changed his principles, nor ever faltered in their fearless advocacy.

Mr. Lawrence was elected to the Assembly by 615 majority. He is a member of the Committee on Banks.

DAVID D. LEFLER.

The little county of Seneca elects one member of Assembly. It is situated between two of the beautiful inland lakes of western New York, from one of which it takes its name — and since the days of ANDREW JACKSON's first candidacy has been one of the Democratic counties of the State, which seldom falters — having been one of seven counties, which stood firm in the Democratic column in the memorable canvass of 1861. It is frequently called the "fast anchored isle of Democracy,"— in view of its isolated position as the only Democratic county in the Seventh Judicial District, and surrounded, as it is, on all sides by strong opposition majorities.

The fertility of its soil attracted the attention of soldiers of the army of General SULLIVAN in their march across it, in the celebrated Indian Campaign, near the close of the Revolutionary struggle, and soon after the restoration of peace, many of these veteran warriors returned and located lands in Seneca county. The three military townships of Ovid, Romulus and Junius, comprising the greater portion of the present county, were set apart as bounty lands for soldiers of the Revolutionary War — many of whom became actual settlers. To this element were added many settlers from Long Island, New Jersey and Pennsylvania; two of the towns having been settled principally with Pennsylvania Germans.

DAVID D. LEFLER, deriving his descent from such patriotic stock, was born in the town of Covert, Seneca county, where he now resides, on the 5th day of September, 1825. Both his paternal and maternal grandfathers served in the War of the Revolution,— and both lived to the age of about one hundred years.

Mr. LEFLER's father is a native of Pennsylvania, and still living at the advanced age of ninety-two years; his mother, now in her eighty-ninth year, is a native of New Jersey. His father, a mechanic in humble circumstances, was unable to extend to his son DAVID the advantages of a liberal education. Leaving home at the early age of thirteen years, with but a few shillings in his pocket, young LEFLER entered upon the battle of life for himself with indomitable energy, and a determination to succeed. For a time he engaged himself to a farmer to chop cord wood and split rails, and afterwards for several years worked on a farm in summer and attended school in winter, working nights and mornings for his board. His education was finished at a select school at Farmer Village, then under the charge of Rev. PHINEAS C. HEADLEY, who has since acquired considerable reputation as an author and a divine. After teaching school several terms, he selected the avocation of a farmer, (having married at the age of twenty-three years) at first working lands upon shares. By strict industry and application to business he soon became the owner of a fine farm, and gradually enlarged his business by adding to it the purchase of live stock, farm produce and wool, to which latter branch of this business he now devotes the greater portion of his time.

As a public spirited citizen he has always been ready to unite in all local enterprises calculated to advance the interest of the community in which he resides. He was the first President of the Trumansburgh and Seneca Falls Telegraph Company, and has always been a prominent member of the County Agricultural Society.

In politics, Mr. L. was an early admirer of HENRY CLAY and DANIEL WEBSTER, and of the doctrines advocated by them, and on arriving at his majority united his political fortunes with the Whig party, then in the minority in Seneca county, casting his first Presidential vote for TAYLOR and FILLMORE, in 1848. A conservative in his political views, on the organization of the Republican party, he identified himself with the conservative branch of that party. In 1858 he received the Republican nomination for Sheriff of Seneca county, and made a handsome run, although defeated by the Democratic candidate.

During the late war he was a member of the Senatorial War Committee, by appointment of Governor MORGAN, and was Chairman of the Town War Committee, in which capacities he rendered very active and efficient services in promoting enlistments and in raising money to carry on the same—giving liberally of his own means. At the close of the war he took issue with the majority of his party on its reconstruction policy and the question of the civil and political status of the Southern States. In the fall of 1866, he entered heartily into the canvass, and warmly supported the Hon. JOHN T. HOFFMAN and his colleagues on the Democratic State ticket. At that election, owing greatly to his efforts and influence, his town, which for many years had been strongly Republican, gave Judge HOFFMAN 36 majority, and at the election of 1867, this majority was increased to 66.

At the Democratic nominating Convention of Seneca county, in October, 1867, Mr. L. was nominated for Member of Assembly, receiving the votes of more than two-thirds of the Delegates on the first ballot, and after a somewhat exciting canvass, was elected by a majority of 575; the largest majority ever given in that county for a Democratic nominee for member.

After the organization of the Legislature, Mr. L. was assigned by the Speaker to the Chairmanship of the Committee on Public Lands, and is also a member of the important committees on Railroads and Sub-committee of the Whole. As a legislator, he is prompt, industrious and watchful of the interests of his constituency, and is deservedly popular and influential with his fellow members.

As a son, husband and father, he is kind and devoted; as a politician and man of business, frank, decided and outspoken; as a neighbor and citizen, genial and warm-hearted — and the poor, the orphan and the fatherless, know no better friend than DAVID D. LEFLER.

JOHN F. LITTLE.

Mr. LITTLE was born July 13th, 1839, in the town of Reading, Steuben county (now Schuyler). His parents were farmers, and, like all boys brought up in agricultural sections, he was employed in the labor of the farm. Manifesting at an early age a desire for study, and more information than was to be obtained in the common schools of the country, he was permitted to attend the high schools and academies of that section of the State, when the labors of the farm did not require his time at home, and was thus alternately employed on the farm of his parents and attending school until he arrived at the age of eighteen. He then abandoned agricultural labor, and for ten years was engaged as a teacher in the schools of his native county, in which capacity he succeeded well, and gained some reputation as an educator in the public schools. He then gave up teaching as a business, and entered upon the study of the law, pursuing it studiously until the breaking out of the rebellion in 1861, when he at once became enlisted in the success of the North. During the first year of the war, a great portion of his time was spent in obtaining volunteers for our army by acting as a recruiting officer, and in making war speeches throughout his county. The reverses to our arms and the necessity of at once filling up our depleted armies, in the summer of 1862, again called him forth from his studies, which he had in the spring of that year resumed, and again he took the field; and after assisting by his time and money in raising the quota of his county, he entered the army as First Lieutenant in the 161st Regiment of New York Volunteers. His regiment being assigned to the "Banks Expedition," was sent with that command to the "Department of the Gulf," and took part in every battle and skirmish in that Department, commencing with the siege of Port Hudson and ending with the capture of Mobile, and in the meantime he was promoted to a Captaincy in his regiment. At the close of actual hostilities, his executive abilities having attracted the attention of his superior officers, he was selected from a large command, and, with a proper garrison, was sent to Marianna, a large town in the interior of Florida, to establish a military post and administer the law as a civil officer, being charged with the duties of an officer of the "Freedmen's Bureau," and of administering the oath of allegiance and amnesty.

Order being restored to that section of the State, he was relieved of his command and ordered to report at Tallahassee, the Headquarters of the Department of Florida, then under the command of Major-General JOHN G. FOSTER, by whom he was assigned to duty as Provost Marshal and acting Mayor of the city, the multifarious duties of which position he discharged to the entire satisfaction of his superior officers, until his health failed him, and for a time he was prostrated by disease superinduced by the exposure incident to active campaigns. On his partial recovery, his commanding officer, believing that a change of climate would be of value in restoring him to health—he having been in the extreme South continuously for over three years, never having had a day's leave of absence—ordered him to Washington in charge of the witnesses in the WIRZ case from the Department of Florida.

On his arrival at Washington he discharged his duties, and his short visit North having failed to restore his health, the war being at an end and his regiment having previously been mustered out of the service, he was, at his own request, by the War Department, ordered to Elmira, N. Y., where, on the 17th day of October, 1865, he was honorably mustered out and discharged. Returning to the home of his father, he was for several months prostrated by sickness from disease contracted during his service in the army. As soon as his health would permit, he again resumed the study of law, and was, on the 6th day of December, 1866, admitted to the Bar, and at once commenced the practice of law in the village of Bath.

From a boy, Mr. LITTLE has taken an active interest in the politics of the country, and at a very early age became active in the local politics of his county, always acting with the Democratic party. In the fall of 1867 he was placed in nomination by the Democratic party for the office of member of Assembly in the First Assembly District of Steuben county. The District was largely Republican, having the previous year given the Republican nominee a majority of about 600; but by his efforts and those of his personal and political friends, he overcame the majority against him and was elected by a majority of nearly 500. He is a member of the important

Committees on Judiciary, Canal Fraud Impeachment, and Salt.

Mr. LITTLE is tall, slim, and attractive in person. There is considerable native humor lurking in his composition, and he is genial and pleasant in his disposition. He ranks as one of the foremost young men in the Assembly. His perceptions are clear, and his manner of of presenting his thoughts forcible. He is an able debater and cogent reasoner. There is no hesitancy, no mere reading in his oratory. His utterance is distinct and his voice pleasant. He is thoughtful and observing. His attachments are warm and his friends numerous, and they rejoice at the evidences of his prosperity.

JAMES LOUGHRAN.

Mr. LOUGHRAN was born at Hamden, Delaware county, N. Y., February 1st, 1831. His education was obtained solely in the common school of his native town; and after acquiring an ordinary proficiency in the rudimentary branches, he learned the clothier's trade, which he continued to follow as an occupation until the year 1853, at which time he engaged in mercantile business, at Windham, Greene county. Mr. L. is still a successful merchant of that place.

At the age of twenty-one, he joined his political fortunes with those of the Whig party. When, however, that once powerful organization became dissolved, as new interests sprang up, he allied himself with the Democrats. He has ever since been a steady adherent to their principles and modes of action. Nor has the warmth of his devotion to his party gone unrewarded. Pleasant proofs of appreciation have, from time to time, been extended to him by the conferring of offices of trust upon him. In the spring of 1854, he was elected Justice of the Peace; and so well did he administer the duties of that office that he was re-elected; and in fact, he has held the position during every subsequent term, down to the present time. In 1862, he was a member of the Board of Supervisors. Last fall he ran for Member of Assembly on the Democratic ticket, and was elected by a majority of 925. He is a member of the committees on Privileges and Elections and Roads and Bridges.

He is unambitious to be among the leaders of his party in the House, and seems always disposed to do his duty conscientiously.

WILLIAM LOUNSBERY.

Mr. LOUNSBERY represents the First Assembly District of the county of Ulster. He was born in the town of Marbletown, in that county, December 25th, 1831. His paternal ancestors are of Welch descent, and some of them were among the earliest settlers of Ulster county. Nearly all of the name now living in this country, trace their origin to the Ulster family. A great uncle (Colonel JOHN LOUNSBERY) was a member of the Senate, and of the Council of Appointment, during the gubernatorial administration of DE WITT CLINTON; another great uncle (Col. EBENEZER LOUNSBERY) was a member of the Senate in 1838, '39. Both served in the war of 1812, in which they acquired their military rank. His father, JOHN LOUNSBERY, was a member of the Assembly in

1853, and was classed as a Hunker, in the political divisions of the Democracy of that period.

Mr. LOUNSBERY has enjoyed excellent educational advantages, which he has not failed to improve. He graduated, in 1851, at Rutgers College, obtaining the third honor of the graduating class. He studied law at the Law School of the University of the city of Albany, and was admitted to practice in 1853; and immediately opened an office in the village of Kingston. By his careful preparation of, and faithful attention to, the causes at first entrusted to him, he soon obtained the confidence of the public and a handsome share of business. About two years since he entered into copartnership with Hon. ERASTUS COOKE, of Kingston, and the law firm of COOKE & LOUNSBERY now occupies a commanding position at the Ulster bar, and does a very large share of its business.

Mr. LOUNSBERY has been connected with the editorial fraternity, having been from 1857 to 1861, associated with Mr. S. S. HOMMEL in the proprietorship of the Ulster Republican — now the Kingston Argus — then, as now, the recognized organ of the Democracy of Ulster county. This was a period of sharp political controversy, and Mr. LOUNSBERY, in such intervals of leisure as were allowed him by his profession, entered into the contests of that period with spirit and zeal. His editorial articles, like his efforts at the bar, were marked by smoothness and elegance of style, clearness, directness and force, and added greatly to the effectiveness of that journal as a party organ. Mr. LOUNSBERY is no mere slave to his profession. He finds time to glean in the broad fields of general literature, and hence he naturally became a member of the Ulster county Historical Society, and took great interest in preparing papers to be read before it. The same literary tastes led him to accept invitations to make addresses before the Kingston Literary Associations, and the Ulster County Agricultural Society. All of these literary productions exhibit fine scholarly tastes and attainments; a clear and practical habit of thought, and great felicity of expression.

With this large and varied experience in law, politics and literature, backed by a laudable ambition and an ardent temperament, Mr. LOUNSBERY naturally became a leading member in the present Assembly. He was selected as a candidate by the Democracy of his party with great unanimity, and was elected by the largest majority ever given in the District for the same office.

His abilities were appreciated at Albany as well as at home, in the organization of the Committees of the Assembly. He is Chairman of the Judiciary Committee, a position of great responsibility. He is also a member of the Committee on Claims. He gives the closest attention to legislative matters, and evidently intends to make himself entirely familiar with the interests and needs of the Empire State. He is fond of social enjoyments that partake of a literary character, is well fitted to take part in conversation, and greatly delights in a good joke or a witty repartee.

JOHN B. MADDEN.

Mr. MADDEN is a native of Ireland. He was born at Carronakelle, in the county of Galway, June 13th, 1823. His father was an extensive land-holder, and was classed as a "gentleman farmer." His position of comparative wealth afforded him the opportunity of giving his son a classical education. Accordingly the youth was duly prepared for a collegiate course, and entered the College of Esker, in his native county. Subsequently he became anxious, like thousands of others of his countrymen, to try his fortune in the New World. Convinced that so long as England might continue her peculiar mode of governing Ireland, there would be little chance of accomplishing much for himself, he resolved to emigrate to America, where the rights of men are better respected, and every citizen has a voice in relation to the administration of the Government. He accordingly took passage for the United States, and landed in New York in the month of July, 1845.

As soon as he could properly do so, he took the first steps toward becoming a citizen of the country of his adoption; and in the Autumn of 1850 he cast his first vote. Like a great majority of the men who have come from Ireland, he joined the Democratic party, and worked vigorously for the promotion of its interests. Mr. MADDEN continued to live in New York from 1845 to 1855, being engaged in mercantile pursuits. At the end of that time, he purchased property in the town of Newtown, Queens county, where he has ever since resided.

In the spring of 1860, he was elected Justice of the Peace by a majority of thirty-six votes; and re-elected in 1863, by 700 majority. In 1867, though there were two Democratic candidates in the field against him, he was again elected to fill the same position by 400 majority. Last fall, Mr. MADDEN was tendered the nomination for member of Assembly, and his great local popularity was shown by a majority of 1,198, the largest given in his district during the past ten years. He is a member of the Committee on Privileges and Elections, and Chairman of the Committee on Charitable and Religious Societies, and is an active and intelligent member.

FRANCIS AVERY MALLISON.

Mr. MALLISON, one of the representatives of the county of Kings, was born in Rome, Oneida county, March 13, 1832, of Connecticut parentage. His father was of that hard worked and poorly paid class, the Methodist clergy, and was a teacher in Rome. SARAH WARNER was the maiden name of his mother. She was from Plymouth, Conn. Their son was educated in the Oneida Conference Seminary, the Polytechnic School at Chittenango, Madison county, and the Seminary at Lowville, Lewis county.

Mr. MALLISON traveled in the west in 1849 and in the south in 1851 and 1852, acquiring valuable information relative to the characteristics of the people in those sections, and the value and products of the territory. He was for seven years telegraph operator in Central New York. In November, 1859, he settled in Brooklyn, and was at once engaged as a writer upon the City News, a daily paper, and was subsequently employed on the Daily Times. For three years he has been connected with the Brooklyn Eagle, the organ of the Democratic party of Kings county. He writes under the *nom de plume* of "O'Pake." His contributions are widely admired, and have added largely to the popularity and circulation of the very influential journal with which he is now connected. He was confined in Fort Lafayette four months and two days for copying the bogus proclamation of President LINCOLN, commonly known as the HOWARD proclamation, which was published in May, 1864, and for printing which the offices of the New York World and the Journal of Commerce were closed by military order. He was sent to the Fort May 21, and released September 23, 1864.

The manner of his release is mentioned by Mr. CARPENTER, in one of his papers containing recollections of President LINCOLN, published in the New York Independent, in which he says that "HOWARD, the proclamation forger — a Republican — was pardoned out of Fort Lafayette, while MALLISON, his confederate, who was a Democrat, continued incarcerated. A Brooklyn gentleman mentioned the fact to Mr. LINCOLN. He was busy at the time, but said very earnestly, 'Don't leave the city till I fix that;' and at the first leisure moment he wrote and placed in the hands of the gentleman an order for MALLISON's unconditional release." This may or may not be true, but no one will suppose that President LINCOLN intentionally kept Mr. MALLISON in confinement because of any difference in politics. He was too just, not to say kind hearted and humane, for that. And we are pleased to know that Mr. MALLISON accords with us in this view.

Mr. MALLISON was admitted to practice law in the Supreme Court of the State, in December, 1866. He has been a member of the Democratic General Committee of Kings county for several years, and is a popular, active and successful politician. He has never held office before. He received a majority of 2,683 for member of Assembly. He abounds in humor, and is the wit of the House.

JOHN F. MANN.

In the life of Mr. Mann we have another instance of what native talent and tact, backed up by energy and perseverance, will do in enabling even the most humble of our race to rise in the scale of manhood, and in obtaining wealth and influence. He was the son of a carpenter, and was born at Lowville, Lewis county, New York, September 21, 1824. Three years after his birth his parents removed to New Bremen, in the same county, making their home in a log house, surrounded by an entire wilderness. When old enough to labor he assisted his father at the business of house carpenter, receiving in the meantime, such education as the common schools of his locality could furnish, and obtaining it in those intervals when his services could most easily be dispensed with by his father. At the age of twenty-one he commenced attending the Lowville Academy, and by teaching occasionally and working at his trade when nothing better presented, he succeeded in paying for such tuition as that institution could give. At the age of twenty-six he secured a place as clerk in a store, and served faithfully in this capacity for four years, carefully saving all his wages not absolutely needed for personal expenses. He then commenced keeping store on his own account. He was successful in business, and has secured for himself a fine competence, and can now enjoy the fruits of his early self-sacrificing toil.

In 1855 Mr. MANN was appointed Postmaster at New Bremen, his place of residence, and has held the office ever since, with the exception of about six months. He also acted as Census Marshal in 1855. He was formerly a Whig, and became one of the earliest members of the Republican party. He is quite active in political matters, and has often been chosen to represent his locality in district and State conventions. As he is and has been in business transactions, so he is and has been found in political matters — straightforward and honest. He was elected on the Republican ticket to represent Lewis county in the Assembly. He is a member of the Committee on Public Printing. He takes no part in debate, but in a quiet way is very attentive to his duties.

ANGELL MATTHEWSON.

Mr. MATTHEWSON was born in Pulaski, Oswego county, New York, June 8th, 1837, where he received a good academic education. At the age of fifteen he commenced learning the printer's trade, in the office of the Pulaski Democrat. At twenty-one he was foreman of the job department of the Daily Palladium, in Oswego, and a year later was city editor of the Palladium. In 1859, he went to Utica, where he was employed in the Daily Herald office until January 4th, 1860, when he went to Fort Plain, Montgomery county (his present residence), where he soon after purchased a half interest in the Mohawk Valley Register.

September 15th, 1861, he commenced raising a company for the War, in which he took a Second Lieutenancy —

Hon. LORENZO CROUNSE, District Judge of Nebraska, being Captain, and Capt. S. WALTER STOCKING, now Clerk in the Executive Deparment of this State, First Lieutenant. This company rendezvoused at Elmira, in September, 1861, where it was attached to the 1st New York Light Artillery, as Battery "K" of that regiment. May 18, 1862, Lieutenant MATTHEWSON was appointed Post Adjutant, at Camp Barry, Washington, D. C.

May 30th, 1862, at Bolivar Heights, near Harper's Ferry, with a single piece of artillery, he routed the enemy's sharp-shooters, and engaged a four gun battery for half an hour, handling his gun with such judgment and skill that the only damage sustained was the disabling of one of the wheels of the gun carriage by a solid shot from the enemy, while the enemy's loss, as reported by Major GARDNER, of the 5th New York Cavalry, was seven killed and upwards of fifty wounded. For his services on this occasion, he was appointed Ordnance Officer on the Staff of Major-General FRANZ SIGEL, June 7th, 1862, and afterward served in the same capacity on the Staffs of Generals COOPER and AUGUR.

November, 1862, he was promoted to First Lieutenant, and assigned to duty with Battery "D" of his regiment.

May 23d, 1863, he was appointed Adjutant of his regiment, and May 25th was appointed Acting Assistant Adjutant-General of the Artillery Brigade, First Corps, Army of the Potomac, which position he held one year.

July 1st, 1864, he was promoted to Captain of his company, for meritorious service at North Anna River, Va., May 23d, 1864, where he was shot through the thigh with a Minnie ball, while in command of his Battery ("D"), and fighting almost a forlorn hope.

He was in service until the end of the war, three years and nine months, and was mustered out at Elmira, New York, the 17th day of June, 1865.

He was engaged in the following battles: Harper's Ferry, Cedar Mountain, Rappahannock Station, Fredericksburgh, Chancellorsville, Gettysburgh, Mine Run, Wilderness, Spottsylvania, North Anna River, Siege of Petersburgh, Weldon Railroad, Hatcher's Run and Lee's surrender, at Appomattox Court House.

July 1st, 1865, he became sole editor and proprietor of the Register newspaper, at Fort Plain, and still conducts that paper; being also one of the proprietors of the Canajoharie Radii.

In the fall of 1866, he received sixteen votes in the county Democratic Nominating Convention, for member of the Assembly; and last Fall (without asking or seeking), was put in nomination and elected by the largest majority (seven hundred and twenty-four) ever received by any member from Montgomery county; running two hundred and eighteen votes ahead of the State ticket.

In the field, Mr. MATTHEWSON was brave, and received frequent commendations from his superior officers. He is active and energetic, pushing to success vigorously everything he undertakes. He is a calculating and wise financial manager, and in the Assembly is an observing, industrious and efficient legislator. He is an easy and graceful writer, possesses fine social qualities, and his personal character is above reproach.

JAMES McKIEVER.

Mr. McKIEVER is the member from the Fourteenth Assembly District of New York. For the past three years this district has been represented by Hon. THOMAS J. CREAMER (now Senator), whom the present member delights to call his friend. Mr. McKIEVER is a member of the Tammany Hall Democracy, and is an active worker in its ranks, and a steadfast believer in its principles. He is a native of Ireland, having been born in Tyrone county, October 23, 1832, and has resided in New York city most of the time since coming to this country. He is a ship-carpenter by trade. In 1861, he held the office of Constable, and in January, 1864 was appointed Marshal to the Board of Supervisors, but resigned immediately afterwards. He was elected to the Assembly by a plurality of 1,258. He is a member of the Committees on Commerce and Navigation and Charitable and Religious Societies. He is modest and unassuming in manner, and has many friends both at home and in the Legislature.

EDMUND MILLER.

Mr. MILLER, who represents the county of Chemung in the Assembly, was born in Southport, November 1, 1808. His father is of German descent, and his mother a native of Connecticut. In 1783, during the French and Indian war, his grandfather was taken prisoner by the Indians in Northampton county, Penn., and brought to the head of Seneca Lake, where he escaped and returned home. He subsequently settled in Southport, and his son, the father of EDMUND, who was a farmer, lived and died upon the farm now occupied by the latter.

Mr. MILLER's education was confined to the common schools, but those advantages were thoroughly improved. He has held all the various offices in his town, and has been Supervisor for many years, and was re-elected while a Member of the House. His varied experience, ripe judgment and practical common sense render him an invaluable Member of the House. He is a farmer, cattle dealer and lumberman. He was elected member by a majority of over five hundred, running three hundred ahead of his ticket. His competitior was GEORGE W. BUCK, who had been chosen the preceding year by a majority of 110.

He is a member of the Committee on Claims and Chairman of the Committee on Agriculture. He has always been true to the Democratic party, and of great service to it. He is a successful politician and a careful legislator.

JAMES C. MORAN.

Mr. MORAN, who represents the Thirteenth Assembly District of New York, was born in the Ninth ward January 22, 1839, and has always resided in that city. His ancestors immigrated to this country from Ireland. Mr. MORAN obtained his education in the public schools of the city of New York, and is a carpenter by avocation. He has never before held a political office, but has been an active Democratic politician in his ward and district for the last ten years. He ran on both the Tammany and Mozart tickets, and was elected by a plurality of 636, and a majority of 248. He serves on the Committees on Public Printing, and Trade and Manufactures. As a member of the House, he is remarkably quiet, but always attentive to his duties.

MICHAEL C. MURPHY.

Mr. MURPHY, though still young, has experienced many exciting adventures, and has won military distinction in defending his adopted country. He is a native of Kilmallock, Limerick county, Ireland, where he was born March 7th, 1839. When about eight years of age, he came to America, arriving in New York city, November, 1847. When he reached a suitable age, he learned the printer's trade. At the opening of the civil war in this country, Mr. MURPHY, in common with hundreds of others from the same avocation, enlisted in the army. April 20th, 1861, he was commissioned as Captain in the Ellsworth Regiment of Fire Zouaves. After the release of General CORCORAN from the rebel prison, Captain MURPHY resigned his commission in the Regiment of Zouaves, and joined the "Irish Legion," as Captain. He was promoted January 4th, 1863, to a Lieutenant-Colonelcy of the 2d Regiment of the "Legion." He was closely identified with the movements of General CORCORAN's command, until he was dismissed from the service by order of General MEADE, to date from June 9th, 1864, for sending a flag of truce to the skirmishing line of the enemy, in an endeavor to save the lives of one hundred and five privates and seven officers, who were wounded and lying between both lines. This took place May 24th, 1864, while he was in command of the advance line of the Second Division of the Second Army Corps. When this dismissal was brought to the notice of General GRANT, and the facts of the case were clearly presented to him, he justified the course of Lieutenant-Colonel MURPHY, who was immediately restored to his rank, by order of President LINCOLN. He left the service in March, 1865, in consequence of ill health. He was a valorous officer, and a man true to his country.

The Fenian raid upon Canada, which set the English Cabinet in a flutter, made the Canadians quake with sudden fear, and caused her Majesty's troops to suppose that the time for field duty had come, will long be remembered as a preliminary movement which, though it failed to accomplish the purposes of the Irish people, nevertheless caused John Bull to cast an inquiring glance toward the Emerald Isle, and wonder if Erin was really in earnest. Mr. MURPHY was General of that portion of the Fenian army, in May and June, 1866, which was concentrated at Malone, New York, and was intended for the assaulting column against Montreal. Every reader is familiar with the failure of that undertaking, the causes of which it is neither our place nor purpose to discuss.

In November, 1866, Col. MURPHY was elected to the Assembly by the Demcrats of the First District of the city of New York, which is composed of the First, Second, Third and Fifth Wards. His majority was 1,496. He was appointed on the Committee on Militia and Public Defense. He was re-elected in 1867 by a majority of 1,501, and is a member of the Militia and City Committees.

Colonel MURPHY is a practical and proficient legislator. He has, at times, a brusqueness of manner which is somewhat disagreeable to those not entirely acquainted with his kindly nature and warm heart. Notwithstanding this peculiar characteristic, he soon succeeds in winning the good will of those with whom he comes in contact, and impresses himself on them as an agreeable gentleman. He has a fine military bearing and courteous manner.

HENRY C. NELSON.

Mr. NELSON is a native of Sing Sing, Westchester county, and was born July 29, 1838. His family is Dutch, but by his mother's side he is descended from the Huguenot family of DELANOY. He was educated in the public schools of New York, afterward entering the Free Academy, where he remained two years. He then went into a law office in the city, and was, in due time, admitted to the bar. He then entered upon the practice of his profession at Sing Sing, where he soon obtained a remunerative practice. He was generally popular, and was chosen to several positions in the village and town. Last fall, he accepted the Democratic nomination for Assembly in the Third District of the county, and received, somewhat unexpectedly to himself, the majority of 991, overcoming a Republican majority of 630. He was promptly assigned a leading position in the House. He is Chairman of the Committee on State Prisons, and a member of the Railroad Committee and Sub-committee of the Whole, thus enabling him to exercise a marked influence in shaping legislation. Having succeeded in carrying a district heretofore Republican, he is very likely to be pressed for re-election, an event which would continue a very estimable gentleman in the legislative councils of the State.

AMBROSE NICHOLSON.

Mr. NICHOLSON is a native of Hinsdale, Berkshire county, Massachusetts, where he was born March 16th, 1801. His father was from Glastonbury, Connecticut, where his grandfather also lived during the Revolutionary war, all of the male members of whose family were in the army during that early struggle of the colonies. Mr. NICHOLSON'S father was in the army of General WASHINGTON when he evacuated Long Island, and continued in that branch of the service to the end of the war. Being only sixteen years old when he enlisted, his health was broken down by the hardships of the service, so that, for the last twenty years of his life, he was a confirmed cripple. He died in 1814, at the age of fifty-four.

Mr. NICHOLSON'S maternal grandfather was NATHAN HIBBARD, who removed from Norwich, Connecticut, and settled in Hinsdale, Massachusetts, when the country was new. He was a leading man in the community, distinguished for his sound judgment and his integrity. He was one of those who resisted "SHAY'S Insurrection," and at one time frightened SHAY'S forces away, by mounting a log on cart wheels, and displaying it on an eminence, so as to present the appearance of a cannon. He had a son, BILLY HIBBARD, who was, for a long time, a traveling preacher of the Methodist persuasion, and somewhat noted for his strength of character, as well as his eccentricities.

Mr. NICHOLSON'S father, at the time of his death, which occurred when this son was thirteen years old, left a family of eight children — five daughters and three sons, of whom he was the youngest. Up to that time he had attended the district school, and had a strong desire to acquire a thorough education. But circumstances were against his so doing, as shortly after his father's death he was apprenticed to learn the tanner's trade. He however used such means as he could find to make up for the lack of more favorable chances, and, at the age of eighteen, he was employed to teach a district school. He followed teaching in the winter time for several years. His tastes, and also circumstances, led him into mechanical pursuits, other than the one to which he was bred. Hence, he became a carpenter, then general builder, and then millwright and machinist. He is now a manufacturer of lumber, doors, sash and blinds and cheese boxes.

Mr. NICHOLSON, for fifteen years, was one of the Superintending School Committee of his native town. He was also town clerk for a number of years, and Adjutant in the militia of Massachusetts twelve years.

After he removed to Russia, Herkimer county, N. Y., he was elected Justice of the Peace, Road Commissioner and Supervisor, notwithstanding the fact that the town was Democratic and he a HENRY CLAY Whig. In 1855 he moved with his family to Trenton, where he resided until 1860, when he removed to Oriskany, Oneida county, where he now resides. Three of his sons were in the Federal service during the Rebellion, leaving in his care alone a somewhat extensive business. They all returned home, but with constitutions impaired by the hardships of war. One of them has since died from causes which no doubt originated in his army life. Mr. NICHOLSON has faithfully served under the banner of the Republican party since its first organization. Without his knowledge or expectation he was nominated for the Assembly and was elected by 434 majority. He is a gentleman of sound, practical views, aspiring to no great personal distinction, and satisfied only with an honest discharge of duty.

DANIEL O'REILLY.

This gentleman has royal Irish blood in his veins, being a descendant of the famous O'REILLYS, of the county of Cavan, Ireland, who were Princes under the Irish monarchy, and participated in the ineffectual struggles of Erin to keep herself an independent government.

He was born in Cavan county, Ireland, in the year 1839. When very young, he left his home, without the knowledge, and, in fact, against the will of his parents, and came to New York city, where he obtained an education in the public schools. After leaving school, Mr. O'REILLY was employed in the manufacture of soda water, for several years. But being, at that time, of a restless and venturesome disposition, he embarked on an expedition to Nicaragua, with the late General WALKER. The romance of his dreams were dissipated by the privations which he had to endure. Instead of General WALKER's marching, with triumphant banners, to the consummation of success, his progress was, inch by inch, disputed, until he found his army dwindled down to a mere handful of men. After many sufferings, Mr. O'REILLY returned to New York.

When the late war broke out, he enlisted in the 170th Regiment, New York State Volunteers, and served until the surrender of the rebel forces. He participated in twenty-one different battles, among which were those of Bristow Station, Mine Run, Chancellorsville, Wilderness, Spottsylvania Court House, North Anne River, Petersburgh, Richmond, &c. After his return from the war, he was elected School Inspector of the Fourteenth Ward of New York, and acted in that capacity until an act of the

Legislature abrogated that office. In the fall of 1866, he was nominated by the Mozart Democracy of the Third District for Member of the Assembly, and was elected against three other candidates, by a plurality of four hundred and eighty-two votes. He was re-elected to the present Assembly by the large majority of four thousand one hundred and thirty-four. He is Chairman of the Committee on Petitions of Aliens, and a member of the Insurance Committee and Sub-committee of the Whole.

Mr. O'REILLY is very popular in his district; is rather bluff in his manner, but possesses a good heart and is a warm friend.

JULIUS M. PALMER.

Mr. PALMER, who represents the Second District of St. Lawrence county, is serving his first term in the Assembly. Mr. PALMER is a native of New York State, and was born in Wilna, Jefferson county, December 11, 1830. He received a good education, and at the age of eighteen went to Russell, St. Lawrence county, where he acquired a knowledge of surveying and followed the business for several years. In 1851, he engaged in trade as a merchant, in which occupation he has been successful, and is a prosperous business man; his partner at present being Hon. BENJAMIN SMITH, who formerly represented the same district in the Assembly during two terms.

Mr. PALMER has taken an active interest in all matters of public concern in the locality where he resides; was chosen Clerk of the town of Russell in 1856, and held the position for six years. He was elected Supervisor in 1862, the duties of which position he discharged for five years, and until he declined further service. During his connection with the Board of Supervisors, Mr. PALMER was Chairman of several important committees, and also of the Commission, appointed in 1866, to equalize the assessment of the county, whose report he wrote, and which has received very general approval. During the war he gave much of his time in aid of all enterprises looking to the support of the government, and, in common with his fellow-citizens, has given his town a record which shows it to be one of the most patriotic in St. Lawrence county. He was Recruiting Agent and Treasurer of the "Russell Volunteer Association." He was appointed Postmaster in May, 1861, by President LINCOLN, and was removed in November, 1866, by President JOHNSON.

Mr. PALMER is an ardent and active Republican, and was chosen to represent his district in the Assembly at the last election, by a majority of 2,121. He is a member of the Committee on the Expenditures of the Executive Department.

Mr. PALMER is a gentleman of quiet habits, of excellent judgment, and of unimpeachable integrity.

DE WITT PARSHALL.

Mr. PARSHALL was born at Palmyra March 23, 1812; and is therefore now in his fifty-seventh year. His parents were of American birth, and had previously resided in Orange county, neighbors of DE WITT CLINTON; and in naming his son, the elder PARSHALL complimented at the same time the illustrious founder of the Erie canal and a brother surveyor, then well known throughout the State, SIMEON DE WITT.

Mr. PARSHALL was "brought up to work." His father, a surveyor and farmer by occupation, and a bustling, energetic, go-ahead man, would tolerate nothing that savored of thriftlessness; and it was in his boyhood that his son learned those lessons of prudence and good management that have been put in practice with such telling results in his maturer life. A common school education, with a few terms at the Canandaigua Academy (where he was the room-mate of STEPHEN A. DOUGLAS), were all that were afforded him in the way of educational advantages. Leaving the Academy, he chose the profession of the law, and entered the office of the late General WILLIAM H. ADAMS (at Lyons), then in the height of his fame as an able and eloquent counsellor and advocate. Mr. PARSHALL was in study as diligent as in work, and in good time was admitted to the bar; but the demands of other claims upon his attention, prevented him from commencing practice until 1840, at which time he had reached the age of twenty-eight years. He connected with his practice (which soon came to be very large) a real estate agency — in which department of business he was, however, himself the best patron. Buying depreciated farms at low figures, he would repair the buildings and fences, reinvigorate the soil, and put the property in the best possible condition — of course, realizing a handsome profit when he came to sell, as he deserved to do. This branch of business he has continued to the present day; and it is estimated that he owns now, and has owned, since 1840, in Wayne county, something like ten thousand acres of land, in various farms, valued at from $500,000 to $600,000. The village of Lyons is largely indebted to Mr. Parshall's enterprise; he having owned, at one time and another, more than half the land the village stands upon; and besides about fifteen houses now owned by him, he has built or refitted upward of seventy-five more; selling them, with building lots, at fair prices and on accommodating terms, to mechanics and laborers; thus increasing the population of the village and adding to its material prosperity. In addition, he owns at present four blocks of stores in Lyons — one just completed, the handsomest in the county, and a lasting monument to his enterprise and liberality — and others are projected for the coming season. Of farm property, Mr. Parshall now owns more than two thousand acres; one parcel being the well known "Shaker Tract," on Sodus Bay.

In 1852 Mr. Parshall commenced the business of banking — starting "The Palmyra Bank of Lyons," afterward "The Lyons Bank," and now "The Lyons National Bank." This bank is doing a very large business, its capital being $100,000, and its circulation $90,000. Mr. P. has, besides, extensive banking interests (as well as real estate) in Buffalo, where he has a son engaged in that business; and also much valuable real estate in the States of Michigan and Iowa. In politics Mr. Parshall is a Republican of the strictest sect, and has been one since the organization of the Republican party, previous to which time he acted with the Democratic party. He has several times been elected Supervisor of the town and President of the village; but never until now has he been prevailed upon to accept any other official position. He was nominated for the Assembly because of his peculiar fitness for the place; because of his close identification with the interests of his district and county; because of his well-known executive ability; and because the people *would have it so*—running largely ahead of his ticket at the election. His constituents know him for a man of deeds rather than of words—a man of work rather than of theories—a man of facts and not of fancies; and they do not expect windy speeches from him. But they do expect to find him one of the hardest working, most attentive and most influential Members in the House—alive to the public interests, industrious in advancing them, and free from suspicion.

Personally, Mr. PARSHALL is a man of fine presence, of commanding stature, with shoulders scarcely stooped by years of bending over his desk; keen eye; hair and beard bleached with the frosts of advancing years; and countenance indicative of the most robust health. Mr. PARSHALL'S appearance is one that strikes a stranger favorably, and though a plain man, and making no attempt to curry favor with his fellows, his straightforward manner, his close attention to business, and his constant endeavors to enhance the thrift of his village and county, have won for him the confidence and respect of all who know him. Emphatically he is a self-made man: one of those who have won success and deserved it, too.

GEORGE J. PENFIELD.

Mr. PENFIELD was born March 24th, 1826, in Camden, Oneida county, New York. He is the youngest son of FOWLER PENFIELD, of English descent, who took part in the war of 1812, on the western frontier, and who was the second son of JESSE PENFIELD who distinguished himself in the Revolutionary war, having entered the service at the age of seventeen. He served in the army, over seven years, and was in the battle of White Plains, and all the other memorable battles of the Revolution; he then removed from the State of Connecticut to Camden, New York, where he lived to a good old age.

On the maternal side, Mr. PENFIELD is of French and Holland descent, of the families bearing the names of DE MILT and WORMSLEY, that fled from the persecutions instituted against the Christians, having left their property to be confiscated, and landed on Manhattan Island, when New York was but a small village. BENJAMIN DE MILT was a man of almost unbounded liberality; he donated an extensive library to the Mechanics' Library of New York city, and appropriated a large amount of money to that institution. His maiden sisters bequeathed a great portion of their estate to benevolent institutions; and the authorities of New York honored them for the deed, by giving one of the Dispensaries their name.

Mr. PENFIELD had few advantages for acquiring learning. From boyhood to the age of twenty-five, he was employed in farming pursuits. Before he was twenty-one, he removed, with his father and family, to Westchester county, New York.

For twelve or thirteen years, Mr. PENFIELD conducted a lucrative business, in the town of New Rochelle. On the breaking out of the war, he aided in fitting out the first regiment of volunteers which went from Westchester county, and which participated in the disastrous battle of Bull Run. He, and other patriotic gentlemen in that vicinity, pledged themselves to the support of the families of the soldiers who went out at that time; and they faithfully redeemed their pledge. And, in fact, all through the war, Mr. PENFIELD was among the foremost of those who assiduously exerted themselves to fill the quotas of men, which were demanded for the purpose of filling up our broken columns in the field. In 1862, he was elected Secretary of the Westchester county Mutual Insurance Company, and was subsequently chosen President of it. He has also held various town offices. He is now a member of the Board of Education, and one of the Trustees of the village of New Rochelle; and he has twice represented his town in the Board of Supervisors, having been elected by the Democratic party. He is President of the Savings Bank in New Rochelle; and, as a business man, displays eminent characteristics. He very materially aided in securing the erection of a new church edifice for the congregation of which he is a member, also in improving the public schools, in order to meet the growing wants of his town, and in accomplishing the incorporation of the village of New Rochelle.

Mr. PENFIELD was a member of the preceding Assembly, and performed his legislative work acceptably to his constituents, and with credit to himself. He was re-elected to the present House by a majority four times larger than that he received in 1866. He is Chairman of the Committee on Insurance Companies, and a member of the Committee on Affairs of Villages.

Mr. PENFIELD is of irreproachable character, and a useful citizen. As a legislator, he has made an honorable record, and is highly esteemed by his fellow-members for his uniform courtesy and gentlemanly bearing.

EDMUND L. PITTS.

Mr. PITTS is a native of Yates, Orleans county, New York. He is not yet twenty-nine years of age; but he has a maturity of mind which is rarely found in one so young. When a lad, he attended the academies in the vicinity of his home, and was considered to be a remarkably brilliant scholar. A desire sprang up in his mind to go through college; and, therefore, the mysteries of *amo-as-at* and *bonus-a-um* were in due time mastered, the classics and mathematics duly conned, and, after a time, the boy found himself prepared for the Sophomore year in college. During these terms of study, he had an able instructor and reliable friend, Professor CHARLES FAIRMAN, now Principal of the Medina Academy, of whom he speaks in warm terms of gratitude. When Mr. PITTS was fifteen, he carried off the first prize for declamation at a public exhibition, and, from our knowledge of him, he has not yet relaxed his study in that direction. But the question of a collegiate course was abandoned, because his father, though now in comfortable circumstances, was then scarcely prepared to take the responsibility of meeting the bills which would have to be incurred. In the year 1859, Mr. PITTS attended the Law School at Poughkeepsie, and then read law with Hon. SANFORD E. CHURCH, at Albion. Such was the rapidity of his progress, he was admitted to practice in 1860, about fifteen months after he began the study of his profession. In the autumn of 1860, he entered into a partnership with Adna Bowen, Esq., which has continued ever since. Confidence was had in his legal acumen; men trusted the firm with cases of importance, and found that they were skillfully managed; and what was, at one time, a promising beginning, has ripened into a steady success.

When Mr. Pitts was nineteen, he was a Douglas Democrat, and made campaign speeches in favor of that wing of the Democracy; but when he began to studiously weigh the doctrines which he was promulgating, he became convinced of their sophistry, and discarded them altogether. His first vote, he is proud to say, was cast for Abraham Lincoln; and every campaign since he was of age, has found him advocating, from the forum, almost daily and nightly, the enduring principles of his party. In 1862, in convention, Mr. Pitts, without any thought that he was even remotely dreamed of for a candidate to the office, came within one vote of the nomination for Member of Assembly; two years after, however, he was elected to the Assembly, and has continued to represent his district ever since. While carefully watching and urging the local interests of his constituents, he has boldly battled against the "New York ring," and has never hesitated to attack the strongholds of corruption, or to tear away the flimsy gauze of trickery. In 1866 he introduced a very important amendment into the New York tax levy, which met with obstinate resistance from certain parties; and yet, if we mistake not, a subsequent decision of Judge Barnard, in relation to the notorious gas contract swindle, turned upon that very amendment which was finally fought through by Mr. Pitts. He is regarded with confidence by many of the best men of New York city, who recognize in him the exponent of unselfish motives, and the staunch friend of their municipality. In the Assembly of 1866, he was Chairman of the Committee on Privileges and Elections, and was a Member of the Committee on the Affairs of Cities.

Mr. PITTS has attained a height of popularity seldom reached by men at so early an age. The canvass for Speaker of the Assembly of 1867, gave a striking illustration of this. His name was mentioned in that connection even before the close of the political struggle of the year. After the result had become definitely known, and the question of Speakership became more generally agitated, names of men long indentified with legislative action, of conceded ability, and who were among the leaders of the Republican party, were mentioned as being worthy of the honor; but, as the time for the assembling of the Legislature drew near, and previous to the meeting of the Republican caucus, one name after another was dropped, and Mr. PITTS was conceded the candidacy with cordial good feeling and perfect unanimity. On the assembling of the caucus, he was nominated by acclamation. The compliment was well bestowed, and was in accordance with public sentiment. As Speaker of the Assembly, he distinguished himself for his ready perceptions, his intimate knowledge of parliamentary law, acquired by long familiarity with legislation, his impartiality in administering the rules, for which he was warmly commended by his political opponents, and his speedy dispatch of business. He was uniformly courteous, but self-reliant; and in referring bills to the various committees—an act which requires discretion—he seldom made mistakes. The present session he is a member of the Committees on Ways and Means, and Privileges and Elections. He has previously served on the latter Committee, and uniformly has impressed political friends and opponents alike with his impartiality and freedom from partisan bias. In 1866, he reported in favor of three Democratic sitting members, and has always acted with a simple desire to find according to the law and the evidence, insisting that questions of right to hold seats should never be allowed to be made political.

Mr. PITTS is a firm adherent to the Republican party; he has never had any affiliation with frauds and corrupt measures, and his great aim has been to fight down schemes for plunder, and to maintain principles of right, irrespective of men. If he has personal ambitions, as it is natural he should have, he makes them subservient to the general welfare.

In stature, Mr. PITTS is five feet and four inches. He sometimes facetiously remarks that his friends call him five feet only, but he is determined to have the benefit of the *fraction over*. He has a pleasant face, which is full of animation and character, and a voice which is decisive in tone when he is in earnest, but sweeping when he is denunciatory.

JOHN A. PLACE.

The First Assembly District of Oswego county is represented by JOHN A. PLACE. It is composed of the city of Oswego, together with three of the adjoining towns.

Mr. PLACE was born in the town of Foster, Providence county, Rhode Island, in 1823. His parents were of Welsh descent, but his ancestors were among the earliest settlers of New England, and he comes of as nearly pure "Yankee stock" as is often traced in this country. Very early in his life his parents removed to Hartford county, Connecticut, where his schooldays commenced. In 1832, his family removed to Oswego, in this State, then comparatively a small village, in which, and in its vicinity, his home has since continued.

Mr. PLACE enjoyed only the advantages of such schools as his locality afforded, and most of his education was acquired by solitary study. Before his majority, he spent four years in the office of the Oswego Palladium, then a thorough-going Democratic sheet of the SILAS WRIGHT school, in which he thoroughly imbibed Democratic ideas, as they were then maintained by the leaders of that party.

After Mr. PLACE reached his majority, he was engaged for several years in the business of teaching. He very early took to the pen, and contributed many articles on local and political topics, which were published, sometimes anonymously and sometimes as editorial, in the press of his locality. In 1848, he purchased the Fulton Patriot, then the only Cass paper in Oswego county. Mr. PLACE had always held strong anti-slavery sentiments, and obtaining unlimited control of the columns of a newspaper, gave him a long coveted opportunity to advocate those sentiments with the people. He quietly took possession of his office, and it having become current through the village that a transfer had been made, the issue of the first number was looked for with much solicitude by the people. In the meantime he was waited upon by the leading "Hunkers," as the pro-slavery Democrats were then called, and the most flattering promises were made in case the paper continued in the old faith. On the other hand he was assured of loss of patronage and ruin should he not comply. The "free soilers" waited and hoped. The young editor was immovable. Hatred of slavery had taken too strongly hold of his principles to permit him to hesitate, and in his first number he unfurled the banner, for "Free Speech, Free Soil, and Free Men." He advocated the principles of the "Buffalo Platform," and supported VAN BUREN and ADAMS on the national ticket, throughout that memorable canvass. Subsequently, when a "union" was patched up between the "soft" and "hard shell" Democrats, the Patriot, under Mr. PLACE's control, nominally supported the Democratic cause; but he was in every sense of the word "independent," and unhesitatingly repudiated the principles of the party and its candidates, whenever they did not conform to his ideas on the slavery and other leading question of the day. He has always been outspoken upon the temperance question, and has written and published many articles urging the temperance reform.

The organization of the Republican party, in 1855, found Mr. PLACE ready and waiting for the movement. He had long foreseen that the anti-slavery element in the two leading parties of the country, must sometime come together, and he welcomed the movement which resulted in the formation of the Republican party. He was a member of the first convention of that party in his own county; was an ardent supporter of FREMONT and DAYTON, and subsequently of LINCOLN and HAMLIN, and has always been active in the support of the principles of his party.

In 1857, Mr. PLACE was elected School Commissioner of the First District of Oswego county. He was subsequently twice re-elected, each time with increasing majorities. While in office, he addressed himself to the elevation of the standard of qualification of teachers, and to the general improvement of schools. During his term of service, a larger number of school houses was erected in his district than ever before in the same period; the average of teachers wages was nearly doubled, and the general interest in schools was greatly increased.

In 1854, Mr. T. S. BRIGHAM, of Little Falls, having accepted an invitation of the leading commercial men of Oswego to commence the publication of the Daily Commercial Advertiser in that city, invited Mr. PLACE to take charge of its editorial columns; which position he accepted, and has since continued to fill. The leading political, commercial and business articles which have appeared in the columns of that sheet, have been written by him. The Commercial Advertiser has ever been an outspoken and earnest advocate of Republican principles, while it has also diligently discussed and maintained the great commercial interests of the State, and especially of its own locality. The best measure of his ability is the fact that the Advertiser has attained a larger circulation, and is more extensively read than any other paper which has been published in his city.

Mr. PLACE is in the vigor of his manhood. This is his first term upon the floor, and being in the minority politically, he contents himself with looking diligently after the interests of his constituents.

ALEMBERT POND.

Mr. POND belongs to the class of independent thinkers — that is, the class of men who do not ask what Mr. A. believes, or what Mr. B. says, before giving an opinion of their own. Their opinions are their own, and are founded upon a careful examination of questions to be decided, and are not shaped by the mere *ipse dixit* of some other man. He was born August 3d, 1821, at Elizabethtown, Essex county, New York. His father was a native of this State, and his mother of Vermont. When he was five years old, his father died, and he was taken to Schroon, Essex county, and there he remained with an uncle until he attained the age of seventeen. The following nine years of his life were spent at Rutland, Vermont, at the commencement of which time he entered the office of REUBEN R. THRALL, of that place, as a student-at-law. He was admitted to the bar, and practiced there some four years, until 1848, when he returned to the place of his birth, and continued to practice law. After a five years' residence in that place, he removed to Saratoga Springs in 1853, where he has resided ever since, continuing the practice of his profession.

Mr. POND was originally a Democrat, and when the question of slavery began to divide that party, he sided with the Free Soil wing. His strong antipathies to slavery led him to join the Republican party at the very earliest period after its organization.

Mr. POND is not a politician in the partisan sense of the term. He takes no pains to seek political preferment, and is very frank in the expression of his opinions, too much so, indeed, to be a successful politician in this age of the world. Some years since he consented to accept the nomination for County Judge, but was defeated, partly because of his outspoken manner of treating men and public questions, and by the union of the Democrats and Know Nothings against him. But he stands high among those who know him for integrity and honesty, and hence he was with great unanimity selected as the candidate of the Republican party of the Fifteenth Senatorial District for Delegate to the Constitutional Convention, a position for which his excellent knowledge of fundamental principles of law and political economy, his independence of views, and his sincere desire to labor for the good of his race, peculiarly fitted him. He was elected, and in the Convention took a high rank as a reasoner and debater. Last fall he was selected as the Republican candidate for member of Assembly for the Second District of Saratoga county. As he supposed the Constitutional Convention would close its labors before the expiration of the year, he consented to take this nomination, and was elected by 457 majority.

As a lawyer, Mr. POND has taken high rank for an intimate knowledge of cases and precedents, and for great familiarity with all the technicalities of the law, not less than for large acquaintance with its great principles. He is fond of fun, enjoys a practical joke highly, and delights in witticisms and cutting repartees. He is a member of the Committee on Banks, and deservedly ranks as one of the ablest members of the House, both in committee and on the floor.

ALPHEUS PRINCE.

Mr. PRINCE is a prominent member of the Assembly, both from personal appearance and political position. He occupies a seat by the middle aisle, full in view of the Speaker and the House, so that when he rises to make a remark or propose a motion, he never fails to obtain recognition. He has always been a close observer of political affairs, and early became a leading man among the Democrats of Erie county. He has earned his place on the floor of the Assembly, and fills it with ability and dignity.

ALPHEUS PRINCE was born in the town of Verona, Oneida county, in the "Tilden Hill School District," on the 13th of December, 1824. He was sent to school from an early age, and made rapid progress. The school in that neighborhood bore a superior reputation for the proficiency of its pupils, having but one rival among the district schools of the county. His father, Mr. DAVID PRINCE was an estimable citizen, public spirited, industrious, and a most excellent neighbor, who took pleasure both in the pursuits of his own family and in rendering good offices to others. In 1836 he removed to Newstead, in Erie county, where he still resides. Young PRINCE attended the district school in that town, and afterward took an academic course in Clinton, Oneida county, in 1842-3. Owing to his genial disposition he was always popular with his schoolmates, as with his associates in subsequent years. He became a farmer, and was successful in the prosecution of business, but being of an active temperament, engaged early in politics. He was always a Democrat, at first a "Barn-burner" or "Softshell," and afterward a thorough-going party-man. He was a delegate to the National Democratic Convention, at Charleston in 1860, and has repeatedly been a member of the State and local Conventions. As a politician, he always possessed the confidence of the late Dean Richmond, whom he greatly resembles, both in personal appearance and in the strong common sense which he displays regarding political topics. He has always stood well with his party, and is respected by his fellow-citizens, as he never unpleasantly obtrudes his opinions upon those who happen to differ with him. He is "six feet high, and well-proportioned," weighing about two hundred and fifty pounds. He is rivaled in physical proportions only by Mr. Ray, of Ontario, and Mr. Cady, of Oneida. His complexion is clear, and his eye brilliant, so that he is one of the good-looking, as well as leading members of the Assembly.

The only important offices held by Mr. Prince before his election to the Legislature, were Deputy United States Marshal and Deputy Collector of the Port of Buffalo. In 1866 he was elected to the Assembly from the Fourth District of Erie county, receiving 2,609 votes, a majority of 207. Last fall he was again nominated and received 2,546 votes, a majority of 508. His political friends having carried the House, he was at once recognized as one of their leaders. His career this winter will be important both to his own reputation and to the best interest of the State. He occupies the responsible position of Chairman of the Railroad Committee.

SAMUEL M. PURDY.

West Farms, a town in Westchester county, New York, is situated along the Sound, and the Harlem River. Its scenery is picturesque; Bronx River bounding it on the east, and Harlem River on the west, and Mill-Brook winding its way through the central portion; undulating plains, broken, here and there, by ridges and productive and well-tilled farms, all conspire to combine within its limits a great deal of beauty and utility. Mr. Purdy has long been a resident of this town, and ever since he settled among its people, has held an honorable rank among his townsmen. He was born, August 28th, 1824, in East Chester, Westchester county, New York. In youth, he received an ordinary English education, and then studied law in the office of Samuel E. Lyon, Esq., of White Plains. At the age of twenty-five, his law studies having been completed, Mr. Purdy passed the usual examination, and was admitted to practice, settling in the town of West Farms. The people elected him Justice of the Peace, in 1850, and they have conferred that office upon him, each successive term ever since. He was a member of the Board of Supervisors, in the years 1855, '56, '61, '64, '65 and '66, being four times elected without opposition. At his election, in 1866, to the office of Supervisor, out of the 521 votes cast, Mr. Purdy received 513; at the same time he was chosen Justice of the Peace by a vote of 518 to 4. Evidently the electors of West Farms are very well satisfied with Mr. Purdy. Such local popularity is rarely possessed by any man. He enjoys the confidence of the inhabitants in his town and vicinity, who often consult him in business matters, intrust large sums of money to him for investment, and act upon his sagacious suggestions. He is not a public reformer, but he entertains and practices the strictest principles of temperance; and his personal example in this direction, is a potent, silent influence, which wins the regard of the community, and places him on a high plane of morality.

In politics, Mr. PURDY was a Whig, until the election of JAMES BUCHANAN to the Presidency; since that time, he has most scrupulously indorsed the Democratic platforms and nominees. While the conflict with the South was transpiring, his influence, both in an official capacity, and as a private citizen, was used in filling the quotas required, each time when there was a call for troops, thus saving the town from a draft. He was elected to the Assembly of 1867 by a majority of 820, and served on the Committee on Internal Affairs, and has the same position this session. His record in the last Legislature was so satisfactory to the people of his district, that he was re-elected to the present Assembly without opposition, and no doubt will sustain the excellent reputation he has acquired as a faithful and successful member.

WILLIAM B. QUINN.

Mr. QUINN was born on the 18th day of July, 1839, in the Eleventh Ward of the city of New York, of Irish parentage. He received the rudiments of his education in the public schools, entered the New York Free Academy (now the College of the city of New York) at the age of fourteen years, and graduated therefrom with honor in 1859. Having pursued the classical course, he received the degree of Bachelor of Arts, and in 1862 the degree of Master of Arts was conferred upon him. While attending the Free Academy, he commenced teaching school in the public evening schools at the early age of sixteen years, and was engaged in other occupations during his leisure hours, for the purpose of obtaining the means to finish his education. After graduating, he commenced the study of law in New York city, was admitted to the bar in 1861, and immediately entered upon the practice of his profession, and is now engaged in a very lucrative business, especially in matters pertaining to real estate. His office is at 169 Broadway, and he is a member of the firm of "BUCKINGHAM, HAYES & QUINN." He commenced his political career in the year 1860. He never held any public office before being elected a member of the present Legislature. He was nominated by the Tammany Hall and other Democratic organizations to represent the Twelfth Assembly District. He was opposed by an influential German, and although the German element is greatly predominant in his district, was elected by a large majority. He is a member of the Committee on Judiciary, a position for which his fine talents, legal ability and critical judgment appropriately fit him. He is an agreeable, affable and industrious member, possessing qualities fitting him for both popularity and success.

JOHN RABER.

Mr. RABER, Representative of the Sixth District of Kings county, is a native of Prussia; he was born March 2d, 1823. He came to this country when he was ten years of age; and, until 1841, his home was in the city of New York. Though he received but the advantages of an ordinary business education, yet he entered upon the active pursuits of life, determined to battle successfully. His first employment was as a clerk in the agricultural business; in 1850, he was engaged in wire cloth and sieve manufacturing; in 1857, he was interested in the flour and feed trade; and, some time after, was largely engaged in the grocery business. In all of these various undertakings, Mr. RABER has met with the success which follows energy, enterprise and practical knowledge.

Mr. RABER has always been an active and unchanging Democrat. Not being in any sense an office seeker, he was only once before his election to the preceding Assembly a candidate for the indorsement of the people. He ran for Supervisor of the Sixteenth Ward of Brooklyn in 1865, and was defeated through party divisions. But, in 1866, he received the unanimous support of the Democracy, and was elected to the Assembly. He was renominated in 1867. The certificate of election was awarded to his competitor, Hon. JACOB WORTH, but the Committee on Privileges and Elections awarded the seat to Mr. RABER, and he was admitted by the House March 13.

Mr. RABER is a quiet man, speaking seldom and then briefly; and, as a representative, is attentive and devoted to the interests of the public.

LUKE RANNEY.

Mr. RANNEY is of the most unimpeachable Puritan blood of New England. His mother was a lineal descendant of JOHN ALDEN, of Plymouth, and the fair PRISCILLA, who bade the generous youth, when pleading the suit of Captain MILES STANDISH, "speak for himself." ALDEN did speak for himself, and having married her, conducted her to his home, seated upon the back of a bull. It was a noted couple; two presidents of the United States were of that lineage.

Mr. RANNEY is an example of what are usually denominated "self-made men." He was born at Ashfield, Franklin county, Massachusetts, on the 8th day of November, 1815. He was sent to school early. In 1824, his father removed from Massachusetts to Mentz, in Cayuga county. Young RANNEY had an insatiable desire for books, and whatever facilities he lacked for instruction, he sought eagerly to make up by home study in the chimney corner. At the age of eighteen he succeeded in attending a term at the academy in Shelburne Falls, Massachusetts. His father removed to Elbridge, in Onondaga county, and Mr. RANNEY obtained another season of academical instruction, finally qualifying himself as a surveyor.

Having now arrived at his majority, he went to Van Buren county, in Michigan, in company with a brother. Here he remained one year, many miles away from the "borders of civilization." He returned the next year to Elbridge, and in 1839 engaged in teaching in the winter school in Throopsville, Cayuga county. He taught the ensuing winter at Port Byron, and in Throopsville again, a year later. He then went to Hopkinsville, Kentucky, where he spent a year in teaching. He now matured those decided anti-slavery convictions which characterized all his subsequent life. He came in contact with slavery only to hate it. In 1843 he returned to this State, married and settled in the town of Brutus. Five years later, he again made his home at Elbridge, his present residence. While living in the former town, he held the office of Town Superintendent of Common Schools; and upon settling in Elbridge he showed a taste for politics and public business. Upon the formation of the Republican party in 1854, he took the field in support of its measures, and displayed an eloquence which was at once fervid and convincing. He has ever since that been one of the best political speakers in the county. In the year 1857 he was elected Supervisor, and the year after was chosen for the first time to the Assembly. Major-General SLOCUM was his colleague. Both made their mark in the Legislature of 1859. Mr. RANNEY's speech on the Personal Liberty bill, was justly regarded as one of the most able oratorical efforts of the session. He was also an active member of the Select Committee which reported the first "*pro rata* freight bill," requiring railroad companies to charge for carrying freight according to the expense incurred and distance transported. That session the famous "Clinton League" was organized, for the purpose of securing the enactment of the same proposition. He was also a member of the Select Committee that drafted and procured the passage of the bill establishing a Board of State Assessors.

Mr. RANNEY was again elected in 1865. The old issues had been almost forgotten, and he was less conspicuous. His colleagues, Hon. DANIEL P. WOOD and L. HARRIS HISCOCK, may have outshone him, but at the latter part of the session the bill was reported at the instance of Hon.

HENRY R. SELDEN, to authorize the New York Central Railroad Company to charge an increased rate of fare for passengers. Mr. RANNEY, almost single-handed, encountered the ex-judge, meeting argument by argument, and endeavored to show by the statistics of the company that no such increase was necessary. He was defeated by the vote, but had the gratification of beholding his arguments and statistics reproduced in Governor FENTON's admirable message vetoing the measure.

In 1867, Mr. RANNEY was again elected by a majority of 586. He is in a House politically hostile to him, and having little of the work of legislation to perform, he has not been heard from as in former years. But the fire is unquenched, and at a proper opportunity he will not be silent or inactive. Few men appreciate more highly the duties of the representative.

HENRY RAY.

Mr. RAY was born at Fenner, Madison county, New York, on the 19th of September, 1827. His family were from New England, and sustained an excellent reputation. His education was obtained at the district school, and he was a proficient scholar, except so far as his inextinguishable love of fun interfered between him and his books. But he had the wit to make his way.

After marrying, Mr. RAY fixed his home in the town of Phelps, Ontario county. Being ambitious, and of a restless temper, he could not content himself with a commonplace life, but engaged in speculations, which generally proved remunerative. In this way he has amassed a handsome fortune, which he knows well how to enjoy.

In 1866, he was elected Supervisor of the town, receiving a majority of twenty-seven, and was re-elected in 1867. His popularity had become general in the county, and in the fall he was made the Republican candidate for Member of Assembly for the first district. He was again successful, and it is more than likely that he will appear again in 1869, among the other men that do law-making for the State. He is genial, full to the brim of sport, but wide awake when the occasion demands serious exertion. His personal reputation is one of which he may well be proud. He is a member of the Committee on the Affairs of Villages.

JAMES REED.

JAMES REED was born on the 19th of August, 1818, in New Brunswick, New Jersey. His paternal ancestors were Irish, and the maternal ones were German. While yet an infant, Mr. REED was taken to the city of New York, by his parents, where he resided until fourteen years of age, having enjoyed the benefits of a select school education. Then going to Yonkers, he engaged to a butcher, and thoroughly learned the trade, after five years' service. Returning to New York, he went to work in the Clinton Market, remained there a short time, and then went to Peekskill, where he hired out as a journeyman at his occupation. But New York city had too many attractions for him, and he soon returned to it, opening a market on Avenue B, and then in Broadway.

Mr. REED early took an active interest in politics, and was a general favorite among the young Democracy of 1840 and 1844. The first public position ever filled by him, was that of Deputy Clerk of Washington Market, being appointed in 1852, which position he filled with credit to himself and advantage to the city. In 1860, he was elected one of the Aldermen of New York, but was defeated in his efforts for re-election. He was elected to the Assembly of 1867 by a large majority, and though often sick, was very attentive to his duties. A short time after the convening of the present House, to which he had been re-elected, Mr. REED died very suddenly in New York city. The Assembly passed resolutions appropriate to his memory.

JOHN H. REEVE.

Mr. REEVE is one of the steady, steadfast kind of men, possessing strong attachments and a leaning to things as they are, rather than a desire for change; who entertain conservative views and are not easily seduced into new beliefs or betrayed into new experiments, and who have a higher regard for the wisdom of the founders of our republic than for the vagaries of our latter day philosophers. He represents the Second Assembly District of Orange county, and was born in the town of Wawayanda, in that county, April 25, 1818. He has resided in the same place ever since, and now occupies the same farm owned by his father and grandfather before him. His grandfather was a native of Suffolk county, Long Island, and a soldier in the American army during our struggle for National Independence. He took part in, and was wounded at, the battle of Minisink, fought on the 22d day of July, 1779. His father was a soldier in the war of 1812.

Mr. REEVE received such education as could be gained from the common schools of the district in which he resided during the days of his boyhood. Arriving at an age when the choice of an avocation was presented to him, he chose to follow the example of his ancestors and be a farmer.

When old enough to vote, Mr. REEVE sided with the Democratic party, and has ever since maintained his connection with that party. He is not a political manager or office-seeker, and yet he has often been honored with public positions. In 1858, he was elected Justice of the Peace for his town; which office he held for four years. In 1861, he was elected Supervisor, and has been re-elected every year since. In all his official career he has displayed strong common sense and firmness of purpose, allied with great modesty and simplicity of manner. His nomination to the office he now holds was a great surprise to him. He not only had not asked such an honor, but more than this, had not thought of such a thing; and the first intimation he had of it was the announcement of the fact, made to him by a committee sent from the nominating convention for that purpose. He was elected by a majority of seven hundred and two, over GEORGE WIGGINS — the largest majority ever given in the district. His majority in his own town was one hundred and ten; the usual Democratic majority being about forty. He is a member of the Committee on the Affairs of Villages, and also of the Committee on Expenditures of the Executive Department.

ALVIN RICHARDSON.

The Third or Eastern District of Oswego county is represented by ALVIN RICHARDSON. He was born in Whitestown, Oneida county, New York, in 1802. His family removed to Mexico, Oswego county, N. Y., in 1806, his present residence, that section of the State being at that early day little else than a wilderness. Consequently the changes which have taken place in the condition of the society by which he has been surrounded during his life time, have been very great, as his town at the present time is one of the most flourishing agricultural districts in that part of the State, and is inhabited by as intelligent a class of people as can be found anywhere.

The advent of Mr. RICHARDSON's family into his early home was in advance of the schoolmaster in that locality. Consequently, his early scholastic advantages were very limited. He was nearly of age before regular schools were introduced. Self-instruction, natural intelligence and a sound mind, have been made to compensate so far as possible for the advantages now everywhere found, but which, during his minority, his locality did not afford. He was early apprenticed to the blacksmith's trade, a calling which he pursued for several years, but which he has finally abandoned for the more congenial pursuits of agriculture.

Mr. RICHARDSON has many times been entrusted by his townsmen with places of responsibility and trust. He was elected to the office of Overseer of the Poor in 1839, which place he filled several years. For a long series of years he has held the office of Justice of the Peace. He has the reputation of being a good and upright magistrate, and his legal decisions have always been characterized by soundness. He was Postmaster at Colosse, a post village in his own town, for five years, commencing in 1844, and at one time held the office of Deputy United States Marshal, under Hon. P. V. KELLOGG, as Marshal. He has at different times held other positions not necessary to detail in this connection.

Although long past the age at which military services cease to be due from the citizen, by the laws of the land, Mr. RICHARDSON's patriotism was such that in 1861 he enlisted, and offered his services as a soldier in putting down the rebellion. Nothing but the interposition of the regimental surgeon prevented him from going to "the front."

Mr. RICHARDSON was formerly a Whig, but at once enlisted under the Republican banner when that party was organized. Although among the oldest members of the lower house of the Legislature, his intellect is still at its full vigor. As a legislator, he is intelligent, discerning, and carefully attentive to his duties.

SILAS RICHARDSON.

A very important and peculiar element of the Republican party, comprising too some of its ablest leaders and members, is made up of those who, at one period of our political history, were known as Free Soil Democrats. Driven by their antagonism to slavery, they separated from their former political associates, and, seeing no prospects of success in the endeavor to act as a faction of the Democratic party, they coalesced with such of the members of the Whig party as agreed with them in their opposition to slavery, and thus added vitality, and gave force and power to the Republican party. Of this class of Republicans, Mr. RICHARDSON is one. He was born in Kennebec county, in the State of Maine. On arriving to a proper age to choose for himself, he determined to follow the mercantile business. In this he was successful, and gained the confidence of his acquaintances, and was made the candidate of the Democratic party of his native county for Member of Assembly. The Whigs largely preponderated but he was defeated by only a small majority. In common with many other natives of New England, his attention was attracted to the fine business opportunities offered by portions of Northern and Central New York, and, in 1847, he came to Elmira, and engaged in the lumber business. In 1851, he transferred his business to Belmont, Allegany county, his present place of residence. He acted with the Democratic party until 1852, when he joined the Republican party. For five successive years, namely, from 1860 to 1865 inclusive, he represented his town in the Board of Supervisors, the two last years serving as Chairman of the Board.

Much against his wishes, he was made the candidate of the Republican party of Allegany county for member of Assembly, and was elected by a majority of 2,852 over SAMUEL SWAIN, the candidate of the Democratic party.

Mr. RICHARDSON is a shrewd business man, and as such has been successful. He has had good educational advantages, and has learned much from experience and the study of current events. He does not make set speeches, but in committees and through conversation with his fellow members, exercises a large influence. He is a member of the Committee on Public Education.

JAMES RIDER.

An old adage says, "Blood will tell." It is no wonder, then, that the sons of Revolutionary sires, who took part in the great struggle by which this country was freed from a foreign bondage, should bear towards the land of their birth the deepest and strongest feelings of patriotism. It is not alone the stories of the trials their ancestors endured in taking part in this struggle, told to the children at the fireside, instilling lessons of patriotism, that make such children strong lovers of their country. There is that in their very blood and constitution which makes every fiber of their nature throb with patriotic impulses. Of this character is the inherited nature of Mr. RIDER. He was born in the town of Sardinia, Erie county, April, 30th, 1828. His father was a soldier in the war of 1812, and his grandfather a soldier of the Revolution, who served through the whole of that war. His childhood days were spent in laboring upon a farm, and in attending a common school. His first ballot was cast for the Whig ticket. He acted with the Whig party until the rise of the American party, when he became identified with the latter. On the decline of the American party he joined the Republican party, with which he has acted ever since.

Mr. RIDER was elected Supervisor of his town in the year 1861, and again in the year 1862, by an increased majority. He was very active in patriotic services in behalf of the country during the rebellion. He was elected to his present position by the Republican party of the Fifth Assembly District of Erie county, obtaining 126 majority over his competitor, Mr. PHILIP RILEY.

Mr. RIDER takes no part in the discussions on the floor of the House. He contents himself with a quiet discharge of his duties, and bringing to bear upon all questions that strong common sense and an integrity of purpose which, after all, are of more value to the State than that "gift of gab," which makes up in sound and fury what it lacks of logical argument. He is a member of the Committee on Agriculture.

JAMES RILEY.

Mr. RILEY, the member from the Seventh District of New York, was born in that city October 17, 1835, of Irish parents. He was educated in the public schools of New York city. By occupation he is a machinist. In the year 1856, he was engaged in the WALKER expedition to Nicaragua. In the year 1859, he enlisted in the United States Navy, and sailed in the sloop-of-war Brooklyn, under the command of the renowned Captain (now Vice-Admiral) FARRAGUT, during which time he visited nearly all the ports of Mexico and Central America on the Atlantic coast, and was also engaged in the surveying expedition to Chiriqui. Being in the service at the breaking out of the rebellion, he was very actively engaged in hard service during the early part of it, and was at Fort Sumter immediately after the firing on the steamer "Star of the West" by the rebels. Afterward he was at Fort Pickens, in Florida, during the siege of that place; then on blockading service at New Orleans, at the time the well known privateer Sumter escaped from the Mississippi River, and committed such ravages among our shipping. He was discharged from the service in October, 1861.

Mr. RILEY was elected to the Assembly in 1867, from the Seventh District of New York, on the regular Democratic ticket, contending against two other candidates—one Republican and one Independent Democrat—receiving a plurality of 380 votes.

Mr. RILEY is one of the best looking and agreeable members of the House, and is a great favorite among men of all parties. He is a member of the Committees on Militia and Public Defense, and Roads and Bridges.

HARPER W. ROGERS.

Mr. ROGERS, who represents the First District of Columbia county, is, in the strictest sense, a "self-made man." By his natural talents, business capacity, indomitable perseverance, and high integrity, he has not only won public distinction and confidence, but acquired a liberal fortune.

He was born in Queensboro', Warren county, in this State, on the 28th day of September, 1819, and is consequently in the forty-ninth year of his age. He is possessed of a high order of intellect; is cautious, but firm and reliable in his judgment; a sound counsellor; social and urbane in manners; and of a noble, generous nature. Physically, he is a gentleman of commanding presence, and will win respect and confidence in any position to which he is called.

His ancestors were natives of Rhode Island, and ranked among the most prominent of the first settlers. His grandfather, SAMUEL ROGERS, was a Revolutionary soldier, and distinguished himself for bravery and patriotism through that struggle. His father, also named SAMUEL, was in his early life an extensive lumber dealer, but afterwards engaged in agricultural pursuits. He removed from Warren county to Saratoga in 1821; and in 1829 changed his residence to Stockport, Columbia county.

HARPER followed the business of farming until the year 1845, when he removed to the city of Hudson and engaged in mercantile business to a small extent. At about the same time he purchased an interest in a paper mill in the town of Claverack. His educational advantages in early life had been limited to a country district school, which in those days were far more restricted than at the present time. But he possessed a natural capacity for business, and had been imbued with the strictest principles of honor, integrity and industry. With these as his sole capital, judiciously invested and actively employed, both branches of his business prospered under his management, and gradually increased in extent and profit until he found it necessary to relinquish the mercantile branch, from which he retired the present year. Mr. ROGERS now devotes himself exclusively to his paper manufactory, which has grown to be one of the most extensive in the State.

Mr. ROGERS has always been a Democrat of the old school, and although never seeking political honors, he has ever been a prominent man in his party. In 1864 he was elected Mayor of the city of Hudson by a very large majority, although the political preponderance of the city had previously been on the other side. As Mayor he was very popular, and his administration was marked with ability, impartiality and a deep solicitude for the municipal prosperity. He was urged to accept a re-nomination under the assurance that no opposing candidate would be run against him, but, from business considerations he felt constrained to reject the flattering honor. Much against his inclination, he gave way to the urgent solicitations of his party and accepted the nomination for Member of Assembly in the last campaign, after it had been given him by acclamation without his knowledge. His great popularity in the District is shown by the almost unprecedented majority (419) by which he was elected.

Mr. ROGERS has for many years been prominent in some of the most important public enterprises, and liberally contributes to all projects calculated to elevate, improve and add to the religious, moral, and business progress of his adopted city.

SAMUEL ROOT.

ASAHEL ROOT, the father of the subject of this article, emigrated from Farmington, Connecticut, in 1809, to Essex county, New York. Those were primitive times, in the history of that section of the State, and he was among the early settlers of that locality, doing the pioneer work of that period. During the memorable contest between this country and Great Britain, in 1812–14, he entered the service, and at the battle of Plattsburgh, served as Lieutenant. SAMUEL ROOT, his son, was born March 7, 1817, at Elizabethtown, Essex county, New York. His educational advantages were good. Besides attending the common schools of his native town, he pursued his studies at the Westport, New York, and Farmington, Connecticut, Academies. Nor did he relax his hold upon knowledge after schooldays were over; for, linking thought with labor, he arose to the true dignity of toil. Having chosen farming for his occupation, he so far gained the respect of his fellow-townsmen as to be deemed both worthy and competent, besides holding various town offices, to represent them in the Board of Supervisors, which he has done for the past six years, being twice elected without any opposition. He was Chairman of the Board for two years, and evinced fair abilities in the discharge of parliamentary duties in county legislation. As Supervisor, he was very active in raising men to fill the quotas called for by the government; and one full company, recruited in his vicinity, was attached to the 77th Regiment.

Mr. ROOT is a Republican. He was elected to the Assembly by 893 majority. The Speaker appointed him on the Committee on Federal Relations. He is possessed of sound judgment, and is esteemed for his integrity and honesty of purpose. As a legislator, he is prudent and reliable. He is keen in discernment, and affable in personal intercourse.

EDMUND F. SARGENT.

Mr. SARGENT was born in Brattleboro, Vermont, on the 18th of April, 1816. He is descended from an English ancestry, of Puritan proclivities, and inherits largely those qualities of his race which, for many generations, have distinguished it for sterling integrity and uprightness. His father died when he was but six years of age, and he was early cast upon the world, without patrimony or wealthy and influential friends to aid him. As was the case with most boys in his circumstances at that day, his education was limited, being confined to the branches taught in the common schools; and the advantages thus afforded were enjoyed by him only for the winter months during the period of his early boyhood. But these opportunities were not wasted. The lessons of the country school-room were, by his native good sense, applied to the purposes of his life, and what he learned from books, under the discipline of the master, he learned also under the discipline of a sterner teacher — necessity — to apply to business. Respected for his application, for his integrity and manly qualities in his younger days, he came to the full years of manhood in the confidence of all who knew him. At the age of twelve years, he removed from Brattleboro to the town of Bangor, in Franklin county, where he has ever since resided.

Mr. SARGENT has always avoided rather than sought public life. He has held, at different times, most of the important town offices, including that of Supervisor for several terms, the duties of which he discharged with fidelity and to the entire satisfaction of his townsmen. His nomination to the office which he now fills was made without his knowledge, and it was with great difficulty that he was finally prevailed upon to accept the position. He received a vote of 2,770 against 2,037 cast for his competitor, B. S. W. CLARK, Democrat, thus electing him by a majority of 733—a majority larger, by nearly forty votes, than was obtained by any other candidate in his county at that election.

Mr. SARGENT has, until within a few years past, followed the business of farming, at which he accumulated a moderate competence. About three years ago he abandoned the farm, and engaged in the manufacture of starch and flour. In this, as in farming, he has been successful, and is widely known as a thorough, upright and intelligent business man.

JOHN H. SELKREG.

Mr. SELKREG has been a practical printer, and, consequently, has had all the varieties of experience and change appertaining to that occupation. He is editor and proprietor of the Ithaca Journal, a paper which has effectively aided in the achievement of many a hard fought battle, and which still survives, as Mr. SELKREG, by his firm Scotch tenacity, has fully proven.

His parents died when he was a mere boy (the youngest of a family of five children), and left him to the care of the older members of the family. He never attended school after he was eleven years old, and what little education he had gained up to that time, had been acquired in the district school at Staatsburgh, New York, his native place. His disposition, at the age of thirteen, rather inclined to printing, as an occupation; therefore, having left his brother-in-law, with whom he had been living, he began an apprenticeship in the printing office of the Poughkeepsie Telegraph, then published by Messrs. KILLEY & LOW, and which was, at that time, as it now is, the Democratic organ of Dutchess county. He continued there, until the year 1838. Having arrived at that point where he thought himself sufficiently proficient to commence life on his own responsibility, he became a resident of Brooklyn, and, for a few months, entered into a partnership with the firm of Messrs. ARNOLD, VAN ANDEN & CO., publishers of the Brooklyn Eagle. Not being entirely satisfied with his business relations, he returned to Poughkeepsie in 1839, and published the Poughkeepsie Casket, a literary paper. Two years subsequently, he purchased an interest in the Ithaca Journal, and, in connection with Hon.

A. WELLS, continued its publication for several years. He afterward became sole proprietor of the establishment.

The Ithaca Journal was once a Democratic organ of Tompkins county. In 1848, Mr. SELKREG refused to support Mr. CASS, and ran up Mr. VAN BUREN's name. The Hunkers established the Flag of the Union, to break down the Journal; but they not succeeding in the attempt, the "Flag" was lowered, and the Journal still continued to be the exponent of the Democracy. From the year 1850 to 1856, Mr. SELKREG saw that a great change was being wrought in the Democratic party. The repeal of the Missouri Compromise seemed to him an outrage upon political honor. Such was the drift of affairs, he refused to support BUCHANAN, and advocated the claims of FREMONT, thus undoubtedly carrying over the county to the "Path-Finder," inasmuch as the Republican vote ran up in a single year, from 1,460 to 4,030.

From 1857 to 1861, he discharged the duties of Commissioner of Loans. President LINCOLN made him Postmaster of Ithaca, in 1861. He was re-appointed, in 1865, by ANDREW JOHNSON, who, in the most *nonchalant* manner, subjected him to the guillotine, on the 25th of August, 1866, for refusing to adopt Mr. JOHNSON's peculiar views. Mr. SELKREG survived the shock; and, under the warm pressure of his friends, accepted the nomination for member of Assembly, being elected by a majority of 1,472. He was re-elected to the present Assembly by a flattering majority.

He has held several offices of business interest. At one time he was President of the Ithaca and Binghamton Telegraph Company, and he is now President of the Ithaca Calendar Clock Company.

Mr. SELKREG during the session of 1867 was a member of the Committees on Ways and Means, and on Banks, two of the most important Committees of the House. The present Assembly he serves on the former Committee.

Mr. SELKREG possesses a sound, discriminating judgment; has a good deal of dry humor, and is as keen as steel. His vigilance is unremitting. In debate he is forcible, concise and convincing, and always "hits the nail on the head." Short but decisive is his motto. He is a very worthy and influential member, and of unquestioned integrity.

WILLIAM C. H. SHERMAN.

Major SHERMAN was born in Norwich, Connecticut, and is thirty-eight years old. His ancestors were natives of Rhode Island. His parents were wealthy, and gave him a liberal education. In early life he embarked in mercantile pursuits. Before the war he was living in the city of New York, where he was engaged as a commission merchant in the dry goods trade. At the outbreak of the rebellion, he resolved to give his energies to the defense of the flag, and when the Seventy-first Regiment went out to serve the Government, he, being a member of the organization, went with it to the seat of war. Displaying business qualities of a high order, as well as soldierly gallantry and courage, he was soon called to the Pay Department, and being promoted to the rank of Major and assigned to duty as Paymaster, accompanied General SHERMAN in his "march from Atlanta to the sea," and served in that capacity until the return of peace. It is said of him in official circles that he was entrusted with immense sums of money by his superiors in the aforesaid Department, and otherwise given large and important responsibilities, and that in no instance did he fail to justify the confidence in him so placed. His war record is, altogether, high, clean and pure.

After the war, he removed to the vicinage of Newburgh, Orange county. His residence is in the town of New Windsor, about two miles from that city. He has engaged in no business there, and he is known to his neighbors and acquaintances only as a gentleman of leisure, and a prominent member of the best society of the section.

Last fall he was nominated for the Assembly by the Democratic Convention of his Assembly District, because of his availability as a candidate in a closely contested canvass, and of his acknowledged fitness for the office. He was largely supported by the soldiers of his district, in many cases without distinction of party, and by the people of Newburgh in the expectation that, if elected, he would be to them peculiarly useful in the promotion of their local interests.

His career in the Assembly has fully justified these expectations, as he has been very active in furthering the fortunes of bills in which his constituents have especial concern, and has shown himself to be an effective and intelligent legislator. He was awarded the seat by the county canvassers, but his right to it is contested by GEORGE K. SMITH, the Republican candidate. At the time this article goes to press, no action has been had upon the case by the Assembly.

Major SHERMAN's private character is unexceptionable; his manners are open, frank and agreeable, and he possesses more than ordinary strength of body and mind.

RANSOM M. SKEELS.

The name SKEELS or SCHEELE indicates Swedish origin. The immediate ancestors of the subject of this sketch were descendants of that small but noble State, whose soil first resounded with the footsteps of ROGER WILLIAMS, that early pilgrim of liberty. Mr. SKEELS was born in Hartland, Niagara county, on the 29th of August, 1825. He is, therefore, now in his forty-third year. His higher education was obtained in the Wilson Collegiate Institute, of Niagara county. Until the year 1851, after leaving school, Mr. SKEELS was a farmer. In that year and until 1853, he was a Clerk in the Post-office Department at Washington, under Judge N. K. HALL, then Postmaster-General. Returning in 1853, at the end of President FILLMORE's administration, to Lockport, and having a penchant for the quill, he embraced the profession of journalism, joining his brother in conducting the Lockport Courier. In this he continued, to use his own language, "until the Whig party was destroyed by SEWARD and GREELEY." The next year we find him in the West, and connected with the Lafayette (Indiana) American, a newspaper independent in politics. Remaining there a year or so, he again turns his face eastward, and once more he is found in the editor's sanctum of the Lockport Courier, wielding quill and scissors with his usual energy.

In 1860 he turns up in business in Philadelphia. Whether on account of the business depression occasioned by the breaking out of the Rebellion, or because of the staid character of the city of brotherly love, the year 1861 finds this restless spirit again in the village of canal locks in his native county. In the years 1864 and 1865 we find him publishing the Ogdensburgh Democrat, a paper of staunch Democratic principles. Again returning to Lockport in 1867, he purchased the Lockport Daily Union, which he now conducts with signal ability. Although returning to their midst only in June last, his Democratic friends nominated him to the Assembly in the fall, and in a District that gave 150 Republican majority the year previous, Mr. SKEELS was elected by a majority of 246, thus showing a gain of nearly 400 votes. This fact speaks significantly for Mr. SKEELS' "home strength."

Mr. SKEELS, though in his first term, takes a leading position in the Assembly. He is Chairman of the Committee on the Manufacture of Salt and second on the Committee on Railroads—two very important committees. He is also on the Sub-Committee of the Whole.

Mr. SKEELS has been in politics more or less since he was of the age of twenty-one. He was a national Whig, and an ardent admirer of HENRY CLAY. He never believed it was within the province of Congress to legislate for or against slavery, believing with Mr. CLAY that, if Congress assumed to prohibit slavery *north* of a certain line, justice demanded equal legislation to protect slavery *south* of a certain line. He held that federal legislation on the subject would engender hatred and end in war, and the endangering of the liberties of the country; that local self-government was the safer principle. Mr. SKEELS, holding to such a creed, on the expiration of the Whig party, allied himself with the Democracy, and is now in full sympathy with the aims and purposes of the Democratic party.

In physique, Mr. SKEELS is massively built, weighing something over two hundred, and is six feet, lacking a single inch, in height. He has "knocked about" the world sufficiently to have gained an intelligent knowledge on a great variety of subjects, all of which renders him more valuable as an enlightened legislator. To his experience and mental accomplishments, is added a geniality of manner, which, together, render him a power in the Assembly.

FRANCIS SKILLMAN.

This gentleman is a descendant, on the paternal side, of Thomas Skillman, and on the maternal side, of Adrian Onderdonk, both of whom were Committee-Men, during the Revolutionary war, and were confined in the notorious "Jersey" prison-ship, at New York, Mr. Skillman is thus a relative of the Bishops Onderdonk, of New York and Pennsylvania. He was born in Brooklyn, New York, but was reared by his grandfather, in the town of North Hempstead, Long Island, where he has ever since resided, following the avocation of farming. His landed estate is both extensive and valuable, and he is one of the best agriculturists in his town. He has served his full time in the militia of this State as Cornet, Lieutenant and Captain in the Horse Artillery. But, in the midst of his labors, Mr. Skillman found time to devote to the reading of law, to which his attention was turned by his election as Justice of the Peace, nearly twenty years ago, which office he has continuously held to the present time. He discharged the duties of Justice of Sessions for three years; and, ever since he was twenty-one, he has repeatedly held town office of some kind. Mr. Skillman never solicited either a nomination or a vote, and, therefore, when the Democratic party of the First District of Queens county nominated him for the Assembly of 1867, he was taken somewhat by surprise. He was elected by a majority of four hundred and forty-seven, and served as a member of the Committee on Trade and Manufactures. He was re-elected to the present House by a majority of seven hundred and ninety-nine, and is a member of the Committees on Affairs of Villages, and Public Printing.

In his manners, he is a pleasant, unassuming gentleman; and as a legislator, is watchful and industrious.

CALEB L. SMITH.

Mr. SMITH is one of the attentive and unobtrusive, but diligent and serviceable members of the House, and is a member of the Committees on Insurance and on State Prisons. He was born in New York city November 21st, 1829. His father and mother were both Americans. They removed into the country when he was quite young, and he was brought up on a farm, after the manner of those days, working in the summer and going to school in the winter. He learned the carpenter's trade, being apprenticed to it in Brooklyn, in which city he has since resided; and is now living at No. 138 South Second street, in the Eastern District. He has acted with the Democratic party since 1857. He was elected to the Assembly for the Seventh Assembly district of Kings county, comprising the Thirteenth and Fourteenth Wards, the former of which is largely Republican, but he carried both wards, and was elected by a majority of fourteen hundred and seventy. He has lived in the wards of which the district is composed, for the last twenty-five years.

LEWIS E. SMITH.

Mr. L. E. SMITH was born in Livonia, Livingston county, November 25, 1812, and is now the representative of that county in the Assembly. His paternal ancestors originally came to this country from Northumberland, England. His grandfather, OZIEL SMITH, was a native of Rhode Island, and his father, GEORGE SMITH, of Vermont. The latter is still living in Livonia, and is 89 years of age. He removed to Livingston county when he was eighteen years of age. He held a major's commission in the war of 1812, and had command of the boats that were used in crossing the river at the battle of Queenstown, and was taken prisoner there. In 1821, he was elected the first Member of Assembly from Livingston county. One of L. E. SMITH's female ancestors was a Quaker, and in the days when it was thought to be a service to God to persecute those inoffensive but stubborn dissenters, she was driven through the streets of Boston and publicly whipped for her principles. Mr. SMITH's maternal ancestors were from Litchfield county, Connecticut. His mother removed from that State to Western New York with her father, in 1803, riding all the way on horseback.

Mr. SMITH was educated principally in common schools, with some little training in academic schools, where he studied mathematics, surveying, Latin and French, before studying law. He attended the Law Department of Harvard University for a half-year term, while Judge STORY and Mr. GREENLEAF were law professors there. He was admitted to the Courts of Law and Equity of the State in 1842, and also to the District and Circuit Courts of the

United States. He practiced law at Livonia until 1850. In that year, on account of ill health, and a serious injury received by being thrown from a carriage, he retired to a farm, in Livonia, and has since continued to operate it. He was a radical Democrat, prior to 1848, and once run as a Democratic candidate for the Assembly. He was a delegate to the Free Soil Convention which met in Buffalo in 1848. He took a prominent part in the organization of the Republican party, having been Chairman of the first Republican County Convention of Livingston county, and a delegate to the first Republican State Convention, which nominated CLARK and RAYMOND. Mr. SMITH was a Deputy Census Marshal in 1840; has been Town Superintendent of Schools, and was Supervisor 1857-60, and Chairman of the Board two years. Mr. SMITH's unbending integrity of purpose, good judgment and strong sympathy with what he deemed righteous causes, have won for him the highest esteem. He is quiet and dignified in the discharge of his duties, and is a faithful representative.

ELISHA W. STANNARD

In the person of Mr. STANNARD we have one of those plain but intelligent farmers that form so large a portion of the Republican party of Central and Western New York, and who do not follow politics for the loaves and fishes, but who fully believe in the principles of their party, and share in its labors because they hope, by so doing, to advance the best interests of their country. They do not "lay pipe" to get office, but consent to take official position simply in deference to the wishes of their neighbors.

Mr. STANNARD was born at Warren, Herkimer county, New York, October 27, 1819. He has been no "rolling stone," but, with true love for his native place, and with rare contentment for the sphere in which his lot was cast by the circumstances of his birth, he has remained a resident of the same town during his whole life, and passed his days in the quiet and steady performance of the labors of a farmer. He has had no educational advantages beyond that furnished by the common schools of his town.

Mr. STANNARD was formerly a Whig, and went with the Whigs into the Republican party. Before the organization of the Republican party, however, he was a strong opponent of slavery, so much so, indeed, that, in 1848, he voted the Free Soil or VAN BUREN ticket.

The only political office he has previously held, has been that of Supervisor. The town in which he resides is nearly evenly balanced politically, the Democratic party having a slight preponderance of strength, but Mr. STANNARD was elected to the office of Supervisor, on the

Republican ticket, in the years 1861, 1862, 1866 and 1867, always running ahead of the average vote of his party. He represents Herkimer county in the Assembly, and is a member of the Committee on Insurance Companies. He is no public speaker, but he is faithful and conscientious in examining questions and giving his vote.

DAVID G. STARR.

Mr. STARR is a native of Fallsburgh, Sullivan county, New York, where he was born, on the twenty-first of January, 1837. His youth was spent on a farm, where, by vigorous toil, his physical powers were developed in such a way as to enable him to bear the tax which an after sedentary life would impose upon him. The rudimental studies which formed the basis of his education, were followed by higher academic branches, which he pursued, for a year, at the Charlotteville Seminary, Schoharie county, an institution which, at that time, was at the height of prosperity. Before entering upon his professional studies, Mr. STARR went to Hampton, a small village in Madison county, Illinois, situated on the Terre Haute, Alton and St. Louis Railroad, where he taught the village school for some months. Whether or not his object may have been to increase the amount of his finances, it is certain that the practical application of what he had learned, more fully prepared him for after life. At the end of a year he returned home, and, during the following year entered into business speculations. In November, 1857, he began the study of law, in the office of Hon. A. C. NIVEN, at Monticello, New York. Subsequently spending a term at the Albany Law School, he was admitted to practice, in April, 1861, and thereupon settled in Monticello, where he has a lucrative business, and is looked upon as a lawyer of promise. Being a comparatively young man, and unambitious for public notice, his life has been unmarked by thrilling episodes. He has been Clerk of the Board of Supervisors of Sullivan county, four years; and, in 1866, was elected Justice of the Peace. He was a member of the Assembly of 1867, serving on the Committee on Claims, and Sub-Committee of the whole. In the present house he is Chairman of the Committee on Affairs of Villages, and member of the Committee on Public Education.

Mr. STARR has always been a Democrat, and has scrupulously indorsed the platforms and candidates of his party. He is a shrewd politician, popular at home and in the House, and has made a good record as a legislator.

JAMES STEVENS.

Among the many rising young men of the central portion of New York, is the subject of this sketch, who was born in the village of Rome, Oneida county, May 9th, 1836, at which place he now resides. Mr. STEVENS represents the Third Assembly district of his native county, and proves a very serviceable member.

Quite early in life Mr. STEVENS went to California, where he remained several years. He subsequently traveled through Central America, and still later made a tour of the Western States, and then settled in his native place, where he has secured a moderate competence and has been repeatedly honored by his fellow-citizens. He was for years a prominent officer of the Fire Department; is Brigade Engineer, with rank of Major, on the staff of Brigadier-General DERING, and is now President of the village of Rome, having been elected by the largest majority ever given for that office.

Mr. STEVENS is possessed of a fine presence, a good constitution and more than a usual amount of energy. As a business man he has been uniformly successful, a result consequent on good judgment rather than what is sometimes termed "good luck." Possessing a strong and clear mind, a good knowledge of public affairs, and with extended experience in railroad and canal forwarding, Mr. STEVENS, at the age of thirty-one, is prominently before the people of Central New York as a promising business man, a warm supporter of Democratic sentiments, and a politician who has a record of which no one need be ashamed. He is in full health, regular in his habits, and looks forward to a long and useful life. He is Chairman of the Committee on Joint Library, and member of the Committee on Federal Relations, and the Canal Fraud Impeachment Committee.

ROBERT STEWART.

The parents of Mr. STEWART were both natives of Scotland, and came, while young, to this country, in the latter part of the last century. After marriage, they settled in Johnstown, Montgomery county, of this State, and subsequently removed to Fenner, Madison county. In Fenner, in the year 1815, Mr. ROBERT STEWART was born. He received what was regarded in those days as a good education, spending some time after leaving the common schools, at the Oneida Academy, at Oneida Castle. Though reared on a farm, Mr. STEWART early developed a speculative turn of mind. After a few years of dealing in farm produce, he associated himself with his brother, in the mercantile business, in the village of Chittenango, where he has ever since resided. He also engaged largely in the manufacture of woolen goods and of high wines, having branch establishments in Buffalo. The firm of STEWART, GRAVES & Co., of which he was the head, was at one time the most extensive distillers in the State. Mr. STEWART's life has therefore been one of active business, and as such has been very successful. For some years he has been President of the First National Bank of Chittenango.

In politics, Mr. STEWART has ever taken a deep interest. He was always a Whig until that party met its death, and has since been an earnest member of the Republican party. He has held various important town offices, and was a member of the Assembly in 1858. He has been frequently a delegate to the State Conventions of his party, and in 1860 was a delegate to the National Convention at Chicago, which put in nomination ABRAHAM LINCOLN.

Mr. STEWART, as a legislator, attends to his duties as a man of business rather than as a politician. Above the temptations which too often beset legislation, and bringing to the discharge of his duties high intelligence, broad experience and earnest zeal, he ranks with the very best men in the Assembly.

ALBERT E. SULLARD.

Dr. SULLARD is a native of Connecticut, having been born in Columbia, Tolland county, in that State, on the 30th of September, 1819. His father was of French descent, and his mother's ancestors were English. When five years of age his father removed to Franklin, Delaware county, New York, and engaged in farming. He assisted his father in farm labor, attending common school at intervals until sixteen years of age, when he commenced a thorough course of study at the Delaware Literary Institute, in Franklin, which he pursued for four years. At the close of his Academic term, he chose the profession of medicine, and commenced studying with Dr. HINE, of Franklin. He attended lectures at the Albany Medical College, and graduated in 1844. He immediately commenced the practice of his profession, in Franklin, where he has pursued it successfully ever since.

The Doctor formerly acted with the Democratic party; was a "Free-soiler," but united with the Republican party on its organization. He has held several town offices; was

Superintendent of schools for eight years, and Supervisor in 1861, '62. He was elected to the Assembly from the First District of Delaware county, by six hundred and forty-three majority. He is a member of the Committee on Public Health and Medical Colleges and Societies.

At home, Dr. SULLARD is highly esteemed for his many excellent qualities. He is classed as a skillful and successful practitioner. As a citizen he is progressive and energetic. The Academy in his village has found in him a steadfast friend; and its present prosperity and sound basis are due in a large degree to his energy and liberality. Mainly through his exertions it has become one of the best educational institutions in the State.

During the session, Dr. SULLARD has made many friends. Retiring and unassuming in manners but always kind and pleasant, he quietly attends to his duties; always giving his vote intelligently, and for what he believes to be the best interests of his constituents and the public at large.

JACKSON A. SUMNER.

Mr. SUMNER is a member of a family that has occupied a prominent place in the history of New England ever since its settlement. Different members of the family have occupied high places among its merchants, lawyers, ministers and public officers. JOHN SUMNER, the great grandfather of the subject of this sketch, was a captain in the Patriot Army during the Revolution. ROBERT SUMNER, a son of JOHN, enlisted in the same army at fourteen years of age. INCREASE SUMNER, who was Governor of Massachusetts soon after the Revolution, was a near relative of ROBERT SUMNER.

In 1792 JOHN SUMNER and ROBERT SUMNER emigrated from Ashford, Connecticut, to the town of Edinburgh, Saratoga county, in this State, and in that place JACKSON A. SUMNER was born, October 31st, 1831.

Having obtained a fair common school education, Mr. SUMNER came to Albany, and attended first a private academy, and then the State Normal School. In 1852 he accepted an appointment as Chief Distributing Clerk in the Troy Post Office, which position he held until 1857. In 1858 he entered into copartnership with Mr. OSCAR L. HASCY, and engaged in the lumber trade in the city of Albany, which business he still pursues.

Mr. SUMNER has never been much of a partisan, and up to the time he was elected a Member of Assembly by the Democratic party in the Third District of Albany county, had not held any elective political office.

Mr. SUMNER is not given to public speaking, but he is a man of strong common sense, excellent judgment and superior business habits. He is a member of the Committee of Ways and Means, and among his associates on that committee, and indeed among all who have business relations with him, his judgment commands the highest respect. If party managers would be more guided by the advice of such men, legislative enactments would be more in accordance with the needs of the people.

HENRY F. TARBOX.

Henry Fisk Tarbox has a soldier's record — a record which places him on a nation's roll of honor; and it is with pleasure that we take this opportunity of alluding to his participation in the grand work which, through blood, and tears, and agonies, has come to a glorious consummation — the redemption of the Republic. The Spartan mothers were accustomed to take their sons, about to go into battle, and, placing their shields in their hands, say: "Either *this*, or *upon* this." And American mothers, and wives and sisters, for four awful years, responded "Amen!" to the heroic sentiment. The people will remember, from generation to generation, the military bravery of the living and the dead. The latter have given their highest treasures for the salvation of our institutions; and, though they may lie in graves far away from home, their deeds of valor are undecaying monuments. We make this reference because Mr. Tarbox's brother, a member of the same regiment, was killed while leading his men in a charge upon the enemy.

Mr. TARBOX is the son of HENRY and JULIA TARBOX, and is twenty-eight years of age. His father, a man of intelligence, was a bitter opposer of slavery. His mother was a descendant of DAVID BRAINARD, and all her relatives are Radical Republicans. He spent two years at the Genesee College, at Lima, New York, diligently pursuing classical studies, and then commenced reading law. He was admitted to practice in November, 1864, since which time he has followed his profession, at Batavia, New York. Prior to his admission to the Bar, he assisted, in 1862, in raising and organizing the 108th Regiment, New York Volunteers; personally enlisting over forty men for that regiment. He received a commission as Second Lieutenant of Company C; and his brother, D. B. TARBOX, was also commissioned to the same rank in Company B. Each led his company in the battle of Antietam, which transpired within less than a month after the regiment was mustered into service. His brother fell in that fight. Mr. TARBOX remained with his regiment until he was so far disabled by disease, that he was discharged by an order from the War Department. By virtue of a good constitution, he afterward so far recovered from his disability, as to be able to accept the position of Assistant Paymaster. A year and a half subsequently he resigned, and, after completing his studies, entered upon his profession, as previously stated. He was a member of Assembly in 1867. After his nomination Mr. TARBOX took the stump, and rendered essential service to his party in his county. The Republicans gave him a majority of 1,400 over his competitor, who was a Conservative Republican. He served that year as a member of the Committees on Internal Affairs of Towns and Counties, and Colleges, Academies and Common Schools. He was brevetted Major, during the year 1867, by Governor FENTON, and the degree of A. M. was conferred on him by Genesee College in the same year. Mr. TARBOX is an active young man; is an influential member of the House; effective in debate when he takes the floor; vigorous, but thoughtful in action, and wide awake to the interests of the people.

E. CURTIS TOPLIFF.

Mr. TOPLIFF, of Cattaraugus county, is a man whom it will pay to know well. He is descended from a Vermont family. His parents were among the first settlers of Chautauqua county. He was born in 1830, and owing to the poverty of his family his opportunities for education were very limited. But he was ambitious, and at an early age entered the office of Judge COOK, of Jamestown, N. Y., to engage in the study of the law. But gold was discovered in California. Mr. TOPLIFF shut up BLACKSTONE and KENT, and in 1851, that he might get and make his fortune, went to California. Three years were spent there. He made a voyage to South America, and visited the silver mines of Chili. Returning home, he engaged in the lumber business, finding it impossible to engage in a sedentary life. His operations were both extensive and successful, and he had a reputation for enterprise, shrewdness and fidelity. Few men are stronger in their friendships, willing to sacrifice almost anything for his friends, political or otherwise, and we would rather have some one else for an enemy. At this time he was a Democrat in politics, but forsook the party when it adopted the territorial policy of 1854. Since that time he has been a zealous Republican, and one of the most efficient members of the party. In 1861, he was appointed Mail Agent through the good offices of Representative FENTON, his personal and political friend, and retained the position two years. He was elected Supervisor of Salamanca in 1863, and was twice re-elected. In 1865, he became for the first time a member of the Assembly. He soon displayed rare capacity as a working member. President LINCOLN had made his last call for recruits, and the quota assigned to this State was considered to be too large. A committee of the Legislature was sent to Washington, Mr. TOPLIFF being one of the members on the part of the Assembly. He readily comprehended the situation, had a personal conversation with the President, told his story, and the mission was successful. Mr. TOPLIFF was re-elected in 1866, and became one of the most influential members. Forgetting every personal slight, he devoted himself to the vigorous prosecution of every measure which he considered beneficial.

Representing his District several times in State Conventions, he was always a leading spirit. In the present House, being in the minority, his activity has been circumscribed, but he is wary, and ready to detect every false move which his adversaries may make. He is neither easy to out-manage nor to beat. His record has always been good, and he is faithful to the interests of his constituents.

SAMUEL H. TORREY.

Mr. Torrey, the father of the subject of this brief sketch was born in Connecticut, and when quite young emigrated to Western New York. He located at the town of Italy, Yates county. It was then an unbroken wilderness. His integrity and practical sense gave him a position of influence. He was one of those who participated in and shaped the destinies of Western New York.

His son, Samuel H. Torrey, was born on the 4th day of July, 1816. As was quite common at that period he left the parental roof at the age of fourteen years, as an adventurer. Resolute, persevering and indomitable, he surmounted every hindrance and acquired a liberal education. In 1837 he entered the law office of Wilson & Lester of Canandaigua, and completed his legal course in the office of John L. Talcott, of Buffalo. In the year 1841 he was admitted to the Bar and entered upon his professional career at Rushville, Yates county. By industry, honesty and an aptitude in his profession, he gained the confidence and respect of the community and also a lucrative practice. This confidence and respect he still retains. He married a very estimable lady, a resident of Naples, Ontario county, at which place he then located. Circumstances as well as inclination now led him into agricultural pursuits. In this new vocation his self reliance and force of character enabled him to succeed. He became a successful husbandman, and an extensive landholder, and his opinions and counsel in business matters as well as in his profession, are held in high estimation.

His history is an illustration of the omnipotence of resolution, and the workings of American life and American enterprise. Mr. TORREY is emphatically a self-made man. He has always taken a deep interest in the development and advancement of his town, his county, State and the Nation. His earnestness, candor and patriotism have given him a deservedly high rank. He has been forced to accept various positions of trust in his own town, and frequently, when grave questions have been involved, he has represented his district at our State Conventions. In all of these positions he has met the expectations of a confiding constituency. He was a delegate to the National Convention which nominated ABRAHAM LINCOLN for President. He was elected to the Assembly from the Second District of Ontario county, in 1866, serving on the Committees on Claims and Affairs of Villages; and was re-elected in 1867. In the present session he is a member of the Sub-Committee of the Whole, and the Committee on Charitable Institutions. Few men in Ontario county enjoy a greater share of the confidence of the masses than does Mr. TORREY. Genial in temper, truthful in utterance, approachable from inclination, he is a particular favorite. As a speaker, he is forcible and earnest, although seldom taking part in debate, and gives utterance to his convictions without circumlocution. He has faith in what he says, and he manifests this faith by corresponding works. He has acquired an honorable record in the Legislature for his integrity and ability, and wields a creditable influence. The impression is generally obtaining that Mr. TORREY is a rising man.

DEWITT CLINTON TOWER.

Mr. TOWER is one of the Kings county delegation. He was born in Waterville, Oneida county, January 20, 1821. His father, REUBEN TOWER, was one of the most enterprising and liberal men in Oneida county, and represented it in the Assembly in 1828. His son received a liberal education, and graduated at Harvard College in the class of 1842. Mr. TOWER was extensively engaged in the distilling business in Sangerfield, Oneida county, and was Supervisor of the town in 1848 and 1849. He was one of the most popular men in the town, and although he always had a mind of his own, he had the warm friendship of every one, and not a single enemy. He removed to Brooklyn in 1850, continuing as distiller for some time, when he engaged in banking, and is now President of the Mechanics' and Traders' Bank, at Greenpoint. Mr. TOWER is a genial and warm friend, good business manager, and successful financier. He is Chairman of the Committee on Banks.

PETER TRAINER.

Peter Trainer was born in the city of Hartford, Connecticut, May 27, 1833. His early education received careful attention. Besides the usual instruction in the public schools, he also took an academical course at Suffield Institute. Coming to New York he engaged in mercantile business. The war breaking out, he accompanied the New York Volunteers to the field, and rendered valuable service to them in various ways, accepting for himself no rank or position, but acting as an assistant to the quartermaster. Returning home he resumed business as a merchant at No. 1203 Broadway, and has prosecuted it ever since with success. He has not been known as an office holder, except as Trustee of Schools, until his election to the Assembly, for which he received 2,644 votes, or a majority of 514 over Mr. John V. Gridley, Republican. Mr. Trainer is a gentleman of fine personal appearance, obliging disposition and agreeable manner, and makes a popular representative. He is a good school officer in New York, and makes a good Assemblyman. There are few duties which he will not discharge well.

DAVID UNDERWOOD.

Mr. UNDERWOOD has never, hitherto, mingled much in politics. He belongs to that class of men whose minds dwell more particularly upon business affairs, and who thereby gain a vast fund of good, practical knowledge, which is doubly valuable because it has been gathered from experience. Mr. UNDERWOOD claims no more than he deserves in this direction. His English ancestors came to this country before the Revolutionary war, and settled in Massachusetts. Thence, Mr. UNDERWOOD's father removed to Marlboro, Vermont, which is the birth place of the gentleman of whom we are writing. At the age of eleven, the boy, DAVID, came to this State; and, as soon as he became old enough, he interested himself in the manufacture and sale of lumber. This was more than thirty years ago. The growing demand for timber, in consequence of increasing enterprise in our cities and villages, presented fine opportunities for a sagacious man like Mr. UNDERWOOD, to extend his business, until he arose from a position of comparative weakness to one of worth and strength. While engaged in his business, he forwarded a great deal of lumber to distant markets, and thereby had abundant opportunities for learning the wants of the Champlain canal, which has been so much neglected of late, and the claims of which, the men of Northern New York are pressing with an earnestness and a vigor commensurate with the object in view. And there are cogent reasons why their voices should be heard, for the vast resources of that region are not yet properly understood by the public at large. But men of wealth and foresight, who reside in that section of the State, know full well that ampler facilities ought to be afforded for the transportation of the products which come from that quarter. It was with the object to remedy this state of things, that Mr. UNDERWOOD consented to run for the office which he now holds in the Assembly. He was elected by a majority of 1,406, having run 500 ahead of the rest of his ticket. In politics, he has belonged to the Republican party ever since it was formed. As a citizen, he is public spirited, and is respected for his many excellent qualities. He is one of the most energetic and influential men in the village of Fort Edward, where he resides, and probably to no one, more than Mr. UNDERWOOD, is it indebted for its present prosperity and business activity. He is a member of the Committee on Canals, one of the most important in the House. He is also a member of the Committee which impeached Canal Commissioner DORN, and made an able minority report in the matter, in which, while he agreed with the Committee in recommending the impeachment of Mr. DORN, he took the position that the Committee should extend their investigations rigidly to all officers of the canals who have proved recreant to their trusts.

GEORGE B. VAN BRUNT.

Colonel GEORGE B. VAN BRUNT was born at Sylvan Brook, Staten Island, on the 30th day of May, 1829. Both of his grandfathers were soldiers in the war of the Revolution. He was educated in the public schools of New York; and upon the breaking out of the rebellion, enlisted in the 47th Regiment of New York Volunteers, June 3d, 1861. He was not long in achieving rank, being in turn First Lieutenant, Captain, Major, and Lieutenant-Colonel. His regiment was attached to the Department of the South, consisting of the States of South Carolina, Georgia and Florida. His record is that of an industrious, courageous and efficient officer — and he took part in every engagement in which the regiment participated.

After his discharge, he received the appointment of Deputy Surveyor of the port of New York, in December, 1864. Being in early manhood a Whig, and afterward a zealous Republican, he was dismissed from office in April, 1867. He opened an office immediately as a Real Estate Broker, at No. 146 East Fiftieth street; and in the fall was nominated for the Assembly in the Twentieth District, receiving a plurality of 106 votes over HENRY CLAUSEN, Mozart Hall Democrat. He is a staunch Republican, preferring principle to position, and doing yeoman's service in whatever he undertakes. He is an effective member of the Assembly.

THEODORE VAN VOLKENBURGH.

Mr. Van Volkenburgh, when twelve years old, was deprived of his father, by death, and was thus left, with his mother, in quite straitened circumstances. He was born in the city of Albany, April 1st, 1835, and attended public and private schools until he was sixteen years of age. He then, though so young, began to teach school; and succeeded so well that he continued in the same place for three years in succession. At the end of that time, anxious to become more proficient as a student, he entered the Albany Academy. Not long afterwards he left that institution, and attended the State Normal School. Having passed through the different grades of study to the senior year, he was obliged to leave his studies, in order to begin the business of life.

Mr. Van Volkenburgh married when he was twenty-one, and immediately thereafter engaged in farming, an oocupation which he still follows. He is a Democrat. His party elected him as Assessor for the town of Watervliet, in 1863, and he held that office for three years. Last fall he was nominated, by acclamation, for candidate for Member of the Assembly for the Fourth Assembly District in Albany county. He was elected by a majority of 328. He is on the Committees on Insurance and Petitions of Aliens.

Whatever Mr. Van Volkenburgh has attained, has been accomplished by his own perseverance and foresight. Being left without any influential relatives to advise and advance him, he was, fortunately perhaps, obliged to work out his own course.

CHARLES H. WEED.

Mr. WEED is of genuine Yankee blood, and has had some of the roving Yankee's experience. His parents were natives of Plymouth, Litchfield county, Connecticut, who emigrated to Cazenovia, Madison county, in the year 1808, at which place he was born December 2d, 1810. He obtained a very good common school education, and then became one of the seven pupils with which the Oneida Conference Seminary was opened, forty-five years ago. He has lived to see it one of the most flourishing institutions of learning in the State. From the age of eighteen to twenty-two he spent the summers in labor upon his father's farm, and the winters in teaching school. In 1832, he went into the State of Ohio, and spent some time in teaching school, and then accepted the position of clerk in a store. He remained in the State of Ohio three years, and then returned to this State and engaged in the mercantile business in Onondaga county. In 1854, he was appointed Superintendent of one of the divisions of the Erie Canal, which office he held for two years, discharging its duties to the entire satisfaction of the Canal Board.

In 1856, Mr. WEED removed to Weedsport, Cayuga county, N. Y., and engaged in the distillery business. In 1862, his distillery building was destroyed by fire, involving a loss of $50,000. In 1866, he purchased the "Putnam Mill" site and erected a large flouring mill, and had just commenced running it when it was set on fire by an incendiary, subjecting him to a loss of $15,000.

During the rebellion, Mr. WEED was very active and efficient in raising recruits for the Union army and in filling the quotas of his town.

He was elected a member of Assembly from the First District of Cayuga county by the Republican party, obtaining 796 majority over OLIVER WOOD. He is a member of the Committee on State Prisons. In committee and on the floor of the house he is active and vigilant, and though not a great talker, what he says is to the point, for he is a man of sound judgment. Socially, he is genial and affable, and possesses the qualities which secure and retain valuable friendships.

D. GERRY WELLINGTON.

Mr. WELLINGTON was born in Cazenovia, Madison county, January 8, 1838. He was educated in the Oneida Conference Seminary, from which he graduated in 1859, and entered Union College, where he passed the Sophomore year, and then entered the Albany Law School, from which he graduated in 1861. Being a laborious and apt scholar, he was of course thoroughly proficient in his studies. In the fall of 1861, he opened an office in the village of Hamilton, Madison county, and is now engaged in the successful practice of law in that village. In the fall of 1862, his patriotic impulses led him to abandon his growing practice, and he enlisted as a private in the 176th Regiment New York State Volunteers, and was immediately elected Captain of Company E. His modest distrust of his qualifications for the position, led him to decline it, but he yielded to the earnest desire of the company that he should hold a leading position in their ranks, and accepted the position of First-Lieutenant. The regiment went into camp at Jamaica, Long Island, and remained there until January, 1863, when it embarked in the BANKS expedition for New Orleans. He was taken prisoner at Lafourche Crossing, Louisiana, January 23, 1863, and was taken to Camp Ford Tyler, Texas, where he remained a prisoner until July 24, 1864 (thirteen months), when he was exchanged. He was honorably discharged from the service in the following August. He immediately resumed the practice of his profession. He was nominated for Justice of the Peace of the town of Hamilton in 1865, and was indorsed by the Democratic party, thus receiving the unanimous support of both parties. He held the office thus flatteringly bestowed until elected to the present Assembly. If any other evidence was needed of his personal popularity than was shown in his election as Justice, it is found in the vote he received in his native town during the canvass for member. The Democratic State ticket received 126 votes in the town, and of that vote he received 65, leaving his Democratic opponent but 61, thus beating him in his own party alone by a majority of four. Mr. WELLINGTON is a quiet but active member of the House, and is a member of the Railroad Committee. When he has anything to say, he presents his points clearly and forcibly, and hence, very effectively. He is strong in the regards and esteem of all who have formed his acquaintance.

JARED A. WELLS.

Mr. WELLS' place of nativity is New York city; but owing to the death of his mother, which occurred in 1834—when he was about a year old—he was adopted by an uncle residing at Rockland Lake, N. Y., with whom he remained until he was eighteen. During this time, he had acquired a common school education. He was then sent to a boarding school, at Pennington, N. J., and subsequently to a like institution at East Greenwich, R. I. About the time of his return home from the latter place, his uncle and aunt died. They had filled the places of parents to him, and he felt keenly their sudden decease. Mr. WELLS soon left the place of his adoption, and returned to the city of New York, where he remained in the mercantile business until the summer of 1861. In that year, he closed up his affairs in New York, and removed to Petersburgh, a quiet, rural town in Rensselaer county, New York. He was immediately recognized as a gentleman of worth. In the Spring of 1863, the citizens of that town elected him to the office of Justice of the Peace; in the Fall of 1865, he was elected Justice of the Sessions, and re-elected the next year. He was nominated for Member of the Assembly, in the present Legislature, against ALBERT S. PEASE, and was elected by 673 majority, being the only successful Republican candidate for the Assembly in his county.

Mr. WELLS has always been an advocate of Republican tenets. His convictions of the true mission of his party were firm before the war; and while the Rebellion was in progress he gave substantial aid in putting it down by furnishing a substitute, though he himself was not drafted.

Mr. WELLS served nine years in the 12th New York Regiment State Militia, and also for three years held the position of Captain of Company "A," 97th Regiment, New York State National Guard, Colonel SCHUYLER GREENMAN commanding. He resigned, however, and was honorably discharged from the service. He is an agreeable acquaintance and an upright man, and is the possessor of good mental powers and a kindly heart. He is a member of the Committee on Agriculture.

STEPHEN H. WENDOVER.

Mr. WENDOVER was, until recently, interested in the forwarding business; he represents the third generation of his family continuously engaged therein. His grandfather, who was a native and resident of New York city at the outbreak of the Revolution, was related to PETER WENDOVER, one of the framers of the first State Constitution of New York, and primarily suggested the idea of the National Flag as it now is.

Mr. WENDOVER was born in the town of Stuyvesant, Columbia county, New York, on the 28th day of July, 1831. His boyhood was unbroken by any stern necessities, or pinching privations; his father, a gentleman of competence, educated him with a view to business, and gave him all the facilities necessary to prepare him for commercial pursuits. Placing his son in the Kinderhook Academy, an institution situated at Kinderhook, Columbia county, New York, he gave him all of the benefits which that school afforded. In 1848, Mr. WENDOVER, then seventeen years of age, left the Academy, and became a clerk in his father's business, to which he succeeded in 1855, and which he conducted with fine business skill.

Mr. WENDOVER never, until the autumn of 1866, allowed his name to be used for the candidacy for office; but at that time, his Republican friends, in view of the political strength of the probable competitor, urged him to run for the Assembly, and he was elected by seventy-two majority. His strength before the people, and which is eminently deserved, is shown by his re-election last fall, in a very close district. He served in the last Assembly on the Committee on Commerce and Navigation, and the present session on Trade and Manufactures. Mr. WENDOVER, on first acquaintance, is somewhat reserved; but among his friends he is genial, and is uniformly polite to everybody. He is emphatically a discerning, large-hearted man. He is safe as a counsellor, and reliable in action. His integrity is spotless, and his services invaluable. He is a tower of strength in the right.

WILLIAM L. WILEY.

Mr. WILEY, member from the 19th District of New York, was born in the First Ward of that city on the 18th of March, 1825. His ancestors, several of whom were soldiers in the Revolutionary war, came to this country from Scotland, in 1735, and became residents of that ward, where they continued to reside for nearly a century.

At the outbreak of the Rebellion, Mr. WILEY took strong ground in favor of the Government, and was associated with General SICKLES in raising the Excelsior Brigade. He acted as Quartermaster, and to his great energy, knowledge of the men of New York, and executive ability, may be attributed, in a large degree, the rapid and successful organization of that brigade. After having aided in placing it in the field, and at about the time it left New York, Mr. WILEY's presence became necessary in the celebrated HOPPER will case, he being one of the heirs, a case that was severely contested in the courts for four years, from the Surrogate's Court to the Court of Appeals, and by the latter decided in his favor. Throughout life Mr. WILEY has been an active uncompromising Democrat. He has been conspicuous in the organizations of that party, and by his energy, sagacity and labors has contributed his full share to its success. He is one of the city surveyors of New York.

Mr. WILEY is a gentleman of commanding presence, great power of conversation, quick, keen eye, honest purpose, which he pursues with an unyielding determination, and is fully acquainted with city affairs. He has been for many years a very intimate and familiar friend of JAMES GORDON BENNETT, editor and proprietor of the New York Herald, and it is said there are few men in New York on whose judgment Mr. BENNETT relies with more confidence than upon Mr. WILEY's.

OLIVER S. WILLIAMS.

The father of Mr. WILLIAMS was in the war of 1812. Having been drafted in 1813, he served his time; and, in 1814, he volunteered into the service. He was engaged in the battle of Fort Erie, and was taken prisoner by the British forces; being held until the declaration of peace.

Mr. WILLIAMS was born in Middlesex, Yates county, New York, May 11, 1823. In connection with farming, he has also pursued mercantile business for a number of years, and dealt considerably in cattle, sheep and wool. From comparative indigence, he has acquired a good competence.

He has held the various offices of Justice of the Peace, Commissioner of Highways, and Supervisor. He has always been elected by the Democrats, with whom he has heartily acted. Mr. WILLIAMS, last Fall, was first nominated on what was termed "The People's Ticket," which was made up by a portion of the Republicans, dissatisfied with the action of the Republican Convention, which had placed in nomination for the Assembly, Hon. CHARLES S. HOYT. This "People's Ticket" was duly indorsed by the Democrats, though it was formed of men from both parties. The result of this coalition was the election of Mr. WILLIAMS by a majority of 162. He is on the Committees on Internal Affairs, and Manufacture of Salt, and is an attentive member.

ABNER I. WOOD.

Mr. Wood was born, February 4th, 1813, and is, therefore, one of the oldest men in the Assembly. At the time of his birth, his parents resided in Clifton Park, Saratoga county, New York, where his father carried on the business of shoemaking and tanning, until the winter of 1835, when he removed to Clarkson, Monroe county. He is of Irish descent—three generations in his lineage dating back to birth under the skies of Erin. His grandfather, in the paternal line, when but fifteen years old, enlisted in the service of his country, and served three years in fighting the French and Indians, in the old border wars. When this period of strife had passed, he settled in the town of Amenia, Dutchess county, became a Baptist preacher, and preached to the same congregation until his death, which occurred in 1810.

His facilities for education were very meagre. Even such advantages as a common school could give were his, only until he attained the age of twelve years. At fifteen years of age, he commenced learning the trade of shoemaking, with his father, and continued in that occupation until 1844, since which time he has been a farmer. He removed from Clarkson to Brockport, Monroe county, in January, 1841, and after residing there four years, again changed his residence to Parma, in the same county, where he has since continued to reside.

In 1850, Mr. Wood was elected Assessor of his town, by the Whig party, which office he held three years. He had voted with that party since attaining his majority, and maintained the same party relations, until the formation of the Republican party. He served his town as Supervisor, during the years 1858, '59, '60 and '65, his faithfulness as such officer being fully attested by these repeated elections. In the fall of 1865, he was elected Member of Assembly, by a majority of seven hundred and fifty-one over the Democratic candidate. He was re-elected the following year by a majority of eight hundred and fifty-eight, his own town speaking his popularity at home, by giving three hundred and ten of the very flattering vote. He served on the Committees on Canals, Charitable and Religious Societies, and Expenditures of the Executive Department; of the latter he was Chairman. Last fall he was re-elected for the third time.

Mr. Wood is an efficient representative. He possesses a cordial social temperament, and is at all times courteous and obliging. A man of good personal presence, his unpretending manner readily wins respect and confidence; and he blends always with his action, the convictions of an earnest, Christian gentleman.

FRANK H. WOODS.

"A man with noble ancestry," says Pauline, in Bulwer's Lady of Lyons, "is like a representative of the past;" but like the supposed prince to whom this eulogy was applied, the gentleman whose name stands at the head of this sketch is by no means "a pensioner upon the dead." Without the favor of wealth or the advantages of parental distinction, he began life a poor boy, almost wholly dependent, from the very beginning, upon himself for a livelihood; yet, by dint of hard labor and the diligent exercise of a will which "never surrenders," he has gradually ascended in the scale of usefulness and honor, until he has attained a position second, perhaps, to but few men in either branch of the present Legislature.

Mr. WOODS is a native of the First Ward, in the city of Albany, where he has always resided. He is only about twenty-five years of age, and was educated in the English department of the Albany Academy, from which he graduated with considerable distinction. Since the age of twenty-one, he has devoted himself exclusively to the practice of the law, for which he was regularly educated, and has already established a reputation for legal tact and ability of which much older heads might well feel proud. He is now President of the incorporated Fire Department of Albany, and was recently one of the Vice Presidents of the Young Men's Association, and in both of these positions has exhibited a degree of popularity which has rendered him almost invincible as a candidate before the people. This is especially shown by the magnificent canvass which he made for the position he now holds in the Assembly. At the election the year previous the Republican candidate carried the district by about seven hundred majority, while Mr. WOODS defeated the then successful candidate in the same district, at the last contest, by a majority nearly as large. The brilliancy of his future career is therefore promising, and unless some unforeseen misfortune should yet befall him, he will have acquired a reputation at the close of his legislative labors which will scarcely be excelled by that of any other young man in the State.

Mr. WOODS is, by instinct, a Democrat. From his earliest youth he has battled manfully in the cause of his country as a humble representative of the Democratic party. But few men excel him, especially upon the stump, and it is seldom, indeed, that a State or Presidential canvass passes in which his voice is not heard. As a member of the House he speaks only occasionally, but always to the point, and logically. His sound judgment and good business qualifications will doubtless render him a safe legislator, and he will always be found cautious, deliberate and intelligent, committing himself to no rash measures, but acting solely in reference to the best interests of his constituents and the benefits of the people of the whole State.

In social life Mr. WOODS is equally popular and well-liked — a prince of good fellows, with an open hand and generous heart for all his friends. He is very easily approached, being utterly devoid of that awkward stiffness which spoils the personal demeanor of most public men; and is always sure to make friends of all with whom he comes in contact. In his personal appearance he is equally attractive; with his fine, glossy black hair, his black, piercing eyes and black mustache, and his ruddy, good-natured face. His countenance is always expressive and intelligent, and altogether he is such an one as the fair delight to entangle in their meshes and compel to worship at their shrine.

Mr. WOODS is Chairman of the Committee on Privileges and Elections, and a member of the Committee on the Judiciary.

TRUMAN G. YOUNGLOVE.

Mr. YOUNGLOVE's ancestors were of English extraction; his paternal and maternal grandfather were both soldiers during the Revolutionary war, and both drew pensions to the time of their death. His paternal grandfather was a native of Connecticut, but early in life emigrated to Vermont, in which State he reared his family. His parents, about the year 1800, removed from Vermont to Edinburgh, Saratoga county, New York, where the subject of this sketch was born October 31st, 1815. The family subsequently removed to Onondaga county, where Mr. YOUNGLOVE's youth was spent, obtaining such an education as were afforded by the common schools of the day, and the best select schools in Fabius and Salina, and assisting his father in his business, which was tanning and shoemaking.

After working at his trade for some years, Mr. YOUNGLOVE resolved to devote himself to professional life, and commenced a course of preparatory study at the Galway Academy, then under the charge of Professor ALEXANDER WATSON, a teacher of remarkable aptitude and success. While prosecuting his studies, he taught a district school one winter in Fabius and two in Galway. As a student, he was noted for his diligence and proficiency, and the thorough manner in which he mastered the various branches of study assigned to him. He was always among the first in his classes, not because he strove to excel, but because he loved knowledge for its own sake; and, in his eagerness for its acquisition, often outstripped even the ambitious, seldom failing to win the honors accorded to fine scholarship. He early cultivated a taste for historical reading, and the lessons of the past have still for him a freshness of interest unsurpassed by current events of the day.

With mental habits well formed, and intellectual powers adequately trained, professional life offered to him its distinctions; and with a view to such life, he studied law with the late Hon. DANIEL CADY, and Hon. TEUNIS VAN VECHTEN, in Albany, where he removed in December, 1846. After completing his studies with these distinguished jurists, he was admitted to the bar in 1847, and at once commenced practice. Patient to investigate all the bearings of a question, persevering in accomplishing his undertakings, deeply versed in the science of law, Mr. YOUNGLOVE had a promising future before him, and would doubtless have attained great eminence in his profession; but soon after commencing practice, he engaged in business enterprises at Cohoes, and has ever since been conspicuously identified with all the interests of that busy and thriving town. He went to Cohoes in May, 1850, and resided there until 1861, when he removed to Crescent, Saratoga county, where he now has an elegant residence.

At Cohoes, Mr. YOUNGLOVE began to display the great executive talent which has made for him a remarkable record. While engaged in a great variety of extensive operations, he is perhaps best known as Secretary and

Agent of the Cohoes Company, an organization that entirely controls the magnificent water-power of the place. The business of the Company consists in leasing the water-power and real estate to the various manufacturing establishments, and the charge of it devolves almost exclusively upon Mr. Younglove. Of this company he is, and has been for several years, a Director. The dam and gate-house of the company, recently constructed mainly under his supervision, are among the finest in the United States, and the water-power thus made available is scarcely equaled by any other in this country. Under Mr. Younglove's skillful and efficient management, the development of this water-power has resulted in making Cohoes one of the most important manufacturing towns in the country. For several years, he had the entire management of the company's large foundery and machine shop, both of which were built under his supervision. In company with another party, he has been for several years engaged in manufacturing straw board, and has had the entire direction of the business. In the meantime, one of the finest and largest mills in the United States for such manufacture, has been erected under his superintendency. He was a Trustee and also the Secretary of the Mohawk River Mills corporation (a company engaged in manufacturing knit goods), during the existence of the company, and for a considerable time had the entire management of its business. Subsequently, at the organization of the Clifton Company, also manufacturing knit goods, he became Trustee and President of it, and so remains. The same is true as respects his relations to the Cohoes Gas Light Company. He has been Trustee, Secretary and Treasurer of the Cohoes Savings Institution, ever since its incorporation by the Legislature in 1851. He is a director in the National

Bank of Cohoes, and has been such from the organization of the Bank as a State institution, in 1859. He is a Director in the Albany City Insurance Company, also a Director in the Troy and Cohoes Railroad Company. He was Water Commissioner of the Cohoes Water Works, and Treasurer of the Water Fund, for six years, and, as such, had the principal management in the construction of the works. His engagements requiring constant professional skill, he has kept up his law library and law reading, and, on all legal points, he is his own best counsellor.

Such eminent success in business is remarkable, when we consider that the man whose native capacities have secured it, had his early boyhood experiences in an entirely different direction, as tanner, currier and shoemaker, and who prepared for a professional life exclusively.

The political career of Mr. YOUNGLOVE dates from his twenty-first year, in which, as a Whig, he was elected Inspector of Common Schools, in Fabius, an office to which he was chosen a second time. In 1845, he was elected justice of the Peace, on the Whig ticket, in the town of Galway, by a majority of twenty-five, when the town was Democratic by eighty. At Cohoes, he was elected trustee of the village, and held the position of President of the Board of Education, for five years in succession, previous to his removal to Crescent. In 1864, he was the Republican candidate for member of Assembly from the First District of Saratoga county, but was defeated by thirty-eight majority, a result caused by the errors of the soldiers' vote, in the field; a number of ballots, evidently intended for him, being cast for the candidate in the Second Assembly District. In 1865, he was put in nomination for the Assembly again, and, although the district was largely Democratic, was elected by three hundred and forty-seven majority. He was Chairman of the Committee on Trade and Manufactures. In 1866, he was returned to his seat by five hundred and fifty-nine majority. He was a member of the Railroad Committee, and Chairman of the Insurance Committee. He was re-elected in 1867, and was placed on the Committee on Internal Affairs of Towns and Counties.

Mr. YOUNGLOVE, in his Legislative career has achieved an enviable reputation; his career has been marked by that earnest and honest attention to duty that has characterized him in all his business operations. Faithful, conscientious, incorruptible, he has always stood up as the champion of right; and no measure ever gained his approval that did not commend itself to his convictions. No breath of suspicion ever tainted his integrity, and the lobby was powerless to influence him against his sense of duty. Clear in his reasonings and correct in his conclusions, his opinions have great weight; and his uniform courtesy has won him many friends. His business talent and experience have peculiarly qualified him to arrive at safe judgments; and his career has been such as to encourage every commercial interest of the State, and foster every sound enterprise.

As a politician, he is keen and sagacious; his conclusions are not so much the result of quick intuition as of a logical method of reasoning from given premises. They are neither hurriedly reached nor hastily expressed.

As a patriot, earnestly supporting the Government in the hour of its greatest need and peril, few men, whose engagements kept them from field duty, have more unsparingly devoted their time and money to a sacred cause, which could only triumph by the offerings willingly laid upon the altar of sacrifice. Soon after hostilities began, Mr. YOUNGLOVE hired and equipped a man to represent him during the whole war. He also contributed largely toward fitting out a company from his county; and by every means in his power encouraged and sustained his country's cause.

In all the relations of life he is most exemplary, and his character is adorned with many virtues. For a long period he has been an active Sunday-school man; being a teacher in Albany; and, both at Galway and Cohoes, was Superintendent of the Sunday school for several years. His personal appearance is commanding, and his countenance reveals a gentle disposition and a benevolent heart. He is one of those self-made men who, forgetful of self, does what he can for the welfare of all around him.

CORNELIUS W. ARMSTRONG.

CLERK OF THE ASSEMBLY.

Mr. ARMSTRONG is of Scotch and English descent. He was born in Hoosick, Rensselaer county, December 18, 1827. He received a first rate common school education, and at the age of sixteen became a clerk, in Penn Yan, Yates county, where he remained about four years, and then removed to Wayne county. He subsequently located in the city of Albany, where he has been engaged in the produce commission business for twenty years. He is one of the most successful merchants of the city, driving his business with energy, and exercising careful judgment in its direction. He is a gentleman of [sterling] probity of character, respected for his many public virtues by all. He is a public spirited citizen, and Albany is deeply indebted to him for its prosperity. He received the honor of an election to the Presidency of the Board of Trade, in 1867, an organization noted for the sterling character of the men it entrusts with responsibilities, as well as for the thrift, liberality and enterprise of its members.

Politically, Mr. ARMSTRONG has always been an uncompromising Democrat of the hard shell school, so that there was never any difficulty in placing him. He was a member of the Assembly in 1858, in which body he was recognized as one of its most able and influential members, and was an acknowledged leader of his party. He was nominated for Canal Commissioner in 1865, on the Democratic ticket, but failed of an election. His systematic business habits keep the Clerk's desk and room in the utmost order, and enable him to discharge the immense amount of labor which devolves upon him with ready despatch and entire satisfaction. His executive talents are of a high order. His voice is penetrating, though not so heavy as some of his predecessors in office. He is prepossessing in appearance, tall and well proportioned.

MEMBERS OF THE SENATE.

NUMBER OF THEIR RESPECTIVE DISTRICTS, AND THE COUNTIES AND WARDS COMPOSING THE SAME.

Lieut.-Governor STEWART L. WOODFORD, *Brooklyn, Kings Co.*

Dist.	Counties and Wards.	Senators.
1.	Counties of Suffolk, Queens and Richmond,	LEWIS A. EDWARDS.
2.	First, Second, Third, Fourth, Fifth, Seventh, Eleventh, Thirteenth, Fifteenth, Nineteenth and Twentieth wards of the city of Brooklyn, in the county of Kings,	JAMES F. PIERCE.
3.	Sixth, Eighth, Ninth, Tenth, Twelfth, Fourteenth, Sixteenth, Seventeenth and Eighteenth wards of the city of Brooklyn, and the towns of Flatbush, Flatlands, Gravesend, New Lots and New Utrecht, of the county of Kings,	HENRY C. MURPHY.
4.	First, Second, Third, Fourth, Fifth, Sixth, Seventh, Thirteenth and Fourteenth wards of the city and county of New York,	WILLIAM M. TWEED.
5.	Eighth, Ninth, Fifteenth and Sixteenth wards of the city and county of New York,	MICHAEL NORTON.
6.	Eleventh, Tenth and Seventeenth wards of the city and county of New York,	THOMAS J. CREAMER.
7.	Eighteenth, Twentieth and Twenty-first wards of the city and county of New York,	JOHN J. BRADLEY.
8.	Twelfth, Nineteenth and Twenty-second wards of the city and county of New York,	HENRY W. GENET.
9.	Counties of Westchester, Putnam and Rockland,	WILLIAM CAULDWELL.
10.	Counties of Orange and Sullivan,	WILLIAM M. GRAHAM.

MEMBERS OF THE SENATE.

Dist.	Counties and Wards.	Senators.
11.	Counties of Dutchess and Columbia,	ABIAH W. PALMER.
12.	Counties of Rensselaer and Washington,	FRANCIS S. THAYER.
13.	County of Albany,	A. BLEECKER BANKS.
14.	Counties of Greene and Ulster,	GEORGE BEACH.
15.	Counties of Saratoga, Montgomery, Fulton, Hamilton and Schenectady,	CHARLES STANFORD.
16.	Counties of Warren, Essex and Clinton,	MATTHEW HALE.
17.	Counties of St. Lawrence and Franklin,	ABRAHAM X. PARKER.
18.	Counties of Jefferson and Lewis,	JOHN O'DONNELL.
19.	County of Oneida,	SAMUEL CAMPBELL.
20.	Counties of Herkimer and Otsego,	JOHN B. VAN PETTEN.
21.	Counties of Oswego and Madison,	ABNER C. MATTOON.
22.	Counties of Onondaga and Cortland,	GEORGE N. KENNEDY.
23.	Counties of Chenango, Delaware and Schoharie,	JOHN F. HUBBARD, JR.
24.	Counties of Broome, Tioga and Tompkins,	ORLOW W. CHAPMAN.
25.	Counties of Cayuga and Wayne,	STEPHEN K. WILLIAMS.
26.	Counties of Ontario, Yates and Seneca,	CHARLES J. FOLGER.
27.	Counties of Chemung, Schuyler and Steuben,	JOHN I. NICKS.
28.	County of Monroe,	LEWIS H. MORGAN.
29.	Counties of Niagara, Orleans and Genesee,	RICHARD CROWLEY.
30.	Counties of Wyoming, Livingston and Allegany.	WOLCOTT J. HUMPHREY.
31.	County of Erie,	ASHER P. NICHOLS.
32.	Counties of Chautauqua and Cattaraugus,	LORENZO MORRIS.

ALPHABETICAL LIST OF SENATORS,

The Counties in which they Reside, Post-Office Address and Politics.

Name of Senators.	County.	Post-office Address.	Politics.
Banks, A. Bleecker,	Albany,	Albany,	Democrat.
Beach, George,	Greene,	Catskill,	Democrat.
Bradley, John J.,	New York,	New York,	Democrat.
Campbell, Samuel,	Oneida,	New York Mills,	Republican.
Cauldwell, William,	Westchester,	Morrisania,	Democrat.
Chapman, Orlow W.,	Broome,	Binghamton,	Republican.
Creamer, Thomas J.,	New York,	New York,	Democrat.
Crowley, Richard	Niagara,	Lockport,	Republican.
Edwards, Lewis A.,	Suffolk	Orient,	Democrat.
Folger, Charles J.,	Ontario,	Geneva,	Republican.
Genet, Henry W.,	New York,	New York,	Democrat.
Graham, William M.,	Orange,	Middletown,	Democrat.
Hale, Matthew,	Essex,	Elizabethtown,	Republican.
Hubbard, John F., Jr.,	Chenango,	Norwich,	Democrat.
Humphrey, Wolcott J.,	Wyoming,	Warsaw,	Republican.
Kennedy, George N.,	Onondaga,	Syracuse,	Republican.
Mattoon, Abner C.,	Oswego,	Oswego,	Republican.
Morgan, Lewis H.,	Monroe,	Rochester,	Republican.
Morris, Lewis,	Chautauqua,	Fredonia,	Democrat.
Murphy, Henry C.,	Kings,	Brooklyn,	Democrat.
Nichols, Asher P.,	Erie,	Buffalo,	Democrat.
Nicks, John I.,	Chemung,	Elmira,	Republican.
Norton, Michael,	New York,	New York,	Democrat.
O'Donnell, John,	Lewis,	Lowville,	Republican.
Palmer, Abiah W.,	Dutchess,	Amenia,	Republican.
Parker, Abraham X.,	St. Lawrence,	Potsdam,	Republican.
Pierce, James F.,	Kings,	Brooklyn,	Democrat.
Stanford, Charles,	Schenectady,	Schenectady,	Republican.
Thayer, Francis S.,	Troy,	Troy,	Republican.
Tweed, William,	New York,	New York,	Democrat.
Van Petten, John B.,	Herkimer,	Fairfield,	Republican.
Williams, Stephen K.,	Wayne,	Newark,	Republican.

ALPHABETICAL LIST

OF THE

MEMBERS OF THE ASSEMBLY,

WITH THE DISTRICTS AND COUNTIES THEY REPRESENT, POST-OFFICE ADDRESS AND POLITICS.

Hon. WILLIAM HITCHMAN, Speaker, New York.

Dis.	Assemblymen.	County.	Post-office Address.	Politics.
2	Ackert, Alfred T.,	Dutchess,	Rhinebeck,	Democrat.
1	Allis, Augustus G. S.,	Onondaga,	Salina,	Republican.
3	Andrews, Alex. H.,	St. Lawrence,	Massena,	Republican.
2	Andrews, William S.,	Kings,	Brooklyn,	Democrat.
	Babcock, Raymond P.,	Cortland,	Scott,	Republican.
2	Balcom, Lyman,	Steuben,	Painted Post,	Republican.
1	Bamler, George J.,	Erie,	Buffalo,	Democrat.
1	Bemus, Matthew P.,	Chantauqua,	Mayville,	Republican.
	Bennett, Chauncey C.,	Broome,	Whitney's Point,	Republican.
2	Bentley, William C.,	Otsego,	Butternuts,	Democrat.
9	Bergen, William G.,	New York,	New York City,	Democrat.
1	Bigelow, Lafayette J.,	Jefferson,	Watertown,	Republican.
2	Bradstreet, N. C.,	Monroe,	Rochester,	Democrat.
	Bristol, William,	Wyoming,	Warsaw,	Republican.
1	Brush, Augustus A.,	Dutchess,	Fishkill Plains,	Republican.
	Buel, Samuel W.,	Fulton & Hami'n	Northville,	Democrat.
2	Burhans, Edward I.,	Delaware,	Roxbury,	Democrat.
2	Burns, Dennie,	New York,	New York City,	Democrat.
1	Burns, Patrick,	Kings,	Brooklyn,	Democrat.
1	Button, Jonas K.,	Cattaraugus,	Franklinville,	Democrat.
2	Cady, Alanson B.,	Oneida,	Waterville,	Republican.
2	Cameron, Winfield S.,	Chautauqua,	Jamestown,	Republican.
6	Campbell, Timothy J.,	New York,	New York City,	Democrat.

Dis.	Assemblymen.	County.	Post-office Address.	Politics.
1	Chapman, William H.,	Oneida,	Washington Mills,	Democrat.
1	Chism, John C.,	Albany,	Guilderland,	Democrat.
	Clark, George,	Schuyler,	Altay,	Republican.
	Clark, William S,	Schoharie,	Sloansville,	Democrat.
	Cook, William F.,	Clinton,	Champlain,	Republican.
2	Cornwall, Andrew,	Jefferson,	Alexandria Bay,	Democrat.
2	Dally, Nathaniel,	Washington,	Hampton,	Republican.
1	Davis, John M.,	Monroe,	Honeoye Falls,	Republican.
3	Dayton, Lewis P.,	Erie,	North Buffalo,	Democrat.
	Decker, John,	Richmond,	Port Richmond,	Democrat.
3	Eaton, Hiram,	Onondaga,	Fayetteville,	Republican.
2	Farley, Benjamin,	Niagara,	Coomer,	Republican.
2	Flach, Richard,	Erie,	Buffalo,	Democrat.
1	Flagg, John L.,	Rensselaer,	Troy,	Democrat.
17	Flagge, Frederick H.,	New York,	New York City,	Democrat.
15	Frear, Alexander,	New York,	New York City,	Democrat.
	Forman, Robert,	Schenectady,	Schenectady,	Democrat.
4	Galvin, John,	New York,	New York City,	Democrat.
2	Gifford, Sanford,	Cayuga,	Sherwood's,	Republican.
1	Gleason, George M.,	St. Lawrence,	E. Pitcairn,	Republican.
2	Glenn, Elijah M. K.,	Wayne,	Macedon,	Republican.
3	Guigon, Theodore,	Ulster,	Pine Hill,	Democrat.
	Halsey, James M.,	Suffolk,	Bridgehampton,	Democrat.
10	Hartman, Anthony,	New York,	New York City,	Democrat.
2	Hasbrouck, Abra'm E.,	Ulster,	Highland,	Democrat.
3	Howard, Harris B.,	Rensselaer,	East Schodack,	Democrat.
1	Hubbard, Myron J.,	Otsego,	Westford,	Democrat.
	Humphrey, Samuel D.,	Putnam,	Patterson,	Democrat.
16	Irving, James,	New York,	New York City,	Democrat.
9	Jacobs, John C.,	Kings,	Brooklyn,	Democrat.
5	Johnson, Christopher,	New York,	New York City,	Democrat.
5	Jones, William C.,	Kings,	Brooklyn,	Democrat.
	Jolland, Frederick,	Chenango,	Greene,	Republican.
3	Keady, Patrick,	Kings,	Brooklyn,	Democrat.
18	Kiernan, Lawrence D.,	New York,	New York City,	Democrat.

MEMBERS OF THE ASSEMBLY. 401

Dis.	Assemblymen.	County.	Post-office Address.	Politics.
	Kinney, Oliver H. P.,	Tioga,	Waverly,	Republican.
	La Bau, Nicholas B.,	Warren,	Luzerne,	Republican.
2	Lasher, James D.,	Oswego,	Fulton,	Republican.
	Lawrence, Thomas,	Rockland,	Nyack,	Democrat.
	Lefler, David D.,	Seneca,	Farmer Village,	Democrat.
1	Little, John F.,	Steuben,	Bath,	Democrat.
	Loughran, James,	Greene,	Windham Centre,	Democrat.
1	Lounsbery, William,	Ulster,	Kingston,	Democrat.
2	Madden, John B.,	Queens,	Long Island City,	Democrat.
4	Mallison, Francis A.,	Kings,	Brooklyn,	Democrat.
	Mann, John F.,	Lewis,	New Bremen,	Republican.
	Matthewson, Angell,	Montgomery,	Fort Plain,	Democrat.
14	McKiever, James,	New York,	New York City,	Democrat.
	Miller, Edmund,	Chemung,	Elmira,	Democrat.
13	Moran, James C.,	New York,	New York City,	Democrat.
1	Murphy, Michael C.,	New York,	New York City,	Democrat.
3	Nelson, Henry C.,	Westchester,	Sing Sing,	Democrat.
4	Nicholson, Ambrose,	Oneida,	Oriskany,	Republican.
8	O'Reilley, Daniel,	New York,	New York City,	Democrat.
2	Palmer, Julius M.,	St. Lawrence,	Russell,	Republican.
1	Parshall, DeWitt,	Wayne,	Lyons,	Republican.
2	Penfield, George J.,	Westchester,	New Rochelle,	Democrat.
	Pitts, Edmund L.,	Orleans,	Medina,	Republican.
1	Place, John A.,	Oswego,	Oswego,	Republican.
2	Pond, Alembert,	Saratoga,	Saratoga Springs,	Republican.
4	Prince, Alphene,	Erie,	Clarence,	Democrat.
1	Purdy, Samuel M.,	Westchester,	West Farms,	Democrat.
12	Quinn, William B.,	New York,	New York City,	Democrat.
6	Raber, John,	Kings,	Brooklyn,	Democrat.
2	Ranney, Luke,	Onondaga,	Elbridge,	Republican.
1	Ray, Henry,	Ontario,	Phelps,	Republican.
6	Reed, James,	New York,	New York City,	Democrat.
2	Reeve, John H.,	Orange,	Wells' Corners,	Democrat.
8	Richardson, Alvin,	Oswego,	Colosse,	Republican.
	Richardson, Silas,	Allegany,	Belmont,	Republican.

Dis.	Assemblymen.	County.	Post-office Address.	Politics.
5	Rider, James,	Erie,	Sardinia,	Republican.
7	Riley, James,	New York,	New York City,	Democrat.
1	Rogers, Harper W.,	Columbia,	Hudson,	Democrat.
	Root, Samuel,	Essex,	Westport,	Republican.
	Sargent, Edmond F.,	Franklin,	Bangor,	Republican.
	Selkreg, John H.,	Tompkins,	Ithaca,	Republican.
1	Sherman, Wm. C. H.,	Orange,	Newburgh,	Democrat.
1	Skeels, Ransom M.,	Niagara,	Lockport,	Democrat.
1	Skillman, Francis,	Queens,	Roslyn,	Democrat.
7	Smith, Caleb L.,	Kings,	Williamsburgh,	Democrat.
	Smith Lewis E.,	Livingston,	Livonia Station,	Republican.
	Stannard, Elisha W.,	Herkimer,	Springfield Centre,	Republican.
	Starr, David G.,	Sullivan,	Monticello,	Democrat.
3	Stevens, James,	Oneida,	Rome,	Democrat.
2	Stewart, Robert,	Madison,	Chittenango,	Republican.
1	Sullard, Albert E.,	Delaware,	Franklin,	Republican.
3	Sumner, Jackson A.,	Albany,	Albany,	Democrat.
	Tarbox, Henry F.,	Genesee,	Batavia,	Republican.
2	Topliff, E. Curtis,	Cattaraugus,	Randolph,	Republican.
2	Torrey, Samuel H.,	Ontario,	Naples,	Republican.
8	Tower, De Witt C.,	Kings,	Green Point,	Democrat.
11	Trainer, Peter,	New York,	New York City,	Democrat.
1	Underwood, David,	Washington,	Fort Edward,	Republican.
20	Van Bruot, George B.,	New York,	New York City,	Republican.
4	Van Volkenburgh, T.,	Albany,	Watervliet,	Democrat.
1	Weed, Charles H.,	Cayuga,	Weedsport,	Republican.
1	Wellington, D. Gerry,	Madison,	Hamilton,	Republican.
2	Wells, Jared A.,	Rensselaer,	Petersburgh,	Republican.
2	Wendover, Stephen H.	Columbia,	Stuyvesant,	Republican.
19	Wiley, William L.,	New York,	New York City,	Democrat.
	Williams, Oliver S.,	Yates,	Middlesex Centre,	Democrat.
3	Wood, Abner I.,	Monroe,	Parma,	Republican.
2	Woods, Francis H.,	Albany,	Albany,	Democrat.
1	Young ove, Truman G.	Saratoga,	Cohoes,	Republican.

www.ingramcontent.com/pod-product-compliance
Lightning Source LLC
Chambersburg PA
CBHW051246300426
44114CB00011B/908